THE PHILOSOPHY OF
JONATHAN EDWARDS

The Indiana Series in the Philosophy of Religion

Merold Westphal, general editor

THE PHILOSOPHY OF JONATHAN EDWARDS

A Study in Divine Semiotics *

STEPHEN H. DANIEL

INDIANA UNIVERSITY PRESS

Bloomington and Indianapolis

*THEORY OF SIGNS & symbols
USED IN COMMUNICATION

The paper used in this publication meets the minimum requirements of
American National Standard for Information Sciences—Permanence of
Paper for Printed Library Materials, ANSI Z39.48–1984.

Manufactured in the United States of America

Library of Congress Cataloging-in-Publication Data

Daniel, Stephen H. (Stephen Hartley), 1950–
The philosophy of Jonathan Edwards : a study in divine semiotics /
Stephen H. Daniel.
p.   cm. — (The Indiana series in the philosophy of religion)
Includes bibliographical references and index.
ISBN 0-253-31609-X (cloth : alk. paper)
1. Edwards, Jonathan, 1703–1758.   2. Edwards, Jonathan, 1703–1758—
Contributions in semiotics.   3. Semiotics—History—18th century.
I. Title.   II. Series.
B873.D36   1994
191—dc20   93-50171

1   2   3   4   5   00   99   98   97   96   95   94

CONTENTS

PREFACE

A new and exciting approach to the history of philosophy has begun to displace the narrative produced by nineteenth-century historiographers indebted to Hegel. Instead of understanding the history of philosophy as a progressive attempt to resolve perennial problems of the human condition, scholars such as Michel Foucault have highlighted the need to inquire into what has been pushed aside or suppressed in the study of the history of philosophy. Such a project reconsiders who count as major thinkers and radically reexamines their works and themes. It provides a means for appreciating why philosophers of the seventeenth and eighteenth centuries who refuse to emphasize specifically modernist topics like subjectivity and autonomy have been pushed to the margins of what is studied today as modern philosophy.

On the surface, this new project has contributed to a wave of fashionable activities concerning the expansion of the philosophic canon, the materialistic deconstructionism known as New Historicism, and the Nietzsche-inspired critique of foundationalist epistemology and metaphysics called postmodernism. But in testing the limits of how far such strategies can be extended in philosophy, these movements have often produced nothing more than deconstructive or poststructuralist "readings" of classical texts. As with earlier Marxist or psychoanalytic approaches, they are sometimes understood simply as alternative interpretations proposed by enthusiasts bent on demonstrating the power of their new toys.

By invoking such contemporary thinkers as Foucault, this book on Jonathan Edwards runs the risk of being understood as merely an application of this new philosophic historiography. Indeed, to some extent it is, insofar as it portrays Edwards' philosophy in other than solely modernist terms. The novelty of this kind of historiography lies not, however, in its offering simply another view of Edwards' thought, but in the way it challenges the dominant practice of considering modern (seventeenth- and eighteenth-century) thinkers in exclusively classical-modernist terms.

Because medieval discourse appeals to the same classical practices assumed by early modernist thinkers, the questions that I address are not concerned with whether Edwards is a medieval or a modern thinker—an issue that vexed scholars several decades ago. Today the problem of modernity (or modernism) reflects the challenge posed by postmodernity, a challenge to the philosophic pursuit of rationality, unity, certainty. From the postmodern perspective, the modernity of Descartes and Locke merely extends the classical (and medieval) presuppositions of philosophy itself, presuppositions amplified by Kant and Hegel. In the Nietzschean critique of classical modernity, the superficial distinctions of classical, medieval, and modern collapse, because all three perspectives embody the same structural presuppositions that support the penchants for self-affirmation and objectivity. Poststructuralist historiography reveals how these structures of thought and reality are ultimately functions of desire and power characteristic of modern humanism. For such a historiography only the antidotes of poetry (Heidegger), irony (Rorty), or play (Lyotard) can be said to correct the totalizing impulse of modernity lost in the fall of philosophy from its rhetorical origins in myth.

This is the new concept of modernity with which discussions of Edwards must now deal. Such a concept alludes to strategies that are suspicious of debates about whether Edwards is a Neoplatonist, a Lockean, or an idealist, for by challenging the fundamental propriety of such positions, postmodernity reveals how the unacknowledged will to truth implicit in the classical–modern perspective has been used to define activities as properly philosophic and to exclude as non-philosophic any activity that does not share such a commitment.

The critics of modernity acknowledge, though, that philosophy (as defined in classical–modern terms) has always included, at its edges and waiting in the wings of its history, the possibility for the metaphorical subversion of the will to truth. That possibility consists in affirming the ontological and logical character of its own rhetoric. It is the temptation to take seriously Edwards' claims that creation is a book, that God is a communicating being, that things are words. In displacing the literal with the figural and symbolic, the paradigm of philosophy embodied in classical modernity is rejected and, with it, the exclusionary practices used to defend against assaults on the privileges of truth. Since the will to truth is central to the definition of philosophy (according to classical modernity), any challenge to the structures by which such a commitment is maintained has to be seen as an invitation to revise philosophy itself. How such a revision occurs in the work of Jonathan Edwards is the theme of this book.

Of course, to displace one way of understanding philosophy with another has the unwelcome effect of changing what constitutes both the history of philosophy and Edwards' place in it. This might explain in part why the study of Edwards in professional philosophy is greeted these days with some suspicion—something that students of American literature or theology might find difficult to understand. But the fact of the matter is that scholars interested in classical American philosophy often strain to include him in the development of pragmatism, and historians of early modern philosophy generally limit their studies to European thinkers. In such an environment, Edwards has been ceded to those for whom his sermons and biblical commentaries occasion as much (if not more) interest than his speculations on ontology or his discussions of freedom. Nonetheless, interest in Edwards' doctrines continues to attract errant historians of philosophy who discover in his writings insights that stand out all the more because of their early modern setting. My efforts are part of that errand into the wilderness.

Much of my initial research for this book was made possible by the support of the faculty development leave program at Texas A&M University. Additional support, in the form of an award from the Honors Program at Texas A&M and a travel grant from the National Endowment for the Humanities, allowed me the opportunity to consult manuscripts and other materials that subsequently proved crucial for the development of my ideas.

Among those to whom I am indebted are Louis Mackey, who first suggested the study of Edwards to me; Miklòs Vetö, who encouraged my occasionally off-beat inquiries; Wilson Kimnach, John E. Smith, and Glenn Erickson, who provided helpful suggestions about how to improve the text; and Ken Minkema, whose hospitality and assistance at the office of the Yale edition of the *Works of Jonathan Edwards* made each visit to New Haven a delight. Ruth Anderson kindly granted permission to quote from the manuscripts of Wallace E. Anderson. No student of Edwards can express enough appreciation to Thomas Schafer for having spent a lifetime clarifying the texts, order, and dating of Edwards' Miscellanies. To him and other Edwards scholars with whom I shared those Thursday lunchtime conversations at Yale's Beinecke Library, I express my heartfelt thanks. Most of the credit for my completion of this book, though, must go to my wife, Breaux, whose love and support make every day a joy.

Full bibliographic information for all citations is provided at the end of this volume.

THE PHILOSOPHY OF
JONATHAN EDWARDS

INTRODUCTION

Of the well-known philosophic minds of the seventeenth and eighteenth centuries, Jonathan Edwards (1703–1758) is perhaps one of the most successful in escaping the historiographic impulse to categorization. With Edwards, many historians are dealing with an unknown quantity, a philosopher whose atomism, idealism, and doctrines of will and beauty frustrate attempts to force him into the empiricist-rationalist continuum that characterizes much of the historiography of modern philosophy.

Part of his elusiveness lies in his appeal to practices that undermine the logical and ontological policies of empiricism and rationalism. Because those policies exhibit the same features found in Platonic, Neoplatonic, or Aristotelian ways of thinking, Edwards' reluctance to adopt them amounts to nothing less than a repudiation of the strategies often taken to define philosophy itself. In terms of those classical notions of logical reasoning or ontological categories, Edwards' doctrines often appear out of touch with those of his contemporaries, and even when he appeals to topics we now acknowledge as philosophically significant, he invokes lines of argument that are seen as more appropriate for a theologian than for a philosopher.

It has become all but a commonplace to say that in order to identify the distinctively philosophic character in Edwards' work, we must situate him somewhere in the empiricist-rationalist continuum, or at least emphasize the Neoplatonic aspects of his thought. By these means (it is argued) we can begin to appreciate Edwards' historical contribution to the topics he addresses.

Such a tactic, however, overlooks how Edwards' philosophy is much more indebted to the Renaissance logic of Peter Ramus and to the ontology of early Stoicism. It is no wonder, then, that once Edwards' ideas are removed from this tradition, they seem to have little bearing on the philosophical debates of the Platonists, Aristotelians, and Lockeans. Accordingly, he is often written off as a historical curiosity.

From the perspective of Stoic-Ramist ontology, the classical-modern problems of epistemology and metaphysics are born out of a misdirected search for some ultimate foundation in terms of which everything else can be understood. According to this Renaissance mentality, the will to discern ultimate principles is itself blind to how the search for them is always already embedded in changing social and linguistic practices that preclude the possibility of there being such foundations.

For example, the classical-modern distinction of thing, idea, and word ignores the policies of discursive exchange by which such a distinction can function in the first place. As long as no one questions the propriety of the thing-idea-word distinction, debates about materialism versus idealism or subjectivity versus objectivity can have some currency. But such debates dissolve once it is shown how the activity of signification undercuts the distinction. Within the Stoic-Ramist-Renaissance mentality (or "episteme" as Michel Foucault calls it), performative, rhetorical practices constitute the network of discriminating behaviors by which the distinction of thing, idea, and word is first made intelligible. Magical incantations can thus bite into the world precisely because every speech is part of a network of practices awaiting social adjudication. As Foucault and Julia Kristeva point out, this way of thinking—common in the Renaissance theory of signatures—unites rhetoric and ontology in a way that is ignored in classical modernity.

In Edwards' appropriation of this Renaissance mentality, reality is understood as essentially communicative, a system of signification in which everything is united as signifier to signified, type to antitype. Even inanimate things "communicate" this movement of intentionality, for their very existence and intelligibility depend on their place in the divine discourse. Every pronouncement is an invitation to ontological revision, and every being obtains but a tenuous grasp on reality as a fleeting anticipation of something else in terms of which it will be fulfilled. Rather than being mere metaphors, expressions about the Book of Nature and about the world as God's communication signal strategies of exchange that permeate and generate discourse.

Studies of Edwards typically overlook this alternative mentality. They describe what he means and how he thinks, but seldom do they ask why he reasons as he does. They assume either an exclusively humanistic notion of communication (the view that individual selves share ideas by communicating) or the Neoplatonic gloss on that notion (the view that God as a subject "emanates" his being in creation). They thus consider communication as subsequent to being, rather than that which constitutes its very possibility.

In criticizing the belief that there is an intelligible self behind communications, Edwards indicts subjectivistic humanism as a fallen way of thinking or speaking. As he shows time and again, this foundationalist assumption of subjectivity frustrates any resolution of the questions that subsequently haunt modern philosophy. In its place he proposes a model of discourse in which communicative exchange and the rhetoric of action form the basis upon which the distinction of subjects is made; this is the discourse of the elect.

The contrast of these two fundamentally different mentalities is a recurring theme in this book. The classical-modern understanding of reality assumes that the world consists of things or "substances" (in logic: subjects) and the features, properties, accidents or relations of those substances (that is, what can be "predicated" of those subjects). The alternative to the mentality of substance and predication is a logic of propositions or (in its medieval formulation) a logic of supposition. This other, Stoic-Ramist, logic provides Edwards the key for developing an antidote to the Platonic-Aristotelian-Lockean logic of predication that characterizes the cognitive procedures of sinful humanity.

In Edwards' use of such a logic, the notion of communication is expanded to include not only the procedures for guiding thought, but also the ontology for determining being. It is in terms of this combination of ontology and logic (in an ontology of signs or "semiotics") that he justifies his arguments about God, the Trinity, creation, freedom, knowledge, and beauty. His claims about how types and antitypes are related, about why human beings individually inherit the burden of original sin, and about how Christ fulfills a central philosophical function in explaining existence, likewise depend on this way of understanding communication. By means of this ontology Edwards identifies the dynamic of being, the rationale for discourse, and the requirement for cogency in reasoning as activities of semiosis.

By drawing attention to Edwards' appeal to a way of thinking commonly associated more with Ramus than with Locke, I do not mean to imply that Edwards ignores the strategies of classical modernity. Indeed, it is a central contention of this book that, for Edwards, the vast majority of human beings reason in terms formalized by predicate logic, representationalist epistemology, and substantialist ontology. In the regenerate, though, the Stoic-Ramist (Renaissance) mentality displaces the perverted assumptions authorized in classical modernity. The ontology of salvation is revealed specifically as an alternative to a set of philosophic practices that characteristically dismiss typological ways of reasoning as unintelligible, indefensible, or mystical. My focus on this alternative is thus intended to correct an overemphasis, rather than to repudiate prior interpretations.

No expositor of Edwards has developed this feature of his thought, especially with an eye toward proposing it as a theme that designates his work specifically as philosophy. This semiotic concept of philosophy does not rely on a metaphysics of substances or a logic of predication. It dissociates Edwards from Emersonian romanticism and draws him closer to the American canon through Charles S. Peirce. It highlights Edwards' sermonic and pastoral immersion in a discourse only partly affected by Cartesian skepticism, Malebranchean Neoplatonism, or Lockean empiricism. And it allows him to reveal a unity among things that other thinkers of his era cannot discern.

By undercutting the focus on subjectivity so characteristic of Cartesian or Lockean expressions of modernity, however, this shift in historiographic approach problematizes the very act of interpretation. To claim that the task of the historian of philosophy is to try to figure out what a thinker had in mind assumes the modernist stance that interior subjectivity precedes and validates what the thinker writes. In contrast, poststructuralist historiography raises the prospect that there might be ways of understanding philosophical texts that do not begin with the assumption that the meaning of a text is to be found in the thought of its author.

This procedure is vastly different from acknowledging that there might be alternative interpretations of a thinker's ideas, for it rejects the assumption that intelligible and accessible ideas behind the text ultimately authorize interpretations. If no thinker or author as such exists apart from the one created by the imposition of a structure, then to provide a critique of the practices that impose structures amounts to a critique of authorization itself. In poststructuralist historiography the authority of an interpretation does not lie in the author or in the historian who recognizes or designates an author, because the very need for authorization betrays itself as yet one more feature of the impulse toward subjection. The prospect of there being something called "Edwards' thought" is thus itself undermined to the extent that we take seriously his repeated self-effacing remarks.

This is not to say that my book is a poststructuralist interpretation of Edwards. Because poststructuralist historiography identifies practices that establish structures by means of which texts are interpreted, it does not itself provide a structure of interpretation. It merely opens up the possibility for recognizing how some strategies of reasoning are made peripheral, minimized, or excluded entirely by modernist emphases on interior subjectivity.

One such set of practices I have identified as semiotics, the study of signs. Marginalized in modernity, discourse structured on semiotic lines (e.g., as found in ancient Stoic propositional logic and reinstated in Ramist logic) has for the most part been lost to those who would now understand Edwards in those terms. To retrieve this semiotic mentality, we must recognize how the logic of propositions to which he appeals differs from the classical logic of predication embedded in modernist discourse.

In order to do that, I have turned to Foucault, Kristeva, and Peirce. These more contemporary scholars reveal what it is like to think in ways other than those that characterize modernity. Their work provides an entrée into a mentality that would otherwise be overlooked or dismissed as incoherent in modernist historiography. By focusing on semiotics, however, I do not imply that it is merely one among a number of possible strategies that I could have selected indiscriminately for the study of Jonathan Edwards. For in spite of their affinities to themes developed in the modernist mentality, Edwards' texts assume practices that are simply unimaginable in terms of modernity. These practices enact a Stoic-Ramist ontology that is not refuted or rejected in modernist accounts so much as it is merely unthought-of. Because such practices are invisible to the classical-modern mentality that guides most of contemporary studies of Edwards, their retrieval is possible only by means of a detour through the study of contemporary accounts of semiotics.

Poststructuralist historiography exposes the exclusionary practices of modernity, highlighting the dominance of a mentality incommensurable with semiotic practices. But poststructuralism does not propose any semiotic mentality as a replacement for the ontology of classical modernity; rather, it discloses how one structuralist, semiotic account of intelligibility has been displaced by another structuralist, semiotic account in modernity. Once we are able to see how the two accounts are incommensurable, we can recognize how Edwards' texts trade on each. Poststructuralist historiography thus clears the way for a revised understanding of Edwards, pointing to what has been blotted out. Contemporary semiotics in turn displays the procedures by which significance is achieved in terms of structures of inclusion and exclusion.

Though many of the principles of semiotics have been elucidated only in the last century, they operate in provocative ways even in the writings of seventeenth-and eighteenth-century thinkers. In fact, without being able to appeal to or assume such strategies, some early modern thinkers would be unable to defend crucial aspects of their philosophies, especially in terms of those arguments that engage epistemological and metaphysical issues. By noting those semiotic strategies, a historian of philosophy can display not only how a discussion intrudes into epistemology or metaphysics, but also how it makes possible the moves made in epistemology and metaphysics as discursive practices.

To show how semiotics identifies strategies by which philosophers initiate the enterprise of modern philosophy is a much larger task than I have set for myself here. Such a project would explore the communicative and textual presuppositions underlying the semiotic nature of philosophical argumentation itself. Often such presuppositions surface in expressions like "the Author of Nature," "the language of vision," "the Book of Nature," or "the language of God." These expressions hint at a discursive economy in which claims of reasoning and argument trade. Rather than being simply intriguing metaphors, they serve as indicators of strategies of communicative exchange.

The appeal to a set of strategic practices such as those found in semiotic analyses occurs specifically as a result of the attempt to determine why a philosophy is structured or developed in one way rather than another. Because the product of such an inquiry displays the inherent rationale of that philosophy, it also indicates why some sets of practices contain different assumptions. As a result of such an inquiry, we are no longer left simply with the assertion that empiricists believe that all knowledge comes solely from experience, or that rationalists assume that knowledge is possible insofar as it is intuitively or demonstratively grounded; for the inquiry invites us to examine why a philosophy should adopt these strictures.

As is apparent from the way I have posed the question in terms of a philosophy rather than in terms of a philosopher, I rule out those answers that appeal to the idiosyncratic psychology of a philosopher as the explanation for why some principles are adopted and others rejected. That tack describes only *how* the philosophy is grounded, not *why* it is grounded in certain principles. To appeal to the claim that "In order to avoid uncertainty, Descartes begins by . . ." or "Locke assumes . . ." is to locate their philosophies in a network of practices without explicating the system of exchange in which such questioning can proceed. It tells us where Descartes or Locke goes on the continuum and even how points on the continuum are distinguished in terms of a taxonomy. However, it does not illustrate why the continuum is structured as it is; it does not indicate why this continuum is preferred.

Indeed, to provide a nonpsychologistic explanation for why some thinkers adopt rationalist instead of empiricist positions is already to raise doubts about the legitimacy of the distinction (apart from its purely pedagogic uses); for if we can reveal the procedures of reflective activity, then all derivative divisions can be explained in terms of, and undercut by, the appeal to strategies that function within and as reflection. A focus on the discursive practices of the classical modern thinkers provides just such a critique of reflective activity. By shifting attention away from debates about materialism versus idealism, or empiricism versus rationalism, the study of signs displays the discursive conditions in which such discussions can take place. With few exceptions, though, semiotic analyses do not provide a more fundamental metaphysical ground for these discussions.

To look for a developed theory of signs in Edwards' thought is thus to miss the point: Because systems of signs function as the means for reflective exchange, they can only be alluded to. Their efficacy lies in how they function in permitting claims of argumentation to proceed. What is noteworthy about Edwards is not so much that he appeals to sign systems in his writings (he has no option not to), but that he so often and thematically makes us aware that he knows he is doing it. In this sense, Edwards' semiotics is much more accessible than that of many of his contemporaries.

At the same time, because Edwards employs three distinguishable but overlapping semiotic practices, his philosophy of signs is more complex than those of many with whom he has been compared:

(1) Throughout his works, Edwards appeals repeatedly to the world as a divine communication. This is often understood as a reference to Edwards' use of a Neoplatonic emanation theory to account for creation, and no doubt there is some truth to this. But with Edwards, the vocabulary of communicative exchange involves the use of a semiotic strategy that resonates with eschatological claims and highlights parallels to God's other form of communication, the Holy Scriptures.

(2) In his more explicit, though tangential, discussions of signs (as in his *Religious Affections*), Edwards combines cause-effect and teleological relations to indicate that epistemological inferences and metaphysical implications are bound up in the functioning of signs. However, because sign relations are not determined by these inferences and implications, any attempt to appropriate the discussion of signs within an epistemology or metaphysics ignores the fact that a theory of signs underlies the possibility for either. Relations of significance (e.g., as signs of divine grace) are in no way legitimated by the endeavor to provide a human rationale for them. Edwards sometimes speaks of signs, then, only to emphasize how a humanistic portrayal of them fails to reveal anything other than the complicity of their own self-referentiality.

(3) Edwards' extension of typology to all relations in the universe transforms what otherwise could be considered one facet of his thought into a key for his work at large. By means of his typology, Edwards supplies the clues for understanding why his strategies of argumentation hold together. As that which discloses his semiotics, therefore, Edwards' typology indicates how he is able to give an account of thought itself.

I begin my treatment of Edwards' philosophy, then, by examining his typology, not because it is the most important feature of his thought, but because it provides an entrée into the problematic of his thought at large. His typology depends for its legitimacy on the same ontology that permeates all the rest of his thought. By showing how signification functions in his typology, I point to signification as the key to understanding other aspects of his philosophical program.

Placing this much importance on typology certainly calls for some comment about how my approach differs from the work of scholars like Perry Miller, Sacvan Bercovitch, Ursula Brumm, and Mason Lowance. As I will argue, following on hints from Wallace Anderson, the study of Edwards' typology until now has centered on how Edwards *uses* typology. I focus instead on the strategy by which his typological claims are justified. To provide the rationale for Edwards' appeal to typology goes beyond his typology to the examination of how his work draws attention to the structures of signification according to which his arguments proceed. These structures identify the requirements for cogency in Edwards' observations and reasoning; as such, they make explicit the conditions for Edwards' discourse.

The study of these practices, designated under the heading of his science of signs or semiotics, extends into all of Edwards' writing. As but one opening into the study of what legitimates the movement of Edwards' thought, typology points to sign relations that mark out how reason itself is possible. Because these structures of significance identify what constitutes reason, they exhibit a transcendental, if not transcendent, order, an order implicit in the typological relations that provide the context for philosophical activity. As Samuel Mather observed, types are a divine, not a human, prerogative: Our discourse is meaningful precisely because it points beyond itself.

This does not mean, however, that *our* meanings are grounded in some transcendent signified, for that would ground the transcendent in human reason and would thus reverse the priority of the grounding. Instead, typological pointing undercuts the impulse to restrict meaning to what is foundational in either transcendent or immanent terms.

To locate Edwards' discourse in such a system of semiotic exchange is thus to place that discourse in a system of signs apart from which "the human" (or for that matter, anything) cannot be thought. Such a strategy reveals a discursive practice with implications not only for Edwards' typological or more explicit metaphysical works, but also for his treatments of moral virtue, original sin, and beauty. In fact, if there is such a logic and ontology implicit in what Edwards' assumes to be the process of reasoning itself, it should come as no surprise that it is discernible in all aspects of his thought and makes his thought that much more intelligible and integrated. That is why I have not limited my discussion to Edwards' moral theory, his theory of free will, his doctrine of beauty, or his treatments of God or sin. Because the definition of meaning itself is under examination, my approach downplays modernist distinctions between metaphysics, epistemology, ethics, and aesthetics as much as it challenges the assumption that the author dictates the strategies that define the intelligibility of thought.

Moreover, my discussion does not participate in the debate about whether Edwards endorses a distinctly medieval theology or a characteristically enlightenment epistemology, for that would leave untouched questions of the primacy of the author and the propriety of comparing different discursive formations. Instead of trying to figure out what Edwards means psychologically, I have focused on the systems of signification that determine how his remarks themselves display the process by which meaning is established and the activity of reason defined. I have thus tried to avoid attributing to Edwards implications of doctrines that were made explicit only much later.

The possibility of anachronism in raising Edwards' name in the context of semiotics is reduced significantly once we recognize how signs play a central role in the Stoic-Ramist mentality. To retrieve a sense of how (for thinkers like Peter Ramus or Paracelsus) the subject is less the manipulator of a system of signification than a function of that system, we must first distance ourselves from classical-modern assumptions about the role of signs, disabusing ourselves of the idea that the Italian humanists (with the possible exception of Lorenzo Valla) represent what I refer to as the Stoic-Ramist or Renaissance mentality. Toward that end, I have suggested that Peirce, Foucault, and Kristeva help us see better the differences between Stoic-Ramist semiotics and classical-modern semiotics.

In turning to Peirce to understand Edwards, I associate his semiotics more with that of Jacques Derrida than with the more classical-modern semiology of Ferdinand de Saussure. However, a deconstructed Edwards would ignore his fascination for the historicity of the sign. To retain that element in his thought, I have relied on Foucault and Kristeva, who alert us to the differentiation of sign systems, a differentiation that constitutes the possibility for history itself.

For those interested in the history of ideas, Miklós Vetö's *La Pensée de Jonathan Edwards* (1987) provides perhaps the best overall treatment of Edwards' place in the Calvinist tradition and in relation to other modern philosophers. Vetö provides a "phenomenology" of Edwards' thought, describing what Edwards means and *how* he thinks. By contrast, I examine *why* Edwards thinks as he does. For example, instead of describing how (for Edwards) grace provides a new sense of things, I hope to explain why understanding what that new sense is requires the adoption of a new way of reading Edwards. To display "the mind of Edwards"—the totalizing, theologico-philosophic apprehension presumed to inform his writings—certainly would give us a better grasp of his often enigmatic writings. But what if his philosophy indicts such a move as an attempt to celebrate his authority by authorizing him as a subject? That is, what if the subjectivity that Edwards depicts as original sin itself characterizes the very way he is studied? In such a case, even the most well-meaning of scholars might fail to see how a new sense of things would require a radically different appreciation of why Edwards writes what he does.

Just how radical a change in our historiographic expectations will affect our understanding of Edwards is yet to be seen; but it certainly draws attention to strategies of study that enact the classical-modernist paradigm that Edwards' philosophy overthrows. For example, in a recently published 1955 dissertation *The Young Jonathan Edwards* (1991), William S. Morris balances Perry Miller's Lockean characterization of Edwards' thought with an emphasis on Edwards' background in scholastic metaphysics. But to trace Edwards' position to his predecessors—a typically modernist move made by other scholars (e.g., Norman Fiering)—merely begs the question of how their positions embody a strategy of reasoning in terms of which Edwards is intelligible.

Insofar as the scholasticism highlighted by Morris or the Neoplatonic metaphysics thematized by Fiering emphasizes the Aristotelian-Cartesian adoption of a substance-accident ontology, it identifies an author as the source of meaning or intelligibility of his or her expressions. In contrast, my study of Edwards does not assume the propriety of discursive practices that characterize such methodologies of modernity. Accordingly, without denying that an understanding of Edwards' thought benefits from references to his predecessors, I focus on the conditions of communicative exchange that make both his thought and theirs intelligible.

The first chapter provides the theoretical framework in which my interpretation is formulated. It describes presuppositions of intelligibility in terms of a doctrine of signs and signification. In later chapters I refer to that doctrine as the Stoic-Ramist-Renaissance treatment of signs, alluded to by Locke and developed in the more recent semiotic work of Peirce, Foucault, and Kristeva. Because the first chapter raises broad questions of current philosophic practices, it may be of less importance to someone interested specifically in Edwards' thought.

Chapter 2 shows how the examination of signification can begin from within Edwards' theory of religious types. It introduces the topic of signification in his own terms rather than those of contemporary semiotics. It portrays his metaphoric appeal to a divine language of nature or a divine semiotics as essential to his invitation to reframe thinking within a discourse of universal signification.

Chapter 3 identifies the historical dimensions of such a discussion. It indicates how questions of philosophic strategy and typology had attracted, long before the eighteenth century, a theoretical analysis in which all existence is considered mental or spiritual insofar as the intelligibility of a thing always implies pointing beyond itself.

Each of these chapters can serve as a point of departure for the subsequent chapters. Separately, they highlight different approaches to the study of Edwards' philosophy; together, they complement one another by revealing how for Edwards meaning or significance is established. This focus on meaning thematizes the project of determining the meaning of Edwards' thought itself. The first three chapters thus suggest a reconsideration of Edwards that questions the assumptions by which his philosophy is identifiable as philosophy.

Edwards' doctrines of the Trinity and the creation of the world are topics treated in chapter 4. Chapter 5 discusses Edwards' treatment of original sin as the loss of signification embodied in selves isolated by Cartesian doubt. In chapter 6, freedom and virtue are defined in terms of relations of signification—relations that are radically transformed in the "sense of the heart" or "consent to Being" that marks the universal semiosis of beauty (the theme of chapter 7). I conclude by noting how, for Edwards, the unity of the sign—lost in modern philosophy—is retrieved in the figure of Christ by the transformation of the classical-modern understanding of propriety.

I

THE PROSPECT OF SEMIOTICS

Shortly before his death in 1981, Wallace Anderson was working on several projects that attempted to explain Edwards' belief that all objects of physical creation represent spiritual things. The general theme of such study, typology, had been of concern to a number of other researchers, but all other study had centered on issues of how typology functions in Edwards' thought, rather than on what would justify his theory of types. By contrast, Anderson identified the central problem underlying typology as that of providing justification for certain maneuvers in Edwards' reasoning. He was confident that the search for the principles guiding typological argumentation would explain how Edwards' typological work could be united with his more explicit epistemological and metaphysical writings. Though he did not have a chance to follow up on these insights, Anderson pointed to the need to discern the philosophical presuppositions in Edwards' writings that would account for how disparate elements of his thought are integrated. As I will argue, that investigation of the nature of reasoning in Edwards' typological thought extends beyond even what Anderson suspected, by revealing how reasoning in general is possible for Edwards.

As Anderson recognized, in trying to provide an account of the rationality of typology, Edwards was responding to a philosophical challenge posed by John Locke. It was not so much a critique of typology itself that engaged Edwards as it was the Lockean invitation to give a rationale for thought in general, including typological thought. For Locke, that rationale could be found only in the science of signs—semiotics—and it is his observation of this fact that furnishes us (and perhaps Edwards) with a key for understanding the problematic of reasoning for Edwards.

However, the Edwardsian project calls for a much more extensive study of the science of signs than Anderson's interest in typological reasoning would have shown. Such a study of the strategies of Edwards' reasoning highlights differences in whole networks of discursive practices. These differences are significant enough to identify them (in Foucault's term) as separate epistemes, mentalities, or fundamental ways of thinking. The purpose of this chapter is to indicate how a discussion of those general sets of discursive practices reveals the semiotic strategies that account for and give meaning to Edwards' writings.

The Invitation of Typology

Though his posthumous notes are sketchy on this point, it is apparent that Anderson believed that something much more was at stake in the philosophy underlying Edwards' typological writings than a retrieval of the Neoplatonic view that all of reality is tied together in a great chain of being emanating from God. "Even if it were granted that all physical objects subsisted only in dependence upon God," Anderson writes, "this would not be sufficient to justify Edwards' claim that nature was a system of representations of spiritual or divine things, nor would it answer the most widespread and pressing philosophical objections his contemporaries would advance against it."[1] The task, as Anderson saw it, was to explain how Edwards' manner of reasoning based on typological presuppositions could itself be justified and then somehow be reconciled with Edwards' so-called idealism (on which Anderson had earlier worked). That reconciliation seemed especially elusive, considering the fact that it required relating suspect theological associations to a metaphysics in which physical realities exist as objects of knowledge by virtue of their divinely granted ability of resistance. Just how this epistemology of resistance could complement a theory of universal typology puzzled Anderson; but he recognized that the key for understanding Edwards' way of thinking lay in such an enquiry.

Most of Edwards' contemporaries would have agreed that God is immaterial, that the physical world depends on God, and that the order of the universe depends on God's wisdom and purpose. As Anderson notes, however, the arguments supporting those beliefs do not support Edwards' extension of typology to include claims, for example, that a serpent's art of luring prey is a shadow of Satan's wiles, or that a general spiritual enlightenment is prefigured by the invention of the telescope.[2] Such expansions of typological procedure appear to exceed Edwards' own restriction that types should be grounded in scripture; otherwise, as he acknowledges, such observations stem merely from human ingenuity.

Exactly what provides the possibility for the comprehensiveness and comprehension of the universal typology implicit in Edwards' thought, Anderson concluded, goes beyond any scriptural evidence. Anderson insisted, though, that a "philosophical assessment of typology" offers a clue as to how Edwards' position could be defended. "By its very nature," Anderson observed, "Edwards' general view required an independent and philosophical defense based upon principles of reason and well-attested facts of experience."[3] Without this defense, Anderson feared, Edwards' theory was liable (as Edwards himself sus-

---

1. Wallace E. Anderson, ed., "Images of Divine Things" and "Types" Notebook, in Jonathan Edwards, *Typological Writings*, ed. Wallace E. Anderson and Mason I. Lowance, Jr., with David Watters, 14.
    2. Ibid., 15, 31–32.
    3. Ibid., 13.

pected) to the charge that it was the product of a man "of a very fruitful brain and copious fancy."[4]

Mindful that such an examination had implications for research on Edwards much more extensive than the study of his typology alone, Anderson sought to reveal the philosophical underpinnings of Edwards' theory, but completed only a few pages of notes toward that end. The notes are instructive in outlining the kinds of questions that can be asked about the philosophical assumptions operating within any typology. They are helpful as much for what they thematize as for what they tantalizingly overlook. Despite their incompleteness, they mark out boundaries of a project unexplored in the scholarship on Edwards' philosophy, though they give little indication as to how that project might be pursued.

Though he did not recognize it, Anderson had identified a distinctly philosophical issue that situates Edwards' metaphysics and epistemology within a context of communicative exchange—one I designate as semiotic—that Anderson had approximated in his allusions to Edwards' scriptural restraints on typological reflection. Though he had the crucial texts before him, Anderson did not follow up on the possibility that Edwards' extension of typology likewise extends the domain of scripturally significant topics to include the scripted in general. Without that move, the examination of the philosophical justification of the centrality of typology in Edwards' thought remains but a promissory note.

Still, unlike any other commentator, Anderson took seriously the philosophical difficulties associated with the claim of typological universality, a claim that Edwards makes without reservation. By calling for a philosophical theory of typology in Edwards, Anderson questioned how Edwards could justify his belief "that the whole universe, heaven and earth, air and seas, and the divine constitution and history of the holy Scriptures, be full of images of divine things, as full as a language is of words."[5] As I will show later, this association of the themes of universe and language is not accidental and provides the key for understanding the relations established by a typology. However, I want to point out not only that Edwards extends typological relations to all reality, but also that his invitation into this universe of scriptural signs itself needs a legitimation that descriptions of his uses of types do not offer.

Among Anderson's unpublished papers is a one-page outline, "A Philosophical Assessment of Typology," in which he specifies the kinds of questions raised by the attempt to unite Edwards' explicitly philosophical writings (e.g., "The Mind") with typological works (e.g., "Images of Divine Things"). By drawing out the implications of that connection, Anderson hoped to reveal the ontological and epistemological presuppositions of typological reasoning:

> Typology supposes that there is a special relation between certain things, and
> that there is a way of discovering that relation and knowing just which things

4. Edwards, "Types" Notebook [mid-1740s], ibid., 152. Cf. Anderson, ibid., 7.
5. Edwards, "Types" Notebook, ibid., 152.

are connected by it. Hence typology seems to have an *ontology*—an account of the nature and foundation of the relation, and an account of the kinds of things that are capable of standing in that relation. And typology has an *epistemology*— an explanation of the procedures by which a certain thing can be truly or reasonably known to be a type of some other thing. In addition to this, one might ask the questions: (1) What is the basis for assuming that any such relation actually exists at all, or exists among the things the theory asserts it does? (2) What is the basis for confidence in the procedures for identifying and correlating the particular types with particular antitypes—what shows that, by following the procedures, we will reach reliable conclusions as to which particular things are types and which are not; and also which is the *true* antitype for a given type?[6]

As Anderson was aware, understanding the first part of an ontology of typology presents the greatest difficulty for the student of Edwards, and Anderson has little to say concerning that. To give an account of the nature and foundation of the relation by which things are connected to one another extends beyond what Anderson took to be covered in the study of types. Because Edwards extended typological relations indefinitely, any analysis of such relations would have entailed a full-scale examination of all ontological relations in order to determine the specific character of typological relations. An ontology of a typological relation would exhibit, as Anderson notes, "the nature and foundation of the relation"; and the claim that something exists or is meaningful in virtue of its participation in such a relation would not by itself explain why that is the case. Something more is needed to explain why this foundation does not itself transcend meaningful discourse; or if it does transcend meaningful discourse, some account would have to be given as to how a philosophical assessment of typology is not therefore made impossible.

Admittedly, a simple way out of the problem to which Anderson alludes would be to concede that no philosophical account of typological relations is possible, and that it is simply a matter of faith, for example, to be able to see in Moses' leading the people of Israel from captivity a type of Christ's salvific mission. Or, if the foundation of the typological relations between "the whole outward creation" and spiritual things cannot be expressed in any meaningful way to human beings, then the acknowledgment of its unintelligibility excludes it as a possible justification for such relations. In either case, all of Edwards' efforts in typological exegesis could fall prey to the charge that he can produce nothing to support his particular interpretations.

Against such negative assessments of the prospects of discerning a strategy legitimating Edwards' typology, I suggest that the key is not in looking for an ontology apart from the communicative exchange contained in typological relations, but in discerning the structures of discursive exchange in which these indefinitely extended relations function. This means revising part of Anderson's

---

6. Anderson's manuscripts on Edwards are on file in the office of *The Works of Jonathan Edwards*, Yale Divinity School, New Haven, Connecticut.

problematic in order to avoid the implication that an ontology must supply a foundation—for example, like Neoplatonism does—that itself is distinct from the relations of ontologically grounded entities.

However, as Anderson admits, Edwards' philosophy presents a special problem in this regard, insofar as it links the methodologies of ontology and epistemology so closely that, as "The Mind" and other writings attest, philosophical idealism lurks behind every Edwardsian pronouncement on metaphysics. But by refusing to treat things in typological relations as ontologically prior to the relations themselves, Edwards suggests a strategy to prevent the subordination of typology to idealism. To use Anderson's words in this semiotic context, the *foundation* of a typological (sign) relation consists in the relation itself. That is, it is of its *nature* to be in such a relation.

Exactly how these hints at a semiotic theory of typology can be justifiably developed in Edwards' work will be discussed in the next chapter. Here I mention them to indicate how even raising the question of the ontology of typology, as Anderson perceptively does, risks the loss of a fruitful answer at the outset. But as long as the epistemological dimension of typology is retained as necessarily bound up with ontology, and as long as both of them are open to nonfoundationalist strategies, the collapse of Edwards' semiotics (of which typology is only a part) into fideism or philosophical idealism can be avoided.

The recognition of the importance of the epistemological does not imply, however, that semiotics falls under epistemology. The case is just the opposite: epistemological discourse, like metaphysical discourse, cannot help but appeal to sign relations as the conditions for both human understanding and meaningful or significant communication.

Locke belatedly recognized that fact; Edwards never seriously questioned it. Edwards certainly would have known how Locke, in the final chapter of his *Essay concerning Human Understanding,* invites a reassessment of the centrality of semiotics by retrieving the Stoic division of science into natural philosophy, ethics, and *semiotike.* Though it is often equated with the epistemology he outlines in the *Essay,* Locke's reference to semiotics extends "the doctrine of signs" beyond a simple analysis of words or the relations of ideas to the study of the order by which thought itself is possible.[7] In this expanded sense, Locke notes, semiotics is "aptly termed also *Logike,* logic: the business whereof is to consider the nature of signs, the mind makes use of for the understanding of things, or conveying its knowledge to others." To understand ideas and words in the context of just such a doctrine "would afford us another sort of logic and critic, than what we have been hitherto acquainted with."[8]

---

7. In the 1682 edition of Ptolemy's *Harmonics,* edited by Locke's friend and former professor John Wallis, "semiotic" refers to the art of musical notation. See Thomas A. Sebeok, "'Semiotics' and Its Congeners," in *Frontiers in Semiotics,* ed. John Deely, Brooke Williams, and Felicia E. Kruse, 255.

8. John Locke, *Essay concerning Human Understanding,* ed. Peter Nidditch, 720–21 (IV.21.4). Cf. John Deely, "John Locke's Place in the History of Semiotic Inquiry," in *Semiotics 1986,* ed. John Deely and Jonathan Evans, 409–411; and Vincent M. Colapietro, *Peirce's Approach to the Self: A Semiotic Perspective on Human Subjectivity,* 27.

Just as Locke had seen the need for his Book III treatment of words only after running up against the limitations of his discussion of ideas in Book II, so here at the end of his essay he points to a project yet to be developed. That project would explain why words, "in their primary or immediate signification, stand for nothing but the *ideas* in the mind of him that uses them."[9] The *Essay* makes the claim that words signify, but it does not present the argument for how they can accomplish this task. Locke does not show how words are connected to the things to which they refer in terms of a "primary or immediate signification," because he does not spell out the theory of signs that would permit such relations.

At the end of his *Essay,* Locke thus stresses the need for a semiotics to account for what makes knowledge possible. As I will point out in regard to Foucault's archaeological analysis of the science of signs, such an enterprise might not have been conceivable in Locke's terms by some of his successors (e.g., Hume or Condillac). For Edwards, however, the proposal of a theory of signs to account for the unity of divine communication and human cognitive and affective practices addresses precisely the question that Anderson raises about the ontological underpinnings of typological reflection. This is not to say, of course, that Edwards' development and use of a theory of signs originates in his reading of Locke; it is only to acknowledge how the introduction specifically of the topic of semiotics in the context of the study of Edwards can occur within an overtly Lockean (and thus Edwardsian) context.

Much of the latter part of this chapter details a semiotic strategy that accounts for the nature of typological relations, especially in the expanded terms in which Edwards elevates typology. Because that discussion provides the theoretical context for the remainder of this book and moves quickly beyond the limits of typology, I mention it here as the kind of investigation occasioned by the attempt to provide an account "of the nature and foundation" of typological relations. It, I maintain, addresses Anderson's first part of a typological ontology.

Concerning the second part of typological ontology—the account of the kinds of things that are capable of standing in typological relations—Anderson notes that "those who accept typology still differ with respect to the ontology they suppose as *definitive* of the theory."[10] Some writers, he comments, limit types to specific historical things and events recorded in the Old Testament; others include the New Testament. Still others are willing to count as types those visible and material things mentioned in the Old (and New) Testament and which we still have available to us. As an instance of this view, Anderson gives Edwards' example of the dove in the New Testament as a type of the

9. *Essay,* 405 (III.2.2). Cf. Norman Kretzmann, "The Main Thesis of Locke's Semantic Theory," in *Locke on Human Understanding: Selected Essays,* ed. I. C. Tipton, 126–28. See also Hans Aarsleff, *From Locke to Saussure: Essays on the Study of Language and Intellectual History,* 28; and Brian Vickers, "Analogy Versus Identity: The Rejection of Occult Symbolism, 1580–1680," in *Occult and Scientific Mentalities in the Renaissance,* ed. Brian Vickers, 110–114.
10. Wallace E. Anderson, "A Philosophical Assessment of Typology," Anderson Ms.

Holy Spirit. Finally, there are those who expand types to include general kinds of visible or material things and characteristics of things not unique to any individual, for example, the stench of death.

Anderson claims that at least one of the keys to understanding Edwards' typology is seeing how Edwards presents arguments responding to one or another of these groups or to those who question the legitimacy of any typological reasoning. Regarding this second part of typological ontology, Anderson outlines a strategy which, he later informs the editorial board of the Yale edition of Edwards' works, could be part of his contribution to the introduction of the volume on Edwards' typology. Because Edwards does not provide a clear statement about the precise nature of typological relations, a more promising approach would identify Edwards' position in terms of objections that would be raised against his application of the type-antitype distinction.

This strategy, Anderson notes, locates Edwards' views relative to factions in the reformed and non-reformed traditions. *Reformed tradition* proponents would acknowledge as types either: (1) only those objects, persons, and events recounted in the Old Testament and fulfilled in the New Testament and subsequent Church history—accepted, for example, by most Calvinists; (2) both Old and New Testament objects, persons, and events later fulfilled in the New Testament and Church history; or (3) Old and New Testament objects, persons, and events plus figurative prophecies and allegories in post-New Testament human history that represent certain eternal, moral, or spiritual truths and realities (a position accepted by many New England Puritans). *Nonreformed tradition* proponents include: (1) Papists and High-Church Anglicans, who treat the Scriptures simply as allegory, "mere divine pedagogy—the mere presentation of truths, rather than the fulfillment of promises and the effective introduction of a new dispensation for man through Christ's sacrifice"; and (2) Lockeans, Deists, and rationalists who reject typology in general as an exercise of human fancy.[11]

As is apparent from his correspondence with the Yale editorial board, Anderson believed that the examination of Edwards' typology could proceed along two quite different lines. Mason Lowance, he says, could treat Edwards' typology in light of the hermeneutical doctrines, rhetorical customs, and scriptural and doctrinal arguments of the various factions of Calvinist Puritans (including their critiques of the abuse of types as allegory). Anderson, in turn, wanted to focus on Edwards' response to the philosophical objections to typology and to "examine how far Edwards depended on the metaphysical and epistemological views he had developed in 'Natural Philosophy,' 'The Mind,' and elsewhere to frame a philosophical defense of typology."[12] Aside from some cursory remarks on Edwards' early scientific writings, though, Anderson was unable to pursue that investigation.

11. See Anderson, ed., *Typological Writings*, 11–15, 20–33.
12. Anderson, "An Approach to Understanding Edwards' Typology," Anderson Ms.

Perhaps without even recognizing it, Anderson had drawn typology into a larger context than the epistemological or metaphysical issues surrounding Lockean and rationalist objections to Biblical exegesis. Had he noted this, he could have seen how the philosophical pursuit of the structures of intelligibility implicit within typological reasoning exceeds the regional discussion of Edwards as a typologist.

In my account, typology becomes only the occasion for a philosophical analysis that reveals a system of communicative exchange which operates throughout Edwards' works. This understanding of Edwards in terms of semiotic practices in turn displays the rationality by which Anderson's goal of relating typology to metaphysics and epistemology is made possible.

The Semiotic Context

The shift to the science of signs as the introduction to the study of Edwards' philosophy turns the focus of that study away from the authority of Edwards as a source of insight to the conditions for locating him within practices that constitute the possibility for expression. Unlike studies that legitimate the author within a company or tradition of other authors, this approach attends to the ways in which Edwards' texts forestall the attempt to retrieve the person behind them. Because the sign system itself identifies what an author is, to search for "the real Edwards" is to mistake the allusion to the system of signification employed in the text as an act of evasion or self-deprecation. As Richard De Prospo points out, such a search for the guarded, seldomly personable Edwards, discovers only a creation of romanticist historiography.[13]

In place of the speaking subject (the cogito that reveals or conceals itself in exercises of its sovereign freedom), the analysis of discursive practices begins on the level of "it is said," not "Edwards said." This shift requires a temporary detour from Edwards' texts through a discussion of the mentality, episteme, or paradigm (in Thomas Kuhn's term)—in short, the complex of social practices and formal structures—that enables his discourse to be considered significant or meaningful.

A *mentalité* or episteme is not, Foucault cautions, "a sort of communal opinion, a collective representation that is imposed on every individual . . . a great, anonymous voice that must of necessity speak through the discourses of everyone; instead we must understand by it the totality of things said, the relations, the regularities, and the transformations that may be observed in them."[14] The domain of discursive practices is neither an arbitrary human construct nor the univocal speech of God, for both humanity and divinity are inscribed through

---

13. See Richard C. De Prospo, *Theism in the Discourse of Jonathan Edwards*, 54.
14. Michel Foucault, *The Archaeology of Knowledge*, trans. A. M. Sheridan Smith, 122; cf. 49, 95–96. See also Michel Foucault, *The Order of Things*, xiv.

such practices. The episteme identifies things in terms of the codes and rules that order relations, and it shows how objects, gestures, nature, and even God himself "speak" in the signs they constitute.

This way of approaching the study of Edwards immediately has the effect of transforming the problematic in terms of which the question of typological relations is raised. It overthrows the common way in which studies of Edwards treat the world as a divine "communication" by rejecting the presupposition that signs are media by which subjects (divine and human) communicate ideas to one another.[15] This shift in mentality exposes how a subject (self, author) is as much a sign as any inanimate object, and how its communicative capacity lies not so much in its ability to use signs as in its functioning within a system of signification. In this way, objects, human beings, and God speak—indeed, exist—in terms of the same strategy of semiotic exchange. The interpretation of the language (or sign system) in which such speech occurs is not itself an interpretation that attempts to go beyond the language or to get outside of the system of exchange. In this sense, there is nothing that provides a foundation or ultimate justification for the episteme. The episteme is the locus of intelligibility, significance, and existence.

As Foucault points out, the assumption that signs represent something else not linked essentially to the sign as such (e.g., ideas) characterizes the mentality of the seventeenth and eighteenth centuries (the "classical" episteme), contrasting with what Foucault calls the Renaissance episteme, in which every thing is linked in virtue of its participation in a system of signs. In the Renaissance episteme, the Book of Nature comprises a network of signs that require deciphering instead of interpretation. In deciphering, *cognitio* remains within the bounded and uniform "consensus" of the world: Meaning consists in the interplay and juxtaposition (in short, the communication) of signs. Interpretation, on the other hand, attempts to transcend the domain of signs in search of some authorial intention behind communication and thus attempts to subordinate signification. Disconnected from the immediacy of the system of signs, interpretation results in an infinite interpretation of the self, the pursuit of a self unregulated by and untied to signs.

This means that in the mentality Foucault identifies as the Renaissance episteme, the task of reading the Book of Nature or the Scriptures is not concerned with the attempt to interpret the mind of God as the author of Nature or Scripture, for that would imply that the notion of God as a self is intelligible independently of the system of signs in which that notion is embedded. Instead, the centrality of signs in the Renaissance mentality undercuts the need to interpret these texts in terms of authorial intention by denying that such a tactic provides any clearer notion of their meaning:

---

15. See, for example, Paula M. Cooey, *Jonathan Edwards on Nature and Destiny: A Systematic Analysis*, 15, 36, 54–58, 160, 230; Sang Hyun Lee, *The Philosophical Theology of Jonathan Edwards*, 57–58; and Stephen R. Yarbrough, "Jonathan Edwards on Rhetorical Authority," *Journal of the History of Ideas* 47 (1986), 395, 399.

> The death of interpretation [Foucault remarks] is to believe that there are signs,
> signs that exist as primary, original, real, coherent, pertinent, and systematic. The
> life of interpretation, on the contrary, is to believe that there are only interpre-
> tations. It seems to me that it is necessary to understand something that many
> of our contemporaries forget, namely, that *hermeneutics and semiology are two
> fierce enemies.*[16]

By affirming the independence of the sign from subjective intentionality, the
Renaissance mentality retrieves it from its classical (and ultimately hermeneutic) subordination to interpretation. Hermeneutics looks for an intention behind
the sign as the ground for signification; semiology locates significance within
signification. The tension they create together in portraying different functions
for signs constitutes a metasemiosis that unites the implicit humanism of the
structuralist semiotics of Ferdinand de Saussure with the displacement of subjectivity in the poststructuralist semiotics of Julia Kristeva or Jacques Lacan.

For Edwards, this metasemiosis holds the mentality of fallen humanity in tension with the apprehension of the semiotic and typological unity of all reality
experienced by the elect. In Foucault's terms, the discrepancy between the two
places the graphics of the world and the discourse of subjectivity one cog out
of alignment and ever so slightly out of parallax. In other words, though humanistic discursive practices can be situated relative to a network of semiotic
exchange, they cannot be integrated into the sign system of the elect as long as
they assume that significance is grounded outside of the system of signification.

For some students of Edwards, this contrast of mentalities might seem
parallel to the ongoing debate about whether Edwards is modern or medieval
in outlook.[17] But the modern-medieval discussion itself adopts the "classical"
attitude toward signs that the recovery of the Renaissance episteme counter-
balances; and attempts to portray Edwards' epistemology as medieval or his
philosophy at large as Neoplatonic merely reinstate the strategies of classical
humanism implicit in Perry Miller's depiction of Edwards as a modern follower
of Locke.[18]

In setting up the problem in this way, an alternative possibility for understanding Edwards emerges. Instead of presenting the medieval-modern
distinction as a contrast between Neoplatonism or Thomism on the one hand
and empiricism on the other, Foucault reorients the discussion according to
how signs are understood. His semiotic approach focuses on how the Renais-

16. Michel Foucault, "Nietzsche, Freud, Marx," in *Transforming the Hermeneutic Context: From
Nietzsche to Nancy*, ed. Gayle L. Ormiston and Alan D. Schrift, 66–67. Cf. Pamela Major-Poetzl,
Michel Foucault's Archaeology of Western Culture, 32–35.

17. For opposing views, see John Opie, ed., *Jonathan Edwards and the Enlightenment;* Michael
J. Colacurcio, "The Example of Edwards: Idealist Imagination and the Metaphysics of Sovereignty,"
in *Puritan Influences in American Literature*, ed. Emory Elliott, 55–106; and De Prospo, *Theism
in Jonathan Edwards*, 18–19.

18. See Perry Miller, *Jonathan Edwards;* John E. Smith, *Jonathan Edwards: Puritan, Preacher,
Philosopher*, 14–28; Mason I. Lowance Jr., *The Language of Canaan*, 6, 250–70; Norman Fiering,
Jonathan Edwards's Moral Thought and Its British Context; and William S. Morris, *The Young
Jonathan Edwards: A Reconstruction*, 3, 78–128.

sance fascination for signatures retrieves an earlier (in fact, Stoic) reluctance to posit a realm of ideas beyond that of signs. However, because the classical (Platonic, Aristotelian) subordination of signs to ideas in most medieval and modern philosophy is hardly attenuated by Neoplatonists like Pico della Mirandola or Ficino, only thinkers who are sensitive to the immanently significatory nature of reality (like Paracelsus) represent the distinctive mentality that Foucault associates with the Renaissance. For him, the distinctively Renaissance thinker is thus not an Italian humanist, but rather a Swiss alchemist. Since much of seventeenth-century empiricism or rationalism reinscribes the practices of classical and medieval thought, Foucault refers to the episteme of early modern philosophy as classical.

In contrast to the mentality of classical modernity, in which ideas are understood to reside in some transcendent realm or in the mind or self, in the Renaissance episteme ideas, minds, and selves are themselves part of the system of signification whereby all things are intelligible. In a semiotic analysis, the self does not disappear when we attend to the discursive practices in which statements have significance; the self is only positioned in the matrix whereby it achieves meaning. This is not to say that semiotics endorses materialism as an alternative to idealism, for materialism's denial of the reality of the distinctly mental equally accepts the propriety of dividing the world of significance along the lines of mental versus physical or supernatural versus natural. Both look beyond the practices of discourse for an underlying reality to ground structures of signification. In doing so, they locate significance outside of signification, thus distancing purpose and value from meaning.

By contrast, much of Edwards' work, even the so-called idealism of his early writings, provides a critique of such attempts to move the question of significance away from the immediacy of the signs in which human beings live. Pregnant with signification, "perfused with signs" (as Peirce says), the universe is for Edwards a communication as much for what it signifies to the saint as for how it includes fallen humanity in the discourse it constitutes. Original sin marks the disruption of the unity of signification and value that the fall into the classical episteme chronicles. The Renaissance treatment of signs resists that turn by recalling the prelapsarian impossibility of a duplicity of subjective aim and objective behavior.

Accordingly, the divorce of the Cartesian subject from the world of signs thematizes the Reformation insistence on human sinfulness. After the Fall, instead of living in a commerce of signs, the self, alienated from its semiotic matrix, struggles to regain access to significance. Made all but impossible by the now classical (especially Neoplatonic) appropriation of a sign system that requires a ground beyond itself, the modern search for meaning becomes one of hermeneutics instead of semiotics.

To describe the fall into the mentality of classical modernity, Edwards situates talk of subjectivity and alienation in a discourse that is itself neither subjective nor alien, because it does not claim to be self-validating or to refer to any transcendent principles. The immanent system of signification constituted by the language of God (expressed in nature and Scripture) does not need to refer to itself or anything beyond itself for legitimacy, for the notion of legitimacy is itself a feature of classical modernity describable only in terms of the divine discursive exchange.

What looks like classical Neoplatonic idealism in Edwards' early philosophic writings thus becomes nothing less than an appeal to a system of signification in which meaning is immanent. Sin is the loss of this sense of immanent meaning within discourse. The semiotics of the Renaissance episteme accounts for what makes discourse (including typological connections) possible; and the seventeenth- and eighteenth-century semiotics of representation (in which thing, idea, and word are not inherently linked) identifies the discursive practices of fallen humanity.

In terms of his semiotics, then, Edwards is less medieval than Renaissance, less Neoplatonic than Stoic. He casts human weakness in terms of Lockean epistemology, and he traces the philosophic difficulties of materialism and idealism precisely to such a mentality. Against this fallen, classical hermeneutic, Edwards contrasts a semiotic system in which relations of signification are immediately accessible in the signs of the language of God. His invocation of the Book of Nature as the language of God draws attention not to the merely metaphoric status consigned to such expression in classical modern discourse, but to the immanent semiotic character of reality thematized in the Renaissance mentality.

To say, as Edwards does, that God is essentially a communicative being is to imply (in the classical, hermeneutic episteme) that as a subject God uses language as a means to communicate ideas to other subjects. By contrast, the Renaissance mentality questions the presumption of subjectivity implicit in that account, and in its place suggests that being itself (including divine being) is always already engaged in relations of signification. This engagement in no way undermines the independence or transcendence of God; indeed, it is what opens the possibility that God can be addressed as a subject with personal characteristics. In the absence of this alternative to the classical understanding of signs, the doctrine of God faces the host of difficulties (e.g., those concerning the predication of divine attributes or divine foreknowledge) generated in classical modern philosophic accounts.

As Kristeva argues, some of these difficulties stem from the Neoplatonic preference for transcendence. She points out, however, that to transcend communicative exchange is to withdraw from the textual matrix in terms of which supposedly transcendent ideas are intelligible in the first place. Ideas are intelligible as functions in practices that define language in virtue of their ability not only to make determinate grammatical relationships, but also to disrupt those relationships through variations of expression.[19] Whatever is signified by an expression does not, therefore, preexist the text; and no text is in-

---

19. See Julia Kristeva, Σημειωτίχή, in *Desire in Language*, ed. Leon S. Roudiez; trans. Thomas Gora, Alice Jardine, and Leon S. Roudiez, 36. Cf. Mark Adriaens, "Ideology and Literary Production: Kristeva's Poetics," in *Semiotics and Dialectics: Ideology and Text*, ed. Peter V. Zima, 188–89.

telligible apart from the permutation of texts or intertextuality by which any text is produced.

This requirement of intertextuality also applies to the self or mind. Just as western grammars mistakenly assume that ideas and words have meaning prior to their appearance in discursive exchanges, so they mistakenly presume that the subject controls at least the intended meaning of an utterance by existing prior to the practices by which expressions become intelligible. Following Jacques Lacan, Kristeva claims that the history and desire of the subject are made objective through the signifying texture of language. Because language contains the potential for grammatical disruption in the form of expressions that refer to no determinate signified thing, it constantly threatens the stability and integrity of the self (since the self is a product of discursive practices).

This threat, characterized by Freud as the unconscious and located by Lacan in language, is not part of a unified self; rather, it is the impulse or drive for signification, the desire that language become a medium of communication for a unitary subject.[20] Ironically, the desire for determinacy and unity is the drive to fulfill and terminate drives. Just as the semiotic impulse within language is resolved when the sign becomes fixed as a symbol, so the subject can become determinate as a structural object of predication. Predication is thus the termination of signifying production, rather than the principle by which it proceeds.

Accordingly, the only way that the subject is capable of realizing its subjectivity and avoids becoming an object of predication is by violating the grammar rules or structures in terms of which it becomes intelligible. This heterogenous character within language is what Kristeva describes as the revolutionary or poetic component of language. It challenges the propriety of autonomous subjectivity and reinscribes subjectivity as the enjoyment *(jouissance)* of the desire for the other.[21] In Edwards' terms, this joy is the ecstacy of the saint's apprehension of God.

Complementing this archaeology of subjectivity, Kristeva provides a historical typology or genealogy of the communicative practices that constitute signification. Though she focuses primarily on the speaking subject, she also discusses the mentalities or "ideologemes" in terms of which subjectivity is formalized. Her chronological divisions do not correspond exactly with Foucault's, but her analysis complements his treatment and shows how elements of Peirce's thought (for example, his distinction of signs into icons, indices, and symbols) can be used to clarify semiotic differences between the Renaissance and classical epistemes.

In thirteenth-century European culture (e.g., literature, painting), Kristeva observes, thought is based on the symbol. The symbol refers to, but does not resemble, an unrepresentable and unknowable universal transcendence. The symbol's ability to communicate meaning precisely relies on its reference to an

20. See Kristeva, "How Does One Speak to Literature?" in *Desire in Language,* 117–20.
21. Julia Kristeva, "The System and the Speaking Subject," in *The Kristeva Reader,* ed. Toril Moi, 28–29; and Julia Kristeva, *Revolution in Poetic Language,* trans. Margaret Waller, 131.

otherworldly context in which distinctions (good-bad, life-death, raw-cooked) are unmuddled by the observed relationships of mundane objects. The terms of these distinctions are neither inherently related to one another nor do they gradually fade off into one another; they are disjunctives that alternately dominate in the "semiotic practice of cosmogony."[22] The function of the symbol is to differentiate objects—not by contrasting them with one another, but by invoking a transcendent other to the system of objects by which they are distinguishable.

As Kristeva notes, the ideologeme of the symbol emphasizes features Peirce associates with the icon. As Kristeva describes it, though, a symbol does not resemble the object it symbolizes (as icons do); it merely alerts us to the fact that the significance of what we experience depends on "unrepresentable and unknowable universal transcendence(s)."[23] In terms of Foucault's account of the classical episteme, the ideologeme of the symbol includes both the Platonic commitment to transcendent forms and the Aristotelian emphasis on immanent forms, insofar as both fail to provide an account of how the referents of symbols themselves come to have meaning.

From the thirteenth to the fifteenth century, Kristeva continues, the shift from the serenity of the symbol to the strained ambivalence of the sign exhibits a recharacterization of the other in terms of the dialogic exchange of irreducible though similar objects.[24] The transcendent referentiality of Gothic cathedrals is replaced by miniatures; comparisons between the otherworldly prophets and the apostles yield to discussions linking the apostles and church fathers. In the displacement of symbolics by semiotics, objects of religious significance become knowable because they can be linked with everything else as members of the same system of exchange. Alternatively, all objects have religious significance, because their meaningfulness lies in their being signifiers or signifieds of one another, always signs of something beyond themselves individually but not of something beyond all signification.

This transcendental (rather than transcendent) sense of the other elevates the semiotic system of exchange, in Kristeva's words, "to the level of theological unity": "The semiotic practice of the sign thus assimilates the metaphysics of the symbol and projects it onto the 'immediately perceptible'. The 'immediately perceptible', valorized in this way, is then transformed into an *objectivity*—the reigning law of discourse in the civilization of the sign."[25] Whereas the metaphysics of the symbol had identified meaning in terms of reference to an other, the ideologeme of the sign recognizes the other within discourse as that which prevents the reduction or "civilization" of the sign into a symbol. Instead of looking for the other in some transcendent realm or in the mind of some subject, semiotics situates oppositional terms "within a network of multiple and

---

22. See Kristeva, Σημειωτίχή, 38. Cf. Adriaens, "Ideology and Literary Production," 197–203.
23. Kristeva, Σημειωτίχή, 38.
24. Ibid.
25. Ibid., 40.

always possible deviations (surprises in narrative structures), giving the illusion
of an *open* structure, impossible to finish, with an *arbitrary* ending."[26] No transcendent forms or transcendental subjectivity provide the ultimate ground for
authorizing meaning, for meaning is understood in terms of a process of textual authorization. In virtue of its place in a tradition of authoritative
commentary, every text thus participates in the intertextuality characteristic of
ongoing semiotic displacement.

In Kristeva's ideologeme of the sign, things are related syntagmatically (to
use Saussure's term) or indexically (to use Peirce's term).[27] That is, they are intelligible horizontally (in history) by means of relations of contiguity and
metonymy. For Foucault, this understanding of meaning characterizes the Renaissance episteme. It emphasizes the immanence of semiotic relations in the
world and avoids the prospect of consigning meaning to an irretrievable
domain. In Kristeva's account, it opens up the possibility for speaking of
otherness in a way that ensures discursive movement. It highlights the ques-
tionable character of the Neoplatonic invocation of an other that transcends
discursive exchange, even while legitimating it. Likewise, it indicts the Aristotelian treatment of what a sign signifies—a concept—by showing how such
a treatment removes the signified from the same domain of discourse as the
sign. Unlike the classical episteme, the Renaissance episteme locates the other
within the system of discourse as the transcendental component of the sign (the
signified) without presuming the transcendence that characterizes the symbol.

As Foucault observes, the medieval Neoplatonic and Aristotelian reduction
of the signifier to a symbol is again taken up in the transformation of the
sign–relation by thinkers of the seventeenth century. In the classical treatment
of the sign, meaning had been tied either to an idea in the mind of God or to
a concept accessible to the human mind. In the hands of thinkers like
Descartes and Locke, for whom the meaning of mind is only accidentally related to discursive exchange, signification is grounded at most on what Kristeva
calls verisimilitude—law-governed associations guaranteed (as Peirce says of
symbols) only by convention.

The removal of the ground of meaning from the exchange of signifiers installs
the ego or transcendent subject as the ultimate determinant of significance and
thus forecloses the possibility of any change of meaning without its authorization. As I will indicate in my chapter on original sin, such a foreclosure essentially
negates the possibility for exchange between the human and the divine; or
rather, it limits it to an economy of sin. If meaning is limited to the symbolic, and
the symbolic is grounded in a referent unimaginable as a signifier, then no discourse is possible, apart from the transgression of the symbolic order.

The Renaissance alternative to this classical preference for the symbolic over
the semiotic treats things as signifiers, not as referents. Always already engaged

26. Ibid.
27. On his distinction between icon, index, and symbol, see Charles S. Peirce, *Peirce on Signs*,
ed. James Hoopes, 181–83, 239–40, 251–52, 270.

in relations of signification, real things (including God and minds) exist only in terms explicable in a semiotic analysis. The thing signified (the *lekton*) is neither a Platonic idea nor an Aristotelian concept located within a speaker's mind. In other words, signs are not terms that function within a logic of predication, for such a logic already legitimates the breach between the subject and what can be expressed of the subject.

In contrast to the classical mentality of Platonism or Aristotelianism, the Stoics think of signs not as things or classes, but as events, the facts that certain sounds or images evoke particular objects. Accordingly, they speak of signifiers and signifieds, rather than signs. A thing signified is located in the "language" of events, and thus it should be understood in terms of propositional logic.[28] Predicate logic, on the other hand, expresses precisely the categorical rigidity that the symbolic casts over the activity of semiotic exchange. It displays the limitations of understanding signs as means of communicating subjective ideas by insisting on the contradictory assumption that those ideas can be meaningful apart from their being either signifiers or signifieds.

For Edwards, the Aristotelian notion of the sign as that which stands in place of a concept more properly describes the fallen condition of subjective, human intellection than it does the nature of things. However, in the divine (Stoic) semiotics that can justify typological claims without being burdened by an epistemology struggling with subjectivity, reality is inherently significant. In it God does not have to add meaning from outside, because even God, as the ultimate signified, the otherness of all objects to one another, participates in the semiotic web.

As Edwards shows in his discussion of the Trinity, this in no way makes God a signifier of some further signified, because neither signifier nor signified need be understood as signs themselves. With St. Augustine, Edwards thus rejects any classical portrayal of God as a sign, since (as the Stoics maintain) signs are not legitimated or made intelligible in virtue of their reference to concepts.[29] Insofar as the communication of signs is understood as the exchange of private thoughts—regardless of whether it involves God or creatures—it simply marks the legacy of the Fall, the sin of subjectivity that the Cartesian cogito authorizes.

If a sign is understood (as in the Stoic-Renaissance account) as a proposition instead of as a predicate, then that which relates the signifier and the signified is not something apart from the relation. No subject or mind is needed to ensure that the signification goes through: reality, on its own and independent of subjects wanting to communicate their ideas, consists of objects related to one another, and those relations constitute signification. The divine appears in such a semiotic analysis as the otherness of every objectivity, as the

28. See Tzvetan Todorov, *Theories of the Symbol*, trans. Catherine Porter, 19–23. For more on Stoic logic, see below, chapter 3.

29. See St. Augustine, *On Christian Doctrine* 2.1.1, discussed in Todorov, *Theories of the Symbol*, 36–44, 291. See also R. A. Markus, "St. Augustine on Signs," and B. Darrell Jackson, "The Theory of Signs in St. Augustine's *De Doctrina Christiana*," in *Augustine: A Collection of Critical Essays*, ed. R. A. Markus, 61–91, 92–147. Cf. Jacques Derrida, *Positions*, trans. Alan Bass, 33, 51.

openness of objects to further relations of signification regulated only by their own characters.

Fittingly, a Stoic-Renaissance semiotics dismisses the centrality of divine subjectivity in dismissing subjectivity as such. Instead of providing a divine teleology based on a model of subjective intention, semiotics offers (in Kristeva's phrase) "a *metonymical concatenation of deviations from the norm* signifying a *progressive creation of metaphors.*"[30] In this ongoing avalanche of metaphorical displacement, the accidents of sheer contiguity that constitute historical relations appear to exhibit no guidance from subjective intentionality. Furthermore, the threat of fate undermines all attempts to impose purpose from outside the system of signs.

The historical contingency of discursive exchange does not rule out the possibility, however, that teleology is immanent, only that teleology is antecedent or requires the prior existence of intentional subjectivity. The semiotic breaks up the intentionality of narrative by threatening the ever-present possibility of unintended signification. The absence of intentionality in no way prevents the process of signification from continuing. It only redefines that process as the juxtaposition of signifiers and signifieds, without presuming the primacy of either thought over language or the symbolic over the semiotic.

As Kristeva insists, signifying practices establish meaning by inscribing the symbolic laws by which signifier and signified are determinately related to and isolated from one another. At the same time, these signifying practices reveal the semiotic as the potential for transgressing those laws. "Although originally a precondition of the symbolic," she writes, "the semiotic functions within signifying practices as the result of a trangression of the symbolic."[31] Apart from the thetic positing of the possibility for transgression, meaning remains indeterminate. By means of such a posit, signifier and signified are separated in the very act of distinction that creates the rupture between subjectivity and objectivity. But because both are conceivable only as functions of the possibility of transgression, neither is intelligible without the consideration of the semiotic process that produces the thetic subject. This prevents the thetic demarcation of the semiotic and the symbolic from reifying the subject as a theological or transcendental ego. The subject, Kristeva concludes, is always both semiotic and symbolic.[32]

The metaphors that form the basis for the subject-object or subject-predicate relations of symbolic thought are themselves characterized as metaphors in terms of those relations. The invention of a metaphor, as Umberto Eco notes, relies on the process of unlimited semiosis whereby language constitutes "a multidimensional network of metonymies," a "subjacent network of arbitrarily stipulated contiguities."[33] Such contiguities are arbitrary from the

30. Kristeva, Σημειωτίχή, 40.
31. *Revolution in Poetic Language*, in *Kristeva Reader*, 118.
32. *Revolution in Poetic Language* (Waller trans.), 25, 48–49, 58–59, 67, 80.
33. Umberto Eco, *The Role of the Reader*, 78. Cf. Jonathan Culler, *The Pursuit of Signs: Semiotics, Literature, Deconstruction*, 201.

perspective of their origination, but once such metonymic concatenations achieve legitimacy as parts of discursive systems of exchange, their arbitrary character is replaced by a retrospective teleological appropriation.

The transformation of a thing from its semiotic matrix of open-ended and indeterminate relatedness into a symbolic and teleological network orders the place of the thing by fixing its relations. This termination of discourse is, in Edwards' terms, the solidification of communication, the resistance to further signification. Such a move to "embody" the sign is, as Peirce admits, itself arbitrary; because "the entire universe is perfused with signs if it is not composed entirely of signs," to identify something as a symbol is to remove it from the immediacy of the experienced relations that characterize other signs.[34] The recognition of that immediacy inhibits the attempt to collapse the prior and mutually distinct though interdependent parts of the signifier-signified relation into a sign that depends for its meaning on its parasitic relation to a concept or idea.

To the extent that an object of experience is incorporated into a system of representation for purposes of communal knowing, its meaning is made more determinate teleologically. Peirce refers to that process of incorporation, "the translation of a sign into another system of signs," as meaning.[35] But unlike Saussure, who treats all signs as arbitrary by treating the signifier-signified relation as arbitrary, Peirce does not conclude that this translation achieves value only in terms of its grounding in an idealism outside of the system of signs.[36] Rather, the action or engagement in the world by which a signifier is realized through its interpretant is possible only within a system of signs.

On the one hand, Saussure adopts the classical understanding of the sign as a component in a scheme to represent an idea. By giving primacy to the conceptual, he rules out the possibilities opened by the Stoic-Renaissance refusal to subordinate signification to thought. Peirce, on the other hand, insists that the meaningfulness or intelligibility of thought relies on the process of translation governed by the discursive exchange of speakers and auditors. That discursive exchange is not directed by human beings; rather, it provides the interpretations by which human beings themselves become intelligible by being signs. In this sense, the self and its thoughts are external and communal productions.

> It is sufficient to say that there is no element whatever in man's consciousness which has not something corresponding to it in the word; and the reason is obvious. It is that the word or sign which man uses *is* the man himself. For, as the fact that every thought is a sign, taken in conjunction with the fact that life is a train of thought, proves that man is a sign; so, that every thought is an *external*

34. Charles S. Peirce, *Collected Papers*, ed. C. Hartshorne, P. Weiss, and A. Burks, 5.448n; and Peirce, *Peirce on Signs*, 258. See Culler, *Pursuit of Signs*, 23–25; and Kaja Silverman, *The Subject of Semiotics*, 16.
35. Peirce, *Collected Papers*, 2.230; and James Jakob Liszka, *The Semiotic of Myth: A Critical Study of the Symbol*, 20–23.
36. Cf. Silverman, *Subject of Semiotics*, 34; Liszka, *Semiotic of Myth*, 54–55; Culler, *Pursuit of Signs*, 24; and Umberto Eco, "Looking for a Logic of Culture," in *The Tell-Tale Sign: A Survey of Semiotics*, ed. Thomas Sebeok, 13.

sign, proves that man is an external sign. That is to say, the man and the external sign are identical, in the same sense in which the words *homo* and *man* are identical. Thus my language is the sum total of myself; for the man is the thought. . . . The individual man, since his separate existence is manifested only by ignorance and error, so far as he is anything apart from his fellows, and from what he and they are to be, is only a negation.[37]

Apart from being integrated into the discursive exchange that provides an (external) interpretant for an individual, the self is simply the negation of intelligibility. The fact that this act of interpretation is not done by a subject using signs, but rather is the process by which practices of significant exchange are specified, all the more throws into question the classical assumption that language can be subordinated to thought. For thought which is unintelligible (i.e., uninterpreted) is no thought at all.

As such, for Peirce a sign does not have an interpreter, a subject for and through whom the sign has meaning. Rather, a sign has an interpretant, a rule of translation that establishes the patterns of action by which an object (the signifier) is related to something else (the signified). The interpretant is a "quasimind" of intercommuncational patterns by which something is recognized as linked to something else.[38] By translating a sign into a symbol—that is, by removing the sign from the generative matrix of discursive exchange and treating it as a component in an arbitrary relation—these patterns identify the sign as a concept. The concept makes the sign more determinate by inscribing it within a teleology. To the extent that a sign is understood purposively, it becomes a symbol. "A symbol," Peirce explains, "is essentially a purpose, that is to say, is a representation that seeks to make itself definite, or seeks to produce an interpretant more definite than itself. For its whole signification consists in its determining an interpretant; so that it is from its interpretant that it derives the actuality of its signification."[39] The interpretant, the discursive practice by which all words, ideas, or things become signs, is thus the teleological criterion for objective realization.

Meaning, in turn, is fulfilled in a concept, where "concept" does not refer to the idea or private thought of any person or mind, but to the material, objective condition for any derivative distinctions. Even though the "symbol-part" of a sign is a concept, it is neither subjective nor separate from its continuing participation in the semiotic process of signification. As in the Stoic account of the sign, the Peircean theory undermines the primacy of the self and in its place substitutes the semiotic network of relations by which everything, including the self, vies for significance.

37. *Peirce on Signs*, 67, 84; and Peirce, *Collected Papers*, 5.313, 5.314. See Colapietro, *Peirce's Approach to the Self*, 42. Cf. Michael L. Raposa, "Jonathan Edwards' Twelfth Sign," *International Philosophical Quarterly* 33 (1993), 159–61.

38. *Peirce on Signs*, 142, 255.

39. C. S. Peirce, *Kaina stocheia*, in *New Elements of Mathematics*, ed. C. Eisele, 4: 261. See Liszka, *Semiotic of Myth*, 20, 22; and J. Jay Zeman, "Peirce's Theory of Signs," in *A Perfusion of Signs*, ed. Thomas A. Sebeok, 37.

This displacement of the self undercuts the classical modern penchant for tracing our insights to human experiences or personal ideas that are supposedly behind or beneath the signs in terms of which we think. As Peirce observes, "All thought must necessarily be in signs."[40] The system of signs precedes all thought, all material difference, all actuality and possibility. Without signs, even divine purpose would have no mooring, no currency of exchange within the system of signification by which to differentiate things. This understanding of divine purpose rules out the possibility of considering God as an intending personality in control of, though distinct from, the world. Instead of challenging the concept of God, however, this approach points out only the impropriety of characterizing God in personalist terms. Indeed, it highlights how, in Peirce's view, God is the ultimate sign, the comprehensive interpretant without which individual signification remains ultimately unintelligible.[41]

In a sense, then, the analyses of Peirce and the more detailed examinations of Kristeva recover a notion of the sign that is lost in the classical substitution of an interpreter for the interpretant. In the displacement of semiotics by hermeneutics, the symbol absorbs the sign by claiming that concepts exist prior to and independently of their expression. According to the classical account, because value and purpose are functions of subjective intentionality, and because no transcendent subjectivity participates in the semiotic exchange of things in the world, value and purpose point beyond signification by pointing beyond a subjective narrative. Within such a classical paradigm, only the Romanticist expansion of transcendental subjectivity can make value and purpose available again in human discourse. This occurs not by means of the Renaissance subsumption of both divine and human subjectivity within a universal system of signification, but by the expansion of subjectivity as the form of a universal symbol.[42] In the context of this Hegelian extension of the cogito's substitution of the sign, Saussure's characterization of signs as arbitrary simply gives up the prospect of relocating teleology within semiology. Peirce's doctrine of the interpretant, by contrast, returns purpose to the field of semiotic exchange by questioning the central role of subjectivity within philosophical idealism.

Of course, such a teleology would depict the lure of divine creativity in terms of metaphorical revisions of syntax that would play havoc with the intransigent semantic structures entombed in predicate logic. In Kristeva's words, the semiotic identifies only the rhythm of transformation, unsettling the identity of meaning and the integrity of the speaking subject. It undermines syntax itself, the guarantor of the consciousness of a signified object or an ego. Appearing

40. Peirce, *Collected Papers*, 5.313; and *Peirce on Signs*, 49, 84, 234, 254, 275. Cf. Zeman, "Peirce's Theory of Signs," 38. For more on Peirce and Edwards, see James Hoopes, *Consciousness in New England: From Puritanism and Ideas to Psychoanalysis and Semiotic*, 198, 203–205, 282–86.

41. See "A Neglected Argument for the Reality of God," in *Peirce on Signs*, 260–67.

42. Cf. De Prospo, *Theism in Jonathan Edwards*, 50–51, 205–221; and Todorov, *Theories of the Symbol*, 221, 285–92.

most explicitly in poetic language, the semiotic identifies the transcendental subject as the structural by-product of the archaic and aboriginal activity of the heterogeneous in the system of thetic, symbolic meaning.[43]

Just as the Kantian-Hegelian reverence for transcendental subjectivity and the Romanticist attachment to self-expression dismiss as irrelevant any account of the world in itself, so the classical episteme's fascination with representing the world displaces the Renaissance reverence for universal significance. But as Richard Rorty points out, the need to hold *anything* in reverence disappears in the postmodern episteme.[44] And that is precisely how the structuralist character of Edwards' divine semiotics distinguishes it from the poststructuralist strategies of postmodernity.

Before examining how the semiotic character of reality expressed in the Renaissance episteme appears in Edwards' doctrines of God, creation, sin, freedom, virtue, beauty, and grace, it is important to get a clear idea of how this theory of signs operates. For as Foucault notes, the mentality of the Renaissance is so remote from much of our own thinking (conditioned as we are by the classical episteme), that to appreciate Edwards requires an understanding of how signs function as "signatures" that pervade reality and thought.

To that end, I have invoked Kristeva's description of signifying practices. Her depiction of the ideologeme of signs corresponds to Foucault's account of the Renaissance episteme. Her particular contribution to his historical taxonomy lies in her clarification of the semiotic strategies that typify different moments in the classical episteme. In the absence of such clarification, Foucault's designation of early modern thought as "classical" seems to ignore ancient and medieval philosophy. However, by drawing on Peirce's distinction of signs as icons, indices, and symbols, Kristeva explains the transition from the ideologeme of symbol to that of sign and then to that of verisimilitude. This, in turn, allows her to differentiate between Neoplatonic (in her terms, symbolic) features of the classical episteme and Aristotelian, Cartesian, or Lockean representationalism. Between these two moments of the classical mentality—that is, between the ideologemes of the symbol and verisimilitude—is the ideologeme of the sign.

By noting how the doctrine of immediate self-knowledge is central in the representationalism of classical modernity, Kristeva can then point out how the mentality of the sign is first and foremost a threat to humanistic or individualistic subjectivity. Unlike Peirce, who mollifies that threat by situating semiotic exchange in a community of interpretation, Kristeva identifies the unconscious, the heterogenity of subjectivity itself, as the semiotic challenge inherent in the

---

43. Kristeva, "From One Identity to An Other," in *Desire in Language*, 135–36; and "Speaking Subject," 31. Cf. Adriaens, "Ideology," 190.

44. See Richard Rorty, *Contingency, Irony, and Solidarity*, 21–22. Cf. Stephen David Ross, *Metaphysical Aporia and Philosophical Heresy*, 284–86, 299–301; and Robert B. Pippin, *Modernism as a Philosophical Problem*, 20–21, 166–67.

desire for representationalist determinacy. Where Peirce's semiotics subverts private intentionality by showing how it is intelligible only in terms of discursive exchange, Kristeva's semiotics highlights the threat posed by the desire for the clarity and distinctness of the symbol. That desire is the longing for an exact match-up among words, ideas, and things, where isolated thought dangerously becomes deed and where all words carry their own magical and incantational invocation of a reality that is purely subjective (indeed, psychotic). At least in the semiotics of the Renaissance episteme, the self is as indeterminate as anything else. Once the self is isolated from discursive exchange, its desire for its own determination requires that it fix all other things in terms relative to itself—what Edwards would have identified as the original sin of pride.

The Renaissance mentality is thus not simply a development of earlier insights of classical thought; rather, it expresses a radical alternative in how intelligibility is defined. Peirce clears away classical presuppositions of representationalist dualism that otherwise would make Foucault's retrieval of the Renaissance mentality difficult, if not impossible. Kristeva extends that enterprise by showing how the classical assumption of the integrity of the self contains the seeds for its own internal disruption. The potential for that disruption, as she makes clear, is inherent to discursive exchange. It is what makes the Renaissance episteme's fascination with the language and textuality of the world—and Edwards' provocative appeal to such a vocabulary—all the more an indictment of the classical subordination of signs to thought.

The Renaissance Episteme

The Renaissance association of the Book of Nature, the heritage of Antiquity, the Scriptures, and the tradition of Biblical commentary reveals a shift from a focus on the symbolic character of things to an appeal to the Ur-text of signs. Like everything else, types and antitypes can be parts of a discursive exchange, because their significance in terms of one another is not limited to their specific relation, but is tied into a system of signification that identifies the web of meaningful discursive practices. Each signifier-signified relation expresses value in virtue of its significance for other sign relations. In this way everything can be said to participate in meaning, insofar as it participates in a semiotic network.

In the Renaissance episteme, resemblance guides exegesis and indicates how the world has been ordered for our benefit. The purpose or order of nature comprises the vast syntax of the world, in which "the plant communicates with the animal, the earth with the sea, man with everything around him."[45] Edwards puts it this way:

> It pleases God to observe analogy in his works, as is manifest in fact in innumerable instances; and especially to establish inferior things in an analogy to

---

45. Foucault, *Order of Things*, 18.

> superior. Thus, in how many instances has he formed brutes in analogy to the
> nature of mankind; and plants, in analogy to animals, with respect to the manner
> of their generation, nutrition, etc.?[46]

The world is simply the universal "convenience" of things, with (as Foucault
notes) the same number of fishes in the water as there are animals on land,
and their numbers correspond exactly to those of the inhabitants of the sky,
just as the same number of the whole of creation is contained eminently in
God. Humanity, as the visible expression or signature of all the figures in the
world drawn together, constitutes the microcosmic sign of the universe.

The system of resemblances unites all aspects of reality in terms of their
mutual communicability. In this universal linguistic web, "The great untroubled
mirror in whose depth things gazed at themselves and reflected their own
images back to one another is, in reality, filled with the murmur of words. The
mute reflections all have corresponding words which indicate them."[47] To learn
the language of that communication—to know, for example, the type of soil
needed for a variety of plant, or that ground walnuts mixed with wine spirits
will ease a headache—requires reading the signatures of similitudes.

> The face of the world is covered with blazons, with characters, with ciphers and
> obscure words—with 'hieroglyphics'. . . . And the space inhabited by immedi-
> ate resemblances becomes like a vast open book; it bristles with written signs;
> every page is seen to be filled with strange figures that intertwine and in some
> places repeat themselves. All that remains is to decipher them. . . . The world is
> covered with signs that must be deciphered, and those signs, which reveal re-
> semblances and affinities, are themselves no more than forms of similitude. To
> know must therefore be to interpret: to find a way from the visible mark to that
> which is being said by it and which, without that mark, would lie like unspoken
> speech, dormant within things.[48]

Signatures require deciphering, because no figure is an exact and indistinguishable resemblance of that of which it is the sign. Because they are written, the
characters of the book of the world are marked legibly as discrete; they are
distanced by the visible and irremedial presence of the sign. Their so-called
strangeness indicates how the forms of resemblance protect the signature as
signifier from being assimilated into the signified.

Interpretation does not attempt to remove the visibility of the signified. Far
from it: by keeping the meaning of the sign-relation within the domain of experience—Edwards' celebrated "idealism"—the scripted (scriptural) distancing
of the signature ensures its historical legitimacy. Indeed, the semiotic resistance
to the attempt to locate meaning in transcendent terms reinstates the propriety
of history itself without reducing history to human history. Interpretation is
needed precisely because signatures do not exist solely to be brushed aside
once their signifieds are identified. Their otherness remains, but it remains

46. *The Nature of True Virtue*, in *Ethical Writings*, ed. Paul Ramsey, 564.
47. Foucault, *Order of Things*, 27.
48. Ibid., 26, 28, 32.

within the semiotic order, the order of experienced signs. In this way, signatures retain the "shadow and image of God" as a natural dowry, marks of the similitudes that guide and determine knowledge about nature, history, and humanity's destiny.

> There is no difference between the visible marks that God has stamped upon the surface of the earth, so that we may know its inner secrets, and the legible words that the Scriptures, or the sages of Antiquity, have set down in the books preserved for us by tradition. The relation of these texts is of the same nature as the relation to things: in both cases there are signs that must be discovered. . . . The heritage of Antiquity, like nature itself, is a vast space requiring interpretation; in both cases there are signs to be discovered and then, little by little, made to speak. In other words, *divinatio* and *eruditio* are both part of the same hermeneutics; but this develops, following similar forms, on two different levels: one moves from the mute sign to the thing itself (and makes nature speak); the other moves from the unmoving graphism to clear speech (it restores sleeping languages to life). But just as natural signs are linked to what they indicate by the profound relation of resemblance, so the discourse of the Ancients is in the image of what it expresses; if it has the value of a precious sign, that is because, from the depth of its being, and by means of the light that has never ceased to shine through it since its origin, it is adjusted to the things themselves, it forms a mirror for them and emulates them; it is to eternal truth what signs are to the secrets of nature (it is the mark whereby the word may be deciphered); and it possesses an ageless affinity with the things that it unveils. It is useless therefore to demand its title to authority; it is a treasury of signs linked by similitude to that which they are empowered to denote. . . . The truth of all these marks— whether they are woven into nature itself or whether they exist in lines on parchments and in libraries—is everywhere the same: coeval with the institution of God. There is no difference between marks and words in the sense that there is between observation and accepted authority, or between verifiable fact and tradition. The process is everywhere the same: that of the sign and its likeness, and this is why nature and the word can interwine with one another to infinity, forming, for those who can read it, one vast single text.[49]

The Book of Nature, the writings of the ancients, and the Scriptures resemble one another in virtue of their textuality, that is, in virtue of their divinely instituted power to signify. Being is signification, marking the presence of something else. Knowledge consists "in relating one form of language to another form of language; in restoring the great, unbroken plain of words and things; in making everything speak"; it provides a commentary on a primal Text "whose return it simultaneously promises and postpones."[50] The infinity of textual commentary and significatory ability marks the presence or embodi-

49. Ibid., 26, 33–34. On signatures as the shadow and image of God, Foucault cites Oswald Croll's *Tractatus de signaturis internis rerum* (1608); French translation, *Traité des signatures* (1624); English translation, *Signatures of Internal Things* (1669). Cf. Daniel Stempel, "Blake, Foucault, and the Classical Episteme," *PMLA* 96 (1981), 389.

50. Foucault, *Order of Things*, 40–41. Cf. Allen G. Debus, *The Chemical Philosophy: Paracelsian Science and Medicine in the Sixteenth and Seventeenth Centuries*, 1:69–70.

ment of God as the Text's invitation to infinite signification and exegesis, not the transcendence of the Text itself.

In Edwards' expression of the Renaissance episteme, the historical type is not subsumed by an eternal antitype, nor are the elect absorbed into God. Each historical individual maintains its own integrity as a real and discrete component in the discursive exchange of signs. That exchange is not a human exchange, just as the history in which humanity is located is not a distinctly human history. The meaning of human existence, like everything else, is not expressed in human terms, because the very definition of what constitutes human as well as divine emerges in the semiotic exchange inscribed as the textuality of existence.[51]

To be precise, within the semiotics of the Renaissance there is no divine discourse, there is no human discourse: there is only discourse. In the exchange of discursive practices, in which signifiers resemble their signifieds and displace other signifiers, history achieves determinateness and significance. To call this a historical process is possible only in after-the-fact terms, because there is no external historical context in which these discursive exchanges occur or in terms of which they are intelligible.

As Foucault notes, the account of this Renaissance mentality must include an explanation of how signatures can identify exactly what they signify and yet be distinguished from their signifieds by a "tiny degree of displacement" in their forms of resemblance.[52] Tied to one another for their meaning, signifier and signified would mirror each other in an identity were they to obey the same law of distribution. But their distribution throughout the world according to different ways in which they resemble other things keeps the similitudes that form the graphics of the world one cog out of alignment with those that form its discourse.

In other words, the actual appearance of a thing in a certain place affects what it is in virtue of its resemblance to other things in its environment. Sharing that environment with other things in part defines the thing and identifies ways it resembles others. The meaning of nature, as constituted in these similitudes, is overlain by signatures differentiated from one another by their figural, historical juxtapositions. Were it not for their historical facticity, signifiers would be assimilated immediately by their signifieds in a coalescence of interpretation and signification. The differentiation of things in terms of signifiers and signifieds constitutes the network of exchanges and practices that stipulate a syntax for the identification of meaning and the designation of reality. By alluding to the prospect of meaning, a semiotics of signatures draws attention to the need for interpretation established by the displacement of signs by one another.

---

51. No one has done a better job of distinguishing the otherness of Edwards' theistic discourse from Romanticist humanism than De Prospo, in *Theism in Jonathan Edwards*, especially 54, 74, 140–43, 200, 205.

52. Foucault, *Order of Things*, 28–29. Also see Foucault, "Nietzsche, Freud, Marx," 60.

In Edwards' account, signifiers and signifieds are identical in terms of their mutual relation of identity. Their similarity, or identity of relation, is the promise that significance, meaning, or (in Edwards' term) beauty can be achieved because of, rather than in spite of, the multiplicity of signifiers and signifieds. In this very un-Platonic doctrine:

> All beauty consists in similarness, or identity of relation. In identity of relation consists all likeness, and all identity between two consists in identity of relation. . . . Two beings can agree with one another in nothing else but relation; because otherwise the notion of their twoness (duality) is destroyed and they become one. And so in every case, what is called correspondency, symmetry, regularity and the like, may be resolved into equalities; though the equalities in a beauty in any degree complicated are so numerous that it would be a most tedious piece of work to enumerate them. There are millions of these equalities. Of these consist the beautiful shape of flowers, the beauty of the body of man and of the bodies of other animals.[53]

Related to one another so intimately that their relations identify their identities, individual things cannot be thought of as individual apart from the variety of relations ("equalities") that at once distinguish yet tie them to one another. Even though these equalities constitute the interpretive harmony by which meaning is defined, the irreducible discreteness of signatures protects the enumerability of their relations.

The universe of signs (the graphics of the world) exhibits the practices (the forms of resemblance) by which order or meaning emerges. But this semiotic of signatures is out of alignment with the discourse by which meaning is defined, because meaning is a product of, not a condition for, the juxtaposition of signatures. As much as they describe the ways in which the world is meaningful, the forms of resemblance by which things are known as meaningful are not necessarily the same forms by which signs resemble one another. If a signifier could be "read" literally as a communication (e.g., as part of a language of vision), then its homology to a signified would identify their communicative association in terms of the resemblance of the interpreted meaning of the signifier and the significance of the sign. "Everything would be manifest and immediately knowable if the hermeneutics of resemblance and the semiology of signatures coincided without the slightest parallax."[54] Semiotics locates significance or meaning in the resemblances of signs, whereas hermeneutics accounts for the resemblance of signs in terms of their meaning or significance. The reason that semiotics and hermeneutics cannot come together on this point stems from the hermeneutic assumption that signs have meaning prior to their resemblances—an assumption that, from a semiotic perspective, cannot be justified.

Because signifiers resemble not only their signifieds, but also other signatures according to different forms of resemblance, an account of the "grammar

---

53. Edwards, "The Mind," #1, in *Scientific and Philosophical Writings*, ed. Wallace E. Anderson, 334–35.
54. Foucault, *Order of Things*, 30.

of beings" requires an exegesis of the syntax that binds signs together in a communicative network. This syntax of signatures identifies a signature as communicating a signification at the same time as designating that signification as another sign. The syntax situates signification solely in a system of signs.

However, even within the system, different forms of resemblance permit different interpretations of significance. In addition to convenience (the association of things in virtue of their adjacency or proximity), the forms of resemblance include emulation (the parallel of attributes of one thing in another), analogy (the resemblance of relations between things), and sympathy/antipathy (the attraction/repulsion of things to one another). Things differ and so achieve meaning, because the signatures by which they are designated enact different forms of resemblance. This inscription of semiotic differentiation marks "that tiny degree of displacement which causes the sign of sympathy to reside in an analogy, that of analogy in emulation, that of emulation in convenience, which in turn requires the mark of sympathy for its recognition."[55] The constant displacement of signs by one another provides for the possibility of discursive development; but it also opens the door to the imaginative flights of fancy that become objects of ridicule for classical thinkers.

In justifying his own typological speculations, Edwards is sensitive to such concerns. He insists that, because his observations are grounded in the nature of things, the connections he highlights should be obvious to anyone who properly considers how creation embodies the divine communication. Insofar as the nature of things is defined in terms of their communicative significance, and insofar as the communicative significance of things resides literally in the resemblances of their figural, textual characters, typological inquiries must permeate the entire philosophic enterprise. This understanding of typology encompasses all other forms of knowing, because it locates meaning in the displacement of signs by one another, amounting to nothing less than a description of discursive activity itself.

In providing such a description, Edwards takes seriously the prospect that, indeed, the Word has been made Flesh, that the communicated presence of an absent infinity is already contained in the signifiability of the sign. As is obvious from his early so-called idealist writings, the creation with which Edwards is concerned does not countenance the radical distinctions of sign and thing or idea and object that support the attempt to move beyond the immediacy of signs. Because all things, including words and ideas, are signs, they resemble one another and are differentiated, in Foucault's terminology, by precisely the same forms of resemblance (convenience, emulation, analogy, sympathy) that link them.

In this infinite play of similitudes the totality of signs forms the text of an unequivocal message, inspiring the infinite task of a commentary that "resembles

55. Ibid., 29. Cf. Vickers, "Analogy Versus Identity," 95–97, 106, 122; and Hugh Ormsby-Lennon, "Rosicrucian Linguistics: Twilight of a Renaissance Tradition," in *Hermeticism and the Renaissance: Intellectual History and the Occult in Early Modern Europe*, ed. Ingrid Merkel and Allen G. Debus, 311–41.

endlessly that which it is commenting upon and which it can never express."
The divine cause of differentiation—for example, how things not spatially adjacent can be analogous—resides in the text of the world as the otherness to
anything in the world, the otherness of textuality. The otherness of the signified cannot be expressed, because resemblance cannot be known in itself.
Commentary produces interpretation within the play of resemblances by super-
imposing a semiology upon a hermeneutics. By providing another text,
commentary discovers meaning in the signifying function of the "language" of
things, revealing the semiotic character of all existence.[56] Once the integrity
of this significatory procedure is established, the presence of God as the lure
of meaning and significance within the world is ensured.

To some, this fashionable poststructuralist vocabulary might seem out of
place in discussing Edwards, but I appeal to it to emphasize both its resonance
with contemporary discussions and with the literal way in which Edwards' talk
of divine communication assumes a network of connections rejected in the
classical episteme. As the scheme underlying Edwards' doctrines of knowing
and being, Foucault's account of forms of resemblance and the semiotic interpretation of signatures identifies the strategy that permeates not only
Edwards' typology, but also other aspects of his philosophy that allude to the
integrity of creation. By grouping these different aspects in semiotic codes
trading in the "language" of God, Edwards thematizes the discursive practices
that characterize his description of prelapsarian existence and the epistemological and metaphysical conditions of the elect.

When Edwards discusses the communicative condition of fallen nature,
though, he invokes the classical understanding of signs. In the classical episteme, language is meaningful or significant only insofar as it represents the
world. In re-presenting things, words lose their kinship with the world. That
kinship, recognized by the Stoic-Renaissance conjunction of signifier and signified in the similitudes of marks and the things they designate, disappears when
language is restricted to the general organization of representative signs.

In the Renaissance episteme, spoken or written language (as that which
marks or is marked) is always already inscribed in the text of the world. The
third element of the Renaissance theory of the sign, resemblance, makes it
possible to see in the first mark the mark of the second; it provides the
Peircean interpretant guiding the process by which the meaning of the text is
made more determinate. In the classical episteme, on the other hand, the
pervasive linguistic characterization of existence is undermined in the transformation of the ordering of signs into a tool for conceptual analysis:

> It is here that knowledge breaks off its kinship with *divinatio*. The latter always
> presupposed signs anterior to it: so that knowledge always resided entirely in
> the opening up of a discovered, affirmed, or secretly transmitted, sign. Its task
> was to uncover a language which God had previously distributed across the face

---

56. Foucault, *Order of Things*, 41, 59.

of the earth; it is in this sense that it was the divination of an essential implication, and that the object of its divination was *divine*. From now on, however,
it is within knowledge itself that the sign is to perform its signifying function; it
is from knowledge that it will borrow its certainty or its probability. And though
God still employs signs to speak to us through nature, he is making use of our
knowledge, and of the relations that are set up between our impressions, in
order to establish in our minds a relation of signification.[57]

The conversational accessibility of God in the Garden of Eden and the linguistic immediacy of Adamic naming are displaced in the Fall by a system of
signs geared to human intellection. No longer bound to a world of resemblances, the relation of signifier to signified is not guaranteed by things,
but resides only in the knowledge relation of one idea to another. Because the
discourse of representation separates language from things in order to mark
thoughts, the divinely authored text of the world is reduced to a metaphor for
how the order of linguistic expression represents relations of ideas. Only
madmen and poets continue to find secret affinities in nature.

The classical order of ideas avoids arbitrariness, however, by relocating significance in forms of representation in which ideas are related to one another
in terms of probability, analysis, combination, or the attempt to establish an
artificial universal language system. The relations of things are fixed by
ordering them epistemologically in terms of differential structures of measure-
ment, taxonomies, and genesis.

Insofar as each idea resembles other ideas (i.e., as a representation), it is a
sign (no longer the signifier component of a signifier-signified unity). The
emergence of the sign disenfranchises the signifier in authorizing the autonomy
of representation. Because it is not tied ontologically to any particular signified
and indicates only "the *representativity* of the representation insofar as it is
representable," the classical sign becomes coextensive with thought as a
whole.[58] In severing the sign from a primary text of the world and limiting it
to a universal science (or *mathesis*) of order, classical semiotics captures what
is signified within the reach of the sign. The sign thus determines the significance or meaning of the signified by means of how the signified is
incorporated into the structures of relation governing representation.

In the classical episteme, no *theory* of the sign is possible because nothing
is prior to or conceivable apart from the sign. Any proposed theory of signs
would constitute simply a self-justifying ideology of representation that would
provide an analysis of meaning in terms of classifications of the arrangement
of signs. By distancing the historical and material immediacy of language from
the immaterial transcendence of meaning or significance, the classical treatment of signs privileges structures of human discourse over the discursive
practices in which those structures arise.

---

57. Ibid., 59. Cf. Eve Tavor Bannet, *Structuralism and the Logic of Dissent: Barthes, Derrida,
Foucault, Lacan*, 145–48.
58. Foucault, *Order of Things*, 64–68, 79. Cf. Major-Poetzl, *Foucault's Archaeology*, 170–73.

Edwards' divine semiotics combines elements of both the Renaissance and classical epistemes. In discussing what makes reality intelligible, he appeals to a vocabulary of divine communication in which discursive exchanges do not rely on autonomous selves intent on overcoming the inherent lack of integrity within signification. Therefore, one of the greatest challenges in reading Edwards' remarks about creation as a divine communication lies in getting beyond the classical assumption that communication occurs between discrete subjects. Retrieving the Renaissance sense of the pervasive textual significance of the world points in the direction of overcoming that hurdle.

Still, the sinful and fallen condition of human experience requires that Edwards turn often to the distancing rhetoric of representation, even if it is only to show how the discursive practices of such a mentality can be subverted by attending to their graphic, rhetorical, or metaphorical features. Without such a semiotic turn, human cognition is effectively isolated from access to any form of signification other than humanist or Romanticist schemes that minimize the need for divine intervention. But by embedding significance in representation, the classical episteme confines the meaning of discourse to relations of representation.

In terms of typology, the classical episteme scarcely offers the kind of ontological support required to justify Edwards' claims. In such a mentality the type would limit the meaning of the antitype, and the antitype's significance would be contained in the type as the means by which the antitype is known. An antitype like Christ would be recognized by means of a type (e.g., Abraham), and the significance or meaning of the type would rest on its connection to the antitype by means of its representation of the antitype. Since no such epistemology could justify the ontological claims for type-antitype relations in the first place, Edwards has to appeal to a strategy other than representationalism. That appeal to semiotics, as Anderson suspected, goes beyond the discussion of Edwards' typology. How far that sensitivity to semiotics extends is the concern of the subsequent chapters.

II

THE DISCOURSE OF TYPOLOGY

Beginning with Perry Miller's 1948 edition of Edwards' *Images or Shadows of Divine Things,* much of the critical scholarship devoted to Edwards' typology refers only in passing to his concurrent references to the language of nature in which types are expressed. Commentators agree that, for Edwards, natural things exhibit a spiritual meaning in terms of what God intends them to communicate, but the fact that nature appears in Edwards' presentation as a language is often assumed to be merely a metaphorical convention. It is argued that, because Edwards speaks of the world as a divine communication throughout his writings, his invocation of the vocabulary of the Book of Nature can hardly be said to have any particular significance for the study of types. Indeed, if his talk of the linguistic or communicative nature of reality reveals more than a rhetorical maneuver, it signals the underlying conditions for the possibility of communal reasoning in general.

No doubt the pervasive presence of relations of signification in Edwards' philosophy includes much more than his typology. I suggest, however, that Edwards bases the justification for his claims of typological relations on a broader theory of communicative exchange. Accordingly, his association of typological relations with "The Language and Lessons of Nature" points to a theory of meaning in which typology unites the significatory and revelatory characters of nature as functions of God's scripted and scriptural activity.

Typology, therefore, is not as central to Edwards' philosophy as it is key to determining the underlying system of relations that legitimate the strategies of rationality employed in his other discussions. Without access to those strategies of communicative signification, we cannot understand *why* typology is connected to his doctrines of the Trinity, original sin, freedom, virtue, or beauty, even if we can understand *how* such topics are related.

This chapter begins with an examination of the syntax of signification that regulates Edwards' theory of meaningful exchange. The second part of the chapter indicates how typology, as the point of convergence of natural and revelational instruction, functions in the system of relations that makes meaning possible. The third section focuses on how Edwards develops a general system of signification in the context of typology, with special attention given to the Scriptural extension of discourse.

The Vocabulary of Nature

Underlying Edwards' repeated references to the world as a divine communication, or to the book or language of nature, is always the assumption that
interlocutors in this discourse are engaged in an educative process of formu-
lating the characteristics of meaningful reality. Aboriginally, there is no teacher,
no student, no language: there is only the exchange of sights and sounds that
become differentiated as communication in the development of semantic and
syntactic relations that identify a community of language users. Even the distinctions of God, nature, and self become meaningful only through the
establishment of elements of exchange in this network of relations. Accordingly, the linguisticality or communicability of a being situates it as a being
relative to other beings. In fact, the constitutive and educative process that establishes these relations at the same time establishes the ontological
characteristics of what it means to be a being.

When Edwards, then, experiments with titles for his "Images of Divine Things,"
he associates "The Book of Nature" with "Common Providence," and the "Language of Nature" with the "Lessons of Nature."[1] Such a move concedes that no
book can be read without guidance, no language can be understood apart from
the lessons by which it is learned. In the process of coming into being, the language permits the distinction of the teacher and the student and thus opens the
possibility for community by means of the discrimination of objects made
meaningful by their being situated in discourse. An object is situated in discourse
by means of the juxtapositions of figural signs. The signs are differentiated in
virtue of patterns of juxtapositions of sights and sounds, and the patterns themselves constitute the bases for semantic and syntactic differentiation.

As Edwards notes in his "Personal Narrative," the sun, moon, stars, grass,
trees, and so on are the "words of nature," figurally distinct from one another,
but alike as simple signs, associated with one another (to use Saussure's term)
paradigmatically as mute signs or words with no meaning apart from their
mutual differentiation. By appearing in some discursive exchange—that is, by
being distinguished syntagmatically from other similar signs—they are situated
semantically and syntactically; only then do they mean something.[2]

The exchange of signs thus establishes the codes for distinguishing meanings
and for combining them to form understandable messages. The "voice of God's

---

1. See Perry Miller, ed., *Images or Shadows of Divine Things,* by Jonathan Edwards, 1; and Wallace E. Anderson, ed., "Images of Divine Things," and "Types" Notebook, in Jonathan Edwards,
Typological Writings, ed. Wallace E. Anderson and Mason I. Lowance, Jr., with David Watters, 9,
34–35. Miller's title for Edwards' "Images of Divine Things" is *Images or Shadows of Divine Things.*
2. See Edwards, "Personal Narrative," in *The Life of President Edwards,* in vol. 1 of Sereno E.
Dwight's edition of *The Works of President Edwards,* reprinted in *Jonathan Edwards: Representative Selections,* ed. Clarence H. Faust and Thomas H. Johnson, 61. Cf. Kaja Silverman, *The Subject
of Semiotics,* 10–11, 104; and Jonathan Culler, *The Pursuit of Signs: Semiotics, Literature, Deconstruction,* 23.

thunder," like the other signs in nature, can communicate and signify only if there is a shared language. Things in the world constitute a mute vocabulary prior to their educating us in the harmonies and juxtapositions that allude to the transcendentality of signs.[3] Within the mutual displacement of signs, the world embodies the transcendental impulse of instruction. The order of things is inherently instructive not because there is some fixed order of intelligibility in which the divine harmony is eternally frozen as a structural architectonic, but because the music of the divine plays on in endless displacement.

This process, by which both subjects and objects are defined, does not assume a fixed content to be mastered, for that would ignore the living character of the language, the openness of the language to semantic and syntactic revision. The openness to conceptual realignments invites the participation of subjects other than God in the co-creation of a community of meaning. The conversation of God is thus more than simply a one-way transmission of God to us; it is the establishment or confirmation of community through communication.[4] As such, the linguisticality of God is the educative lure of all parts of reality toward their own immanent transcendentality.

As in any language, the language of God's speech requires an ability to discern idiomatic differences in actual usage. The more one is sensitive to the beauty of the communicative exchanges characteristic of a language, the more one is able to appreciate creative combinations of expression. Such combinations are relished by those who understand languages (including God's language) not only in terms of their formal structures (*langue*) but also in terms of the idiomatic—and sometimes idiosyncratic—complex of linguistic events (*parole*) that identify languages as developmental.

In his "Types" Notebook Edwards points out that typological thinking is modelled on just such a linguistic practice. He makes clear that the practice he has in mind is not that of formal languages or languages that one can study in order to master diction or expression. The language of types, like the language of God, embodies the "as it were" character of the idiom of a language. Just as the idiom of a language cannot be reduced to rules of grammar, so the discursive exchanges of nature and Scripture cannot be reduced to the categorical formulations characteristic of classical modernity's treatment of language.

> Types are a certain sort of language, as it were, in which God is wont to speak to us. And there is, as it were, a certain idiom in that language which is to be learnt the same that the idiom of any language is, viz. by good acquaintance with the language, either by being naturally trained up in it, learning it by education (but that is not the way in which corrupt mankind learned divine language),

3. See Edwards, "Images," 74. Cf. Richard C. De Prospo, *Theism in the Discourse of Jonathan Edwards*, 85.

4. See Edwards, Miscellany #1338 [after 1755]. Cf. Robert W. Jenson, *America's Theologian: A Recommendation of Jonathan Edwards*, 191–92. Unless noted otherwise, references to Edwards' Miscellanies are to his manuscripts (as transcribed by Thomas Schafer) located in the Beinecke Library, Yale University. Citations from other editions, such as Harvey G. Townsend, ed., *The Philosophy of Jonathan Edwards*, have been silently emendated based on the Schafer texts.

or by much use and acquaintance together with a good taste of judgment, by comparing one thing with another and having our senses, as it were, exercised to discern it (which is the way that adult persons must come to speak any language, and in its true idiom, that is not their native tongue). Great care should be used, and we should endeavor to be well and thoroughly acquainted, or we shall never understand [or] have a right notion of the idiom of the language. If we go to interpret divine types without this, we shall be just like one that pretends to speak any language that han't thoroughly learnt it. We shall use many barbarous expressions that fail entirely of the proper beauty of the language, that are very harsh in the ears of those that are well versed in the language. God han't expressly explained all the types of Scriptures, but has done so much as is sufficient to teach us the language.[5]

The divine education in the language of types concentrates on the development of good taste, the ability to discern the beauty of expression—not in strict adherence to those types explained in the Scriptures, but in the exercise of the sensual comparisons by which discernment itself is possible. The language of types is the proto-language ("the true idiom") of discourse, insofar as it expresses the transcendental character of anything that is discerned. But just as each syntactic determination of elements in a language makes meaning available through fixing the grammatical and semantic possibilities for those elements, so also do acts of discernment display the idiomatic (even poetic) violability of such acts.

The language that types teach us is thus not only idiomatic; it is also a recommendation for idiomaticity. The typological relations identified in the Scriptures set up the idiom in which we learn how to develop facility in discerning relations of signification. But more importantly, the very existence of typological relations demonstrates how divine discourse exhibits beauty and meaning not in terms that transcend the discourse, but in terms of the recognition that every term in the language is known by comparison with others. Therefore, everything is intelligible in virtue of pointing to its own transcendental possibility within idiomatic discourse.

Typological relations cannot be Platonic instantiations of fixed, eternal meanings, because such relations would not acknowledge or respect the revelatory and educative immediacy of spoken and written words. The idiom of a living language embodies such immediacy in its sensitivity to the changing proprieties of words as they are actually expressed in experience. As Edwards insists, "Types are a sort of words: they are a language, or signs of things which God would reveal, point forth, and teach, as well as vocal or written words."[6] Types are much closer to audible or visible marks than they are to concepts, in that they reveal in their presentational order a constitution of meaning grounded in acquaintance with linguistic practices.

5. Edwards, "Types" Notebook [mid-1740s], 150–51.
6. Edwards, "Comment on the Gospel of John 10:34–36," *The Works of President Edwards*, ed. Samuel Austin, 2:486; cited in Paula M. Cooey, *Jonathan Edwards on Nature and Destiny: A Systematic Analysis*, 119.

By treating the world as a domain of types, Edwards extends the notion of linguisticality beyond spoken and written words without, at the same time, subordinating language to concepts or thoughts to which words might be supposed to refer. This does not mean that typology is equivalent to the larger discursive network of significatory relations that identifies typological relations as meaningful. It means that Edwards' invocation of the vocabulary of linguisticality can be justified only by a semiotic strategy that cannot be reduced to a mere rhetorical device. Thus, when Wilson Kimnach refers to the larger patterns of typology in Edwards' account of nature and history as a "divine syntax"; or when Roland Delattre notes that, for Edwards, beauty is central to "the vocabulary and syntax" of the language of God; or when Paula Cooey claims that "nature provides the grammar, and history the syntax" in Edwards' doctrine of divine destiny, each commentator points, knowingly or not, to the strategy that makes possible not only typology, aesthetics, science, and history, but all thought and reasoning.[7]

To say that nature is a communication from God, however, raises the more fundamental question as to what permits Edwards to treat nature as a communication in the first place. Why do things in nature bear an image to things divine? How and why are natural things necessarily linked to divine things? Why does the vocabulary of language and communication figure so prominently in Edwards' discussions? What epistemological and metaphysical importance can relations of signification have in understanding other areas of Edwards' thought?

Such questions only hint at the broader syntax of signification necessary to account for Edwards' typology. For, as Edwards himself was aware, the semiotic strategy that underlies typological relations is certainly not obvious. Much of Edwards' *Religious Affections,* for example, catalogues how external signs are notoriously undependable as indicators of true religious affections.[8] What we experience in the world may signify spiritual realities that transcend our experiences, but there seems to be very little in those experiences to guarantee inferences from one order of being to the other.

As I will argue more fully in the chapter on original sin, the failure of signs to serve as reliable indices for spiritual realities stems from a misunderstanding of the nature of a sign. To the extent that a sign is considered meaningful apart from that of which it is a sign—that is, insofar as a signifier is considered as an independent sign—the unity of the significatory relation disintegrates. Original sin marks this disintegration of signification, this fall from the Stoic-Renaissance concept of the signifier-signified unit into the classical, Aristotelian-Lockean replacement of the signifier with the sign. When no longer

---

7. See Wilson H. Kimnach, ed., *Sermons and Discourses, 1720–1723,* by Jonathan Edwards, 236; Roland A. Delattre, *Beauty and Sensibility in the Thought of Jonathan Edwards,* 206; and Cooey, *Jonathan Edwards,* 12.

8. See Jonathan Edwards, *Religious Affections,* ed. John E. Smith, 193–96. Cf. Jenson, *America's Theologian,* 84–85.

connected internally with what it signifies, a sign loses its ability to indicate anything dependably. The fall into classical modernity thus threatens much more than typology, for it raises the prospect of skeptical challenges to all inferential or discursive proceedings.

Because typological inferences are so susceptible to the charge of imaginative fancy—especially in a postlapsarian environment—Edwards has to reformulate the problematic in terms of which typological reasoning has become suspect. He has to show how the supernatural and the natural are intrinsically related to one another, without reducing either to the other's terms. For to translate the natural into supernatural terms is to make it unintelligible, and to translate the supernatural into natural terms is to efface its very character. In particular, Edwards worries that his doctrine of the typological character of natural things might be taken to imply that, in order to be significant, natural objects must be supplanted by their supernatural counterparts. He admits that natural things are meaningful in virtue of their transcendental or significatory character. But as his repeated celebrations of natural things indicate, he is far from willing to denigrate nature simply to replace it with a transcendent spirituality.

His solution to this dilemma requires that he focus on natural things less as static objects than as events or markers of activity. The more he is able to work us away from the mentality that things are intelligible apart from their actual engagements in history, the more he is able to frame the question of significance in the propositional (rather than predicational) context appropriate for typology.

For example, visions of future events can be meaningful because they tap into typological relations without assuming a connection between the ideational content of the vision and the future event itself. The visions recounted in the Old Testament were not about any future determinate event considered by itself, for its intelligibility as an event seen in a vision depends specifically on its futurity relative to the vision. What makes something a vision is not its anticipation of some future event, but its affirmation that its own intelligibility does not reside in itself.

> We find by the Old Testament that it has ever been God's manner from the beginning of the world to exhibit and reveal future things by symbolical representations, which were no other than types of the future things revealed. Thus when future things were made known in visions, the things that were seen were not the future things themselves, but some other things that were made use of as shadows, symbols or types of the things.[9]

When a future thing is known in a vision, its knowability as something in the future depends not upon the prior existence of the future thing, but on the prospect that the present thing has significance in virtue of something beyond itself. The meaning of something consists in its pointing to an other whose sig-

9. Edwards, "Types of the Messiah," Miscellany #1069 [mid-1740s], in *Typological Writings*, 192.

nificance is intrinsically linked to it within the same semiotic (in this case, temporal) network. This supposition of transcendental fulfillment in typological relations provides the framework for justifying connections between the content of the vision and the actual future event. Without such a framework, any supposed connection is at best accidental and at worst contrived.

The typological character of a thing thus consists in its indication that its meaning depends on something other than itself. What makes it a type is not its antitype, for that would accept as meaningful the prior discrete existence of both things. It is a type insofar as its meaning is understood not in terms of some particular other, but rather in terms of its otherness, its demand that there be an antitype.

Without its signified (the antitype), the signifier (the type) is meaningless. For those bound to the mentality of fallen creation, all claims of signification appear arbitrary: Natural things are simply what they are. Their otherness from other things is purely accidental, and any significance they may have relative to something else is merely a product of subjective fancy. Because they are considered intelligible apart from their association with something else, claims about their significance do not presume any real validity. To some, a newborn's cries might signify our condition of being born to sorrow; or our animal-like birth might be seen as a sign of the ignorance and brutishness of humanity. But such instances of signification are not properly shadows or images of divine things, because they allude to no intrinsic rationale for making the connection.[10]

By contrast, in their spiritual or typological capacity, natural things signify their otherness, their immanent transcendentality. They provide the "proper and true image" of divine things by signifying how their own intelligibility consists in the true thing that is what their transcendentality is an idea of. As Edwards explains, the idea of a thing is perfected only in the idea of the thing as other (i.e., as antitype). Correspondingly, an idea is perfected only by the thing of which it is the idea. As Edwards puts it, a perfect idea is the thing itself:

> Seeing a perfect idea of a thing is, to all intents and purposes, the same as seeing the thing. It is not only equivalent to seeing of it; it *is* seeing of it, for there is no other seeing, but having an idea. Now by seeing a perfect idea, so far as we see it we have it; but it cant be said of anything else, that in seeing of it we see another, speaking strictly, except it be the very idea of the other.[11]

Here Edwards is not simply reiterating a theme typically associated with his supposed idealism. Instead he provides a key for undercutting the theory of meaning implicit in the idealism-materialism dichotomy itself. A perfect idea of a thing is the thing itself. But in seeing the thing itself, we see only an idea

10. See Edwards, "Images," 57. Cf. Ursula Brumm, "Jonathan Edwards and Typology," in *Early American Literature,* ed. Michael T. Gilmore, 81.
11. Miscellany #260 [1728].

of the thing as long as the thing and the thing of which it is an idea are different. If the thing and the idea of the thing are the same, then the idea of the
thing is perfect. The idea, in short, is perfected by the thing.

Unfortunately, this way of speaking assumes the propriety of the distinction
between thing and idea, a distinction which Edwards' entire semiotics throws
into question—which, in part, explains why the passage sounds so convoluted.
In terms of the distinction, the perfect idea of a thing is really the perfected
idea of a thing, which itself needs to be understood as a perfected thing (since
all things, as he notes, are ideas).[12] The perfection of a thing is the thing itself,
the "very idea" of the thing as the other of the thing considered solely as idea.
To consider the other solely as idea, however, is to fall into idealism; and to
consider the thing as the perfection of the idea is to favor materialism. Both
conclusions can be avoided by rejecting the Aristotelian-Lockean dichotomy
of thing and idea from the start.

In place of the idea-thing distinction, Edwards highlights the unity of
signifier and signified, type and antitype, even while retaining Locke's cum-
bersome vocabulary of representational realism, including the ill-fated notion
of substance. "The type," Edwards proposes, "is only the representation or
shadow of the thing, but the antitype is the very substance, and is the true
thing."[13] The type is only a shadow of the other it represents; it is the idea of
otherness, the image of otherness. For it to be the true image of otherness, it
would have to be the other. The antitype is that true image, the image which
at the same time is what constitutes the thing as meaningful. But the other is
not the antitype considered apart from the type; the antitype is the fulfillment
of the *thing* (the interpreted sign) in which both signifier and signified are
functions.

As the fulfillment of the meaning of the thing, the antitype *is* the thing. The
type marks the thing as in need of fulfillment. It signals the more general semiotic constraint, that to be requires being-in-relation. What allows something to
be is its juxtaposition to another, its openness to relations that are necessary
for it to achieve integrity, completion, unity—in Edwards' term, excellence.[14]
Always pointing beyond itself to the displacement of itself as an image of another, each thing signifies its own completion in signifying its own fulfillment
in its other.

In history, the past and present bear the image or shadow of the future, not
so much because the past and present contribute to the future—God recreates
the world at every instant—but because the future is signified in the past and
present as the historical component of temporal otherness. The fact that historical events can be conceived in a Humean isolation from one another testifies

12. See chapter 3.
13. Edwards, "Images," 62.
14. See Edwards, "The Mind," #1, in Jonathan Edwards, *Scientific and Philosophical Writings,*
ed. Wallace E. Anderson, 336; see also Anderson, ibid., 84. For more on these topics, see below,
chapters 3 and 7.

less to their insular intelligibility than to the willingness of fallen consciousness to give up on any hope for discerning meaning or significance in creation.

Of course, such hope would be justified only if history itself is significant, and that would mean that the temporality or historicity of creation has an other of which it is but an image, namely, eternity. From a semiotic standpoint, eternity cannot be a radical other to history: If eternity were completely transcendent, nothing in history would have meaning other than in terms of other historical events, and the process as a whole would lack significance. Historical events are thus intelligible only in terms of other historical events; and they are intelligible as historical events only to the extent that history itself is fulfilled by eternity. Without a rationale for history, there is no reason to presume that events in history must have a rationale. Despite Adam's fall into substantialist representationalism, the immanent transcendentality of history in general and historical events in particular still require an eschatology. As Edwards points out, "Things even before the fall were types of things pertaining to the gospel revelation."[15] The fall does not affect the basic ways in which things are intelligible, only the way that intelligibility is understood. Even when events were knowable as necessarily linked in a pre-Babelic network of semiosis, their historical significance had always already been guaranteed in terms of the transcendental purpose of nature. Whatever religious significance Adam's sin or Christ's resurrection was to have in supplementing the network of relations in which each appeared, that they could have even had prophetic and eschatological significance was a function of the discursive network of typological relations.

It is to that network that Edwards appeals when he speaks of natural objects (e.g., stones) as types, figures, or emblems that exhibit spiritual value. As signs rather than symbols, such things are significant in virtue of their spirituality. But spiritual significance does not require that they refer to, or symbolize, realities of an order apart from their own. Symbols or allegories defer to transcendent counterparts as the realities that make natural objects intelligible and meaningful. In doing so they portray the world as only accidentally significant (as far as its ontological or epistemological status is concerned). By locating the significance of things in the world in things beyond the world, the symbol dispenses with the type in favor of the antitype.

Mason Lowance argues that this transformation of typology into allegorical symbolism is characteristic of the "New Light millennial writers" who extend prophetic power to natural symbols.[16] All natural objects, he suggests, have prophetic and eschatological value because they shadow forth the transcendence of nature. Their very naturalness renders them suspect as essential elements in their own significance and demands that they be considered as symbols. Because objects like stones cannot *naturally* embody spiritual value,

15. Miscellany #479 [1729].

16. See Mason I. Lowance, Jr., *The Language of Canaan: Metaphor and Symbol in New England from the Puritans to the Transcendentalists,* 4–7. Lowance refers to Edwards' typology in general as "symbology" (182–85, 249).

their significance is purchased by denying the essential place of historical displacement and natural differentiation.

However, as I have suggested, the symbolics and semiotics of typology differ substantially in their assumptions about *why* types prophesy. It is thus important to note how the linguistic and communicative grounds of Edwards' typology eschew Lowance's allegorical symbolism. At issue is not only how types can prophesy, but also why they must. As a symbol, a type prophesies its antitype by alluding to an unchanging meaning that both type and antitype express. What distinguishes the type and antitype is their accidental historical differentiation, a differentiation made possible by how each uniquely combines other allusions to transcendent meanings. The deliverance of Israel from Egypt is a symbol of Christ's death and resurrection because both events allude to an act of redemption. In order for the first event to prophesy the second event, it must be a sign or type of it as well; that is, it must allude to the other as *its* historical other, the spiritual completion of its own historicity.

In the context of the sign, though, each natural object is already prophetic. It alludes to an other not because of its connection to some transcendent other that legitimates the prophetic allusion, but because of its immanent spirituality, its immanent demand for completion in an other. The semiotic requirement of the fulfillment of the signifier-signified relation in an interpretation opens up the possibility that the interpretation (in Peircean terms, the interpretant) might be confused with the signified as the other of the natural object. However, that would brush aside the discursive historicity of the sign relations, thus undermining the possibility for prophetic or eschatological significance.

The meaning of a natural object as a sign depends both on those features that distinguish it from other signs irrespective of the actual context in which it appears (its so-called paradigmatic relations) and on those features that distinguish it from other signs adjacent to it in its immediate discursive context (its "syntagmatic relations").[17] Allegorical symbolism makes paradigmatic relations essential to the significance of types and treats syntagmatic relations as accidental: it explains how typological relations could hold without indicating why they must.

However, by maintaining a balance of paradigmatic and syntagmatic relations, Edwards' semiotics shows how natural things are not simply *open* to typological appropriation but, in fact, could not have any meaning or significance without it. Accordingly, the discursive, semiotic relations of natural things cannot be reduced to symbolic relations without at the same time making natural things merely arbitrary "signs" or spurious evidence of spirituality.

Lowance's portrait of Edwards' typology as allegorical symbolism avoids the arbitrariness of the classical theory of signs by preferring the literal and historical exegesis of Scriptural types; but as I have indicated, this precludes the possibility of thinking of type and antitype as mutually dependent components

17. Cf. Silverman, *Subject of Semiotics*, 10–11, 104.

of signification within nature. For Edwards, the relative superiority of antitypes does not presume two distinct orders of being, one material and one spiritual. Both are intelligible as spiritual: the type signals its own transcendentality, the antitype instantiates the otherness of signification.

> The system of created beings may be divided into two parts, the typical world and the antitypical world. The inferior and carnal, i.e. the more external and transitory part of the universe, that part of it which is inchoative, imperfect, and subservient, is typical of the superior, more spiritual, perfect, and durable part of it, which is the end and as it were the substance and consummation of the other.[18]

As the more inchoate provocations to meaning, types adumbrate those things that complete and perfect signification. Antitypes reveal more explicitly their spirituality, but both parts of the created universe are just that—in the universe, not transcendent. The distinction between type and antitype is paradigmatic in regard to the semiotic requirement for distinction or otherness, but syntagmatic in regard to the discursive unity of mutually "spiritual" (othered) terms.

In other words, neither type nor antitype is considered significant in terms of the other. The significance of either transcends the discursive exchange in which their distinction is intelligible. Once withdrawn paradigmatically from the discourse in which their distinction is meaningful, even their distinction no longer makes sense. To say that their differentiation is maintained symbolically in the otherness of God simply overlooks the fact that the notion of intelligibility as significatory and relational includes even the concept of a transcendent God.

From a syntagmatic standpoint, the otherness of God is precisely what unites type and antitype. The other of the type—namely, the antitype—provides the terminus of relatability required for the possibility of meaning. The divine or spiritual element of the relationship appears *in* discursive exchanges as the eschatological promise of the possibility of signification. In order that there be meaning in the world, there must be an other in the world. This otherness is its spirituality, its invitation to fulfillment through divine discourse, the Word, Christ, God-with-us.

Semiotic exchange consummates significatory relations that are neither historical nor ahistorical, neither natural nor supernatural, neither materialistic nor idealistic. All such distinctions collapse retrospectively into the "as it were" interpretations of the products of meaning that belie their origins. Unlike symbolic analyses, semiotics does not begin with the assumption that the relata of distinctions can have any signification apart from the relations in which they are embedded. The code for interpreting the signifier-signified relation is not an interpretation of the relation, just as the code for interpreting the relation of the narrative of history and eternal providence grants no significance to either apart from the other.

---

18. Edwards, "Types of the Messiah," 191. Cf. Miller, ed., *Images or Shadows,* 27; and Brumm, "Edwards and Typology," 83.

Typology thus indicates a broken narrative both at the level of symbols and at the level of signs. At the level of symbols, things in creation appear in a discontinuous history recreated anew from one moment to the next. United only to God as their eternally and infinitely deferred ground, they constitute a text or scripture that is absolutely unintelligible. At the level of signs, things are intelligible in virtue of their differences from one another. They affirm their historicity by denying that they have meaning in themselves, always pointing beyond themselves to an other for signification. In this way, historicity is affirmed in the very act of its own erasure. For if it is significant, it is significant in terms of an other to itself, an eternality implicit within the possibility of historical differentiation.[19]

Two Texts: Nature and Scripture

By referring to an other *to* discursive practice as well as an other *in* discursive practice, Edwards' typology displays the significatory strategies that allow him to consider the world as much a divine communication as are revealed scriptures. Indeed, because the world is scripted as a system of particular things made meaningful in relation to their spiritual fulfillments, it reveals the play of signification without which reasoning and intelligibility lack guidance and regulation. Just as Edwards' philosophical idealism defines existence in terms of determinate patterns of relations, so also his psychology assumes those same patterns, thereby bringing together ontological and epistemological procedures.

As Kimnach points out, Edwards' synthesis of such procedures assumes that natural phenomena are invested with spiritual principles. These principles endow the phenomena with implications for the future; that is, they situate natural things in a universal system of significance. The principles that define what it means for a natural thing to exist (i.e., to be real) also define why the thing must exist in precisely the way it does (i.e., to be true). If true natural types could be positively identified, Kimnach concludes, they would furnish the preacher with "a vocabulary that synthesized instruction, illustration, and proof."[20] Natural types carry their own validation because they embody the principles of meaning in which instruction, illustration, and proof are grounded.

Kimnach's allusion to the preacher's vocabulary hints at the semiotic strategy required to unite the instructive, illustrative, and probative functions of discourse. That strategy presents every existent in terms of its transcendentality,

19. See De Prospo, *Theism in Jonathan Edwards,* 83, 143. Cf. Daniel B. Shea, "Deconstruction Comes to Early 'America': The Case of Edwards," *Early American Literature* 21 (1986–87), 272–73.

20. See Kimnach, ed., *Sermons,* 230; and Wilson H. Kimnach, "Jonathan Edwards's Pursuit of Reality," in *Jonathan Edwards and the American Experience,* eds. Nathan O. Hatch and Harry S. Stout, 108. Cf. Cooey, *Jonathan Edwards,* 17–18.

its instructive and illustrative invitation to further discourse in necessitating a move to an other. The very meaning of a thing points to its fulfillment in those "more spiritual" things in virtue of which the natural thing is significant. The signifiability of a thing allows it to guide us to the thought of an other, to serve as an illustration of an other, and to provide the reason for our endorsement of the intelligibility of an other.

Typological relations thus reveal the patterns of discursive reasoning by inscribing the vocabulary of meaningfulness literally as a communication. Just as the vitality of the preacher's utterances depends on how they point to other, as yet unspoken, words, so things ordered within the speech of God are lively insofar as they indicate others. The very wisdom of God appears "in his so ordering things natural, that they livelily represent things divine and spiritual."[21] The intelligibility of creation depends on an activity of ordering that resists characterization in static or structured terms. If it were static, it would comprise a system of allegorically related (and thus ontologically isolated) entities whose meanings would depend only accidentally on their place in the system. For Edwards, though, things represent "livelily" when they are moving: they move an observer to feel differently in virtue of their own movement toward other things that complement and complete their meaning.

Typological assertions, like any claims of signification, rely on the agreement or harmony of things established in God's communication. That communicative or discursive context creates the possibility of syntactical renovation and creative realignments of relations into new harmonies. It also identifies those alignments already established as guidelines for probative rationality:

> Again it is apparent and allowed that there is a great and reasonable analogy in God's works. There is a wonderful resemblance in the effects which God produces, and consentaneity in his manner of working in one thing and another, throughout all nature. It is very observable in the visible world. Therefore 'tis allowed that God does purposely make and order one thing to be in an agreeableness and harmony with another.[22]

In one sense, all of the effects of God's activity resemble one another equally as expressions in a divine communication; but the variety of their portrayals within that discourse establishes the particular harmonies that serve as foundations for the "consent to being."

As I will show later in discussing Edwards' doctrines of moral beauty and excellence, consent to being, like the discursive exchange in which it occurs, replicates that divine creativity. Here it is important to note that things in nature already exhibit a consentaneity with one another in virtue of the presence of the divine in their constitution. Edwards defers an explanation for how that presence is nothing other than the possibility of harmony with an other. Instead of suggesting that natural significance requires a transcendent ground,

---

21. Miscellany #119 [1724].
22. Edwards, "Images," 53.

he appeals to rhetorical questions that allude to how the transcendentality of natural things maintains their individuality even in their consentaneity with the spiritual:

> Why should we not suppose that [God] makes the inferior in imitation of the superior, the material of the spiritual, on purpose to have a resemblance and shadow of them? We see that even in the material world God makes one part of it strangely to agree with another; and why is it not reasonable to suppose he makes the whole as a shadow of the spiritual world? . . . If there be such an admirable analogy observed by the Creator in his works throughout the whole system of the natural world, so that one thing seems to be made in imitation of another, and especially the less perfect to be made in imitation of the more perfect, so that the less perfect is as it were a figure or image of the more perfect—so beasts are made in imitation of men, plants are [a] kind of types of animals, minerals are in many things in imitation of plants—why is it not rational to suppose that the corporeal and visible world should be designedly made and constituted in analogy to the more spiritual, noble and real world? 'Tis certainly agreeable to what is apparently the method of God's working.[23]

Even in the material world, signatures and resemblances of things appear with such frequency that to ignore them would seemingly be to ignore an essential clue to the structures of reasoning, imaginative association, and self-instruction. Not only is the less perfect incorporated into the system of discursive exchange through its imitation of the more perfect, but the more perfect is made more accessible in virtue of our recognition of their relations. Though completed by and in what it signifies, the less perfect remains an indispensable component in the constitution of meaning. Its place as an imperfect image sufficiently distances it to guarantee the possibility of discursivity within rationality.

When Edwards asks "why is it not rational to suppose" that the corporeal world is constituted in analogy to the more spiritual world, he alludes to the rhetorical stance from which a transcendental account of the activity of reasoning would have to be formulated. In avoiding the irreligious and unjustifiable presumption to describe God's "method of working," Edwards includes the figures and images of the material world as less spiritual elements of the system of semiotic exchange that defines rationality. Because the text of the world instantiates discursive practices which cannot legitimate claims that transcend the system, Edwards can only hint at what is the limit of signification by alluding to an alter-text in terms of which the world can be considered as constituting a discursive network.

That other text from which he draws typological insight, the Scriptures, is structured along the same lines as the natural world. But in the Scriptures typological relations exhibit more explicitly the eschatological character of the system of signification that differentiates the "inferior and shadowy parts" of

---

23. Ibid., 53, 69–70. See also Jonathan Edwards, *The Nature of True Virtue*, in *Ethical Writings*, ed. Paul Ramsey, 564–67.

God's works from those spiritual things that are "the crown and glory, the head and soul, the very end, the alpha and omega of all other works":

> The inferior dispensation of the gospel was all to shadow forth the highest and most excellent, which was its end; thus almost everything that was said or done that we have recorded in Scripture from Adam to Christ, was typical of Gospel things. . . . And this is God's manner to make inferior things shadows of the superior and most excellent, outward things shadows of spiritual; and all other things shadows of those things that are the end of all things and the crown of all things. Thus God glorifies himself and instructs the minds that he has made.[24]

Even though the types of the Old Testament are fulfilled by the antitypes of the Gospel, the relations between scriptural types and antitypes are themselves types of the fulfillment of history. If history is to have meaning, then it must be an image of that which completes it (eternity) and, therefore, cannot be understood apart from a typological eschatology. In learning the proper idiom of typological expression, we must have a guide, for without the guide not only will types in nature be associated with the wrong antitypes, but also natural type-antitype relations will be uninformative in indicating the significance of those relations.

Edwards does not claim that the types and antitypes of the Scriptures provide a lexicon for understanding typological relations, for they constitute only part of the total system exposed in typology. They do, however, provide insight into the instructive role of typological reasoning in general by showing how the mind's activities, like all other things, are moments in our learning the language of being. God instructs in exactly the same way that he creates: He speaks, and thus imprints all existence with the same communicative, intentional character as any other language.

> 'Tis very fit and becoming of God, who is infinitely wise, so to order things that there should be a voice of his in his works instructing those that behold them, and pointing forth and showing divine mysteries and things more immediately appertaining to himself and his spiritual kingdom. The works of God are but a kind of voice or language of God, to instruct intelligent beings in things pertaining to himself. And why should we not think that he would teach and instruct by his works in this way as well as in others, viz. by representing divine things by his works, and so pointing them forth, especially since we know that God hath so much delighted in this way of instruction?[25]

Here Edwards extends the empiricist project precisely by rejecting Locke's relegation of language to a subordinate epistemological position. The order, discrimination, and instructive capacity of things depend on their appearance in the vocal or linguistic expressions of God. The language of God does not represent an already determinate, synchronic order in the mind of God, for the

---

24. Miscellany #362 [1728–29], cited in *Typological Writings,* 51n. Cf. Anderson, ed., *Typological Writings,* 14; and Lowance, *Language of Canaan,* 263.
25. Edwards, "Images," 67.

mind (as that which is intentionally related or points to an other) is itself constituted in the dynamic, diachronic activity of vocal expression.

This identification of language with voice retrieves the Stoic-Ramist understanding of intelligence and rationality as functions of discursive expression. In terms of this mentality, a thing is not intelligible in virtue of its allegorical or symbolic relation to some transcendent idea. Instead, it is intelligible and even identifiable as a thing in virtue of its appearance in an expression or proposition. Since changes in expression affect semantic relations and rules of syntax, minds and things cannot be independent of the discourses in which they are typologically embedded.

To dismiss as merely metaphorical or heuristic Edwards' reference to creation as the voice of God is part of the classical ploy to smuggle in another metaphor (viz., intelligibility consists in vision). According to it, the divine vision situates individuals in relations that remain unaffected by their appearance in the accidental or historical juxtapositions of propositional discourse. By contrast, God's voice identifies individuals in terms of their contribution to the temporal (i.e., historical) melody of the world.[26] In terms of this latter mentality, a thing is significant relative to other things in virtue of its appearance in an ongoing discourse, a discourse which itself is made significant by its own activity of pointing out the transcendental relations in which it functions.

By describing creation as a communicative process, Edwards reveals why types are "a fit method of instruction," consistent with the principles of human nature, and why they tend "to enlighten and illustrate, and to convey instruction with impression, conviction, and pleasure, and to help the memory."[27] The actual constitution of human nature occurs in and as the process of instruction by which impressions and memories are discriminated. It is no wonder that God delights in typological instruction and that human beings take pleasure in it, for in both the immediacy of gratification depends on the experience of participating in the constitution of meaning. Through these discursive or propositional expressions, individuality itself is defined and the possibility of harmony is created.

Through the displacement of the subject in propositional language, the mind comes to know the transcendentality of itself as a moment in the divine speech. The voice of God incorporates intelligence by calling it into differential (and deferential) existence. The differentiation of the natural world from its spiritual complement assumes the deference of the natural world to its spiritual complement. Just as the signification of a thing in the natural world depends on its deferring to an other in nature to ratify its ontological and epistemological status, so also nature as a whole defers for legitimacy to its transcendental other, its own spirituality.

As indicated earlier, the recognition that nature is a language, a speech, or a text provides the clue that signification presumes not only deference to other

26. Cf. Jenson, *America's Theologian*, 20.
27. Edwards, "Types of the Messiah," 191. Cf. Lowance, *Language of Canaan*, 257–58.

elements in the same text, but also deference of one text to another. The text or book of nature could not be read as a text unless there were another text, the Scriptures, in terms of which it is identified as a text open to interpretation. As Edwards points out:

> The Book of Scripture is the interpreter of the book of nature [in] two ways: viz. by declaring to us those spiritual mysteries that are indeed signified or typified in the constitution of the natural world; and secondly, in actually making application of the signs and types in the book of nature as representations of those spiritual mysteries in many instances.[28]

As the means for interpreting nature and history, the Bible establishes procedures for evaluating the legitimacy of reasoning in matters of nature and history. But what serves as the means for interpreting the Bible? Surely the Bible cannot serve as its own ground of intelligibility, and to appeal to a transcendent ground for its meaning is to withdraw the text from any context of meaning whereby its interpretation could be understood.

The answer to this question lies in the recognition of the textuality of both books. As books, both nature and the Scriptures espouse the legibility at the heart of semiotic exchange. What allows nature to be interpreted by Scripture is exactly the same thing that allows Scripture to be interpreted: Both are books. Their very textuality contains the promise that interpretations occur in the intertextual process of discursive (historical) exchange.

The Scriptures are part of the mechanism for interpreting things in nature. That mechanism, formalized in the Renaissance episteme, permits the interpretation of natural things by means of identifying them as typologically significant in terms of other natural things. Such a view had been largely ignored by the typologists with which Edwards is familiar. But that does not keep him from attempting to justify typological reasoning in the very terms that his exposition undermines.

In contrast to those who think that the meaning of a term or the interpretation of an event must be grounded in some system of relations other than the one in which the term or event appears, Edwards discerns a transcendental character in nature itself. Through the Scriptures, he suggests, we become aware of the presence of that character. Because they alert us to the existence of the spiritual and the mysterious in our experience, the Scriptures reveal something essential to the constitution of the natural world. The natural world has meaning in terms of *its* spirituality, *its* textual vocation, *its* calling to serve as a revelation of its own significance. In setting forth people and events as types or antitypes, however, the Scriptures provide only a small vocabulary of signifier-signified relations, only the beginning of a semantics of signification.

---

28. Edwards, "Images," 106. Cf. Michael L. Raposa, "Jonathan Edwards' Twelfth Sign," *International Philosophical Quarterly* 33 (1993), 161; and Lowance, *Language of Canaan,* 3–6, 250–53, 261.

Of much greater importance for Edwards' overall project are the procedures employed in the Scriptures that establish the syntax of typological significa-tion, the strategies for interpreting signs and types as representations of spiritual mysteries. Though the Scriptures indicate particular typological re-lations, they more significantly draw attention to the stipulations for meaning already implicit in interpreting anything as a type. Those few relations that are interpreted in the Scriptures in typological terms thus act as exemplars for the extension of typological interpretation:

> If we may use our own understandings and invention not at all in interpreting types, and must not conclude anything at all to be types but what is expressly said to be and explained in Scripture, then the Church under the Old Testament, when the types were given, were secluded from ever using their understanding to search into the meaning of the types given to 'em; for God did, when he gave 'em, give no interpretation.[29]

The prospect of interpretation itself relies on the possibility that a thing can have meaning. But the meaning or significance of a thing presumes the rela-tion of that thing to another. The impulse to interpretation is contained in the perception of a thing in terms of its indication of something else that makes it understandable. Indeed, the prospect of an interpretation calls understanding itself into being. Insofar as the possibility of an interpretation invents (i.e., comes upon) a thing in disclosing the thing's availability to meaning, it situ-ates it in a discourse defining the process of the thing's understanding. Hence, understanding is itself a product of the typological textualization of both nature and Scripture.

In contrast to its typological appropriation, unguided experience of the world fails to acknowledge its textual character. The prospect of typological relations revealed in the Scriptures textualizes nature; it makes nature into a book that can have meaning. When Edwards speaks of the Book of Nature, then, he invokes the "new sense of things" in which Scripture can complement nature in affirming its typological significance. Apart from the availability of Scripture as an alter-text that calls it into intertextual significance, nature re-mains the disjointed congeries of experiences exhumed in radical empiricism.

This new sense of things need not characterize the experience of only the elect or regenerate, because the substitution of a semiotic for a symbolic under-standing of nature need not occur on both levels of interpretation.[30] True, the elect experience both the significatory integrity of things in nature and the sig-nificance of nature in its totality. But it is also possible to experience the spirituality of things in the world, seeing how things have meaning only rela-tive to one another, without appreciating the immanent transcendentality of the world itself. For this latter recognition, one needs to inscribe the world in an eschatological context, and that requires appealing to an alternative text.

---

29. Edwards, "Types" Notebook, 150.
30. Cf. Miller, ed., *Images or Shadows*, 27; Lowance, *Language of Canaan*, 6; and Anderson, ed., *Typological Writings*, 24.

That alternative text, the Scriptures, portrays nature as a source of revelation in virtue of nature's signification of its own transcendentality. As the figural expression of God, nature draws attention to figuration itself. It opens up the possibility that individual things in our experience might serve as figures shadowing forth other things yet to be experienced. In this way, the spiritual things described in the Scriptures draw attention to the sensible figures used in those descriptions. Their sensual character stands as an affront to the possibility of their transcendentality in spite of what they claim to mean. Their figurality becomes both the prohibition for meaning's transcendence of discourse and the requirement that meaning be disclosed beyond that figure.[31]

Understanding either nature or Scripture thus requires the adoption of a typological attitude toward things; we must recognize how the meanings of things are embedded in the process of their understanding, and how that process of learning the language of nature inscribes the regulations of rationality and prophecy. Edwards avows:

> I am not ashamed to own that I believe that the whole universe, heaven and earth, air and seas, and the divine constitution and history of the holy Scriptures, be full of images of divine things, as full as a language is of words; and that the multitude of those things that I have mentioned are but a small part of what is really intended to be signified and typified by these things: but that there is room for persons to be learning more and more of this language and seeing more of that which is declared in it to the end of the world without discovering all. To say that we must not say that such things are types of these and those things unless the Scripture has expressly taught us that they are so, is as unreasonable as to say that we are not to interpret any prophecies of Scriptures or apply them to these and those events, except we find them interpreted to our hand, and must interpret no more of the prophecies of David, etc. For by the Scripture it is plain that innumerable other things are types that are not interpreted in Scripture (all the ordinances of the Law are all shadows of good things to come), in like manner as it is plain by Scripture that these and those passages that are not actually interpreted are yet predictions of future events.[32]

Having noted in his *Religious Affections* the year before how sign relations provide no guaranteed indicators for the presence of spirituality, Edwards nonetheless insists that relations of significance permeate the universe. But here he makes the telling observation that the world, like the Scriptures, constitutes a language whose elements come into significance and yet are continually being reinterpreted in an ongoing discourse.

Confronted with a system of signification that is open to the internal revision of rules of semantics and syntax, Edwards prefers to focus on the strategies that justify typological signification instead of on the instances of typological relations mentioned in the Scriptures. For without an awareness of how those

---

31. Cf. Stephen J. Stein, "The Spirit and the Word: Jonathan Edwards and Scriptural Exegesis," in *Edwards and the American Experience*, 125–28.
32. Edwards, "Types" Notebook, 152. Cf. Lowance, ed., "Types of the Messiah," ibid., 179.

procedures are themselves intelligible, any typological argumentation or prophetic reasoning based on them remains suspect.

Even so, the language of the Book of Nature or of the Scriptures does not
contain its own justification; no language does. Relations established in the
language constitute the procedures of signification, and in that sense the rules
for signification are both the products of discourse (the interpretations of signs)
and the guides for further discourse (the prophetic allusions to the prospect of
subsequent interpretations). Not only does typology identify the specific ways
in which discursive expressions become regularities and other expressions
become intelligible in terms of those regularities; it also indicates the possibilities for further completions of allusive expressions within discourse. Because
both typological functions reflect characteristics of discourse itself, they reveal
why Edwards' typology relies so heavily on his characterization of nature and
Scripture as divine books or communications.

The Nature of Typological Relations

Though Edwards acknowledges that some types of divine things are more
readily apparent than others, he does not favor scriptural types over those that
appear in nature. In some things, he says, the image of the divine is very lively,
while in others the image is but faint or even contradictory.[33] But the extent to
which something is a type of another thing does not necessarily depend on
any scriptural legitimation.

However, types from the Old Testament merit special consideration, Edwards notes, insofar as "a plain, summary rehearsal or narration of them is
called 'a parable' and 'dark saying' or 'enigma'."[34] As parables they exhibit the
divine wisdom implicit in the historical fulfillment of elements in the discourse
of the universe. Through their allusion to other, future historical (New Testament) events, they serve as exemplars of all other forms of natural typological
relations.

As "a mystical, enigmatical speech signifying spiritual and divine things," the
discourse of Old Testament types confounds the plain, historical (Lockean)
method by which the meaning of history itself is forever deferred from any
system of signification. As narratives fulfilled in other narratives, references to
Old Testament types implicate narrativity itself as part of the enigmatic character of signification. The speech of Old Testament types signifies spiritual and
divine things precisely by calling into question just how plain or evident their
narrations are. Indeed, as "figurative and typical representations," they are often
anything but evident. As "dark sayings" they say what they do not mean. They
present a narration of history made mysterious, made other by a challenge to

33. See, for example, "Images," 114.
34. Edwards, "Types of the Messiah," 217.

the claim of historical narration to supply its own evidential legitimacy.[35]

By appealing to the narrativity of Old Testament types, Edwards transforms their historicity from something over and against eternity into something implicitly and essentially spiritual. This transformation of history into an eschatological system calls into question the propriety of allegorical forms of exegesis. An allegorical analysis presumes that natural events and objects have a literal meaning that is augmented by an allegorical meaning, a meaning indicating the spiritual significance of the events or objects.[36] The problem with such allegorical accounts is that they do not explain what justifies the augmentation. To avoid the charge that typological reasoning is simply the product of a copious fancy, Edwards undercuts the theory of meaning that allows the distinction of literal and allegorical to go unchallenged. If the spiritual is seen merely as an addendum to the natural, then the natural can legitimately be considered autonomous. But if the spiritual is essential to the meaningfulness of the natural, then the spiritual cannot be confused with an allegorical amplification of literal meaning. The supposition of the possibility of literal meaning—that is, meaning limited to what a thing is apart from its function within a discourse—is ruled out as unintelligible; it is the mark of the collapse of understanding, a fall from the possibility of significance.

Considered by themselves, events and objects in nature and history can have no meaning at all, because there is no legitimate or defensible way in which we can consider them by themselves. This insight powers Edwards' so-called idealistic metaphysics and epistemology and, as I will argue throughout my discussion, it explains not only *how* Edwards reasons in matters such as the Trinity, freedom, and moral virtue, but also *why* he proposes his arguments as rational. For if we begin with the notion that experience, history, and discourse are composed of meaningfully discrete components, then reasoning about them (as Hume observes) cannot but be considered the arbitrary productions of imagination.

The complementarity of events in the Old and New Testaments brings into focus how truncated such events appear when they are understood apart from each other. In fact, prior to their juxtaposition they can hardly be said to constitute a discourse at all, inasmuch as the Scriptures often refer to events that (apart from their typological relations) are mentioned for no apparent reason. Simply to assume that there is a reason for everything in the Scriptures would be to affirm a posture of faith without explaining how such a posture posits a discourse as the strategy for all reasoning, including typological inference. By alluding to that strategy, Edwards draws attention to the mentality or episteme that defines the nature of discourse itself.

Even while they point eschatologically to the fulfillment of the history they recount, the Scriptures exhibit in their very textuality the historicity of the discourse they embody. The historicity they reveal, just like the nature they

35. Ibid.
36. See Lowance, ed., *Typological Writings*, 162–66, 177–79.

disclose, is eminently prophetic by being immanently significatory and typological.

As Edwards sees it, the debate about typology is a debate between, on the one hand, those who would reject all typological claims as unjustified tropes of human contrivance (e.g., Lockeans) and, on the other, those who identify scriptural events or objects as candidates for symbolic allegorization. Both perspectives assume that historical events or objects can be conceived discretely; they then differ on the arbitrariness of the relations in which such things are placed.

If the historical relations of things are guaranteed by reference to their places in the mind of God—as Lowance's modified Platonic reading of Edwards suggests—then such relations are hardly arbitrary.[37] But what such relations gain in veracity and ontological status they lose in practical accessibility; for if the typological relations identified in the Scriptures are not part of the discourse of human experience, they will be untranslatable into terms that can motivate historical action.

For this reason Cooey claims that Edwards' doctrine treats types less allegorically than "anagogically," that is, in terms of revealing spiritual significance in a nature already historicized prophetically.[38] She argues that, for Edwards, nature is already embedded in a spiritual creation. Typological relations have meaning and thus can guide not only human thought but action as well, because they are intelligible in terms of an inherently historical discourse. That discourse is not simply the historicized version of a universal and eternal truth. Rather, because history itself is part of the eternal communication of God, history (and thus nature) is not conceivable apart from its spirituality.

As Cooey herself notes in contrasting this interpretation of Edwards with that of Conrad Cherry, nature (for Edwards) has significance because of its eschatological and redemptive dimensions. I have earlier referred to this in discussing the role played by the Scriptures as the alter-text to nature, the indication that creation in its totality is open to significance. As much as Cooey's approach might also point out why we should expect individual things in nature to lend themselves to the overall project of the communication of meaning, it does not explain why particular types (e.g., from the Old Testament) *must* find fulfillment in their New Testament antitypes.

Lowance's explanation, that types are like Platonic emblems of their antitypes, accounts for why certain individuals can shadow forth only certain others and why typological reasoning, for Edwards, cannot degenerate into arbitrary speculation. But this "symbological" interpretation of Edwards fails to explain how Edwards can be confident that there is such a discursive unity underlying the relations of type and antitype. If Edwards were simply to assume that types and antitypes are related, even if by divine fiat, then he

---

37. See *Language of Canaan,* 250, 265; and Lowance, ed., *Typological Writings,* 161, 172–73.
38. See Cooey, *Jonathan Edwards,* 8, 118. Cf. Harold P. Simonson, *Jonathan Edwards: Theologian of the Heart,* 79–80, 146–53.

would fall victim to his own charge of arbitrariness.[39] If type and antitype are inherently related, then their difference must be explained. To explain that difference in Platonic terms, though, is to withdraw the antitype from the discourse of history. In Lowance's account, Edwards' typology spiritualizes history; in Cooey's account, typology historicizes spirituality.

The only other option available to Edwards is to locate difference within the discourse of history by transforming the problematic of historicity itself. History and nature must allow for the presence of spirituality without transcending the significatory strategies that circumscribe their possibilities for meaning. Because the connections among things in nature are established in and as history, the significance of natural things depends on their historicity. This is how, as Perry Miller remarks, the sequences or connections of ideas that creatures have agree with those of God. Furthermore, these connections reflect the same kind of agreement as that between the types of the Old Testament and their antitypes, because both kinds of connections exhibit the same pattern of the cosmos, the pattern by which the cosmos is intelligible and by which types are not confused with tropes.[40]

As purely human inventions, tropes identify such connections in allegories, similes, and metaphors that self-consciously acknowledge their difference from the real connections that characterize nature. To the extent that they re-present those connections in the artificial context of redoubling meaning, they only re-affirm their inability to signify real relations in creation. But because real relations are not representations, they cannot re-present a typological relation. In short, a type cannot be said to *represent* its antitype; if it does, it is simply a trope.

Miller's comment, then, that "the pattern of the cosmos is infinite representation" can be misleading, for Edwards' typology demands precisely the rejection of a representational epistemology, even one that qualifies that representational process as infinite. Infinite representation defers infinitely the possibility of significance, except insofar as the very infinity of that representational deferment signifies infinity itself. But this exception undermines all signification by collapsing into one another whatever distinctions are necessary to establish patterns in the cosmos. However well an object, person, or event represents another, its re-presentation of the other forestalls its own possibility for legitimacy. The appeal to tropes ensures the inaccessibility of the spiritual by presenting the spiritual as so alien or other that it has to be re-presented. Such an appeal also accepts the ontological insularity of natural things, guaranteeing that relations of significance even among natural things remain merely accidental. Tropes, in short, prevent natural things from having a *natural* spiritual significance.

39. Cf. William J. Wainwright, "Jonathan Edwards and the Language of God," *Journal of the American Academy of Religion* 48 (1980), 524–25.

40. See Miller, ed.; *Images or Shadows*, 27. Cf. John E. Smith, *Jonathan Edwards: Puritan, Preacher, Philosopher*, 134; and Lowance, *Language of Canaan*, 259–60.

To suggest, as William Wainwright does, that (for Edwards) natural things are consciously invested by God with specific significations would require that God act in exactly the same way as a human fashioner of tropes. Limited specifically to their eschatological significance as pure inventions of the divine mind, natural things would be circumscribed in their meanings and could thus be made humanly intelligible. In creating the things in nature, God would also be creating both the natural relations of things and the tropes by which those things could be understood.

However, such an interpretation implies that Edwards provides no explanation for why God would create the particular relations identified as typical. To see why a dove typifies the Holy Spirit more immediately than does, say, a flower or a full moon, would require that human beings know the mind of God. And as Edwards points out on numerous occasions, it is hard enough to know our own minds or those of other human beings, much less to know what God is thinking. Wainwright's claim that the Scriptures provide the key for interpreting a world full of types and emblems simply delays the more central question, because it gives no hint about what would justify our interpretations of the Scriptures.[41] If such justification is faith or election, then types collapse back into tropes in virtue of their arbitrariness. If there is some justified ground for the interpretations, then there is something in natural things themselves that reveals it.

Thus, the whole debate about whether Edwards' typology is grounded in the ontological nature of things (the liberal view) or in the historical events recounted in Scripture (the conservative view) assumes a false dichotomy. Neither things nor historical events are intelligible apart from their appearance in the matrix of signification identified appropriately by Edwards as a language or a communication. But to leave the matter standing at that point (as Janice Knight has recently done, linking ontology to God's communication *ad intra* and history to God's communication *ad extra*) is to appeal to metaphors in place of explanations.[42] What is needed is not simply an indication of how the distinction between ontology and history fails to respect Edwards' mixture of the two, but how the very nature of typological relations defines whatever intelligibility each might have.

By focusing on the relations of things to one another as the locus of meaning, Edwards resists the modernist temptation to situate the significance of a thing in the mind of its contemplator. In doing so, he avoids the classical-modern problems of skepticism about other minds by rejecting the very Lockean epistemology that questions how he can avoid the slide of typological claims into tropes. If he had adopted Lockean empiricism to address the issue of types, he would have been unable to avoid the charge of arbitrariness in interpretation. Because he prefers a semiotic account over one in which iso-

41. Cf. Wainwright, "Edwards and Language of God," 527.
42. See Janice Knight, "Learning the Language of God: Jonathan Edwards and the Typology of Nature," *William and Mary Quarterly,* 3d ser., 48 (1991), 534–43, 546–47.

lated subjects communicate with never more than tentative success, Edwards provides a much stronger case for his typology.

The problem with types in general, like the problem with signs of spirituality addressed in the *Religious Affections,* is that they are confused in the classical modernist (e.g., Lockean) account with tropes because of an unwillingness or inability to reject the fall into representational ontology and epistemology. The Romanticist psychology of Emerson and the Transcendentalists serves only to universalize that sin by expanding subjectivity to encompass nature as a representation of its own activity.[43] The Romanticist move makes creation humanly intelligible, but it does so by translating nature into a system of tropes.

Instead of dissolving the strangeness of God's communication, Edwards' insistence on the pervasiveness of types calls for reforming the problematic that sets up the possibility of confusing tropes and types in the first place. Tropes can be arbitrary precisely because the figurative associations they establish are accidental to the meanings of the things they describe. Types, on the other hand, are relations that situate a thing in a context by which it achieves significance, without which it would neither be intelligible nor exist in any sense.

Through his doctrine of types, Edwards thus raises serious doubts about the propriety of placing individual minds at the center of intelligibility. While this does not undermine the importance of mind in his philosophy, it does require a re-understanding of his idealism in ways that discount semblances with Berkeley or the Romantics.

The key to such a reformulation, as I have suggested, lies in his suspicion of subjectivity. Once the subject is eliminated as a pole over against which nature is placed or through which nature is understood, the system of signification in which the subject is but a part retrieves its status as the domain in terms of which mind functions. Significatory exchanges or discursive practices then become the means for situating the subject and for identifying policies of reasoning. Depending on the structure (or logic) of those exchanges or practices, what constitutes discourse itself can change. As the next chapter will show, a shift in the logic of discourse is precisely what characterizes the regenerate mentality of the elect.

43. Cf. Lowance, *Language of Canaan,* 270; Lowance, ed., *Typological Writings,* 180; and De Prospo, *Theism in Jonathan Edwards,* 78, 200, 205.

III

THE LOGICS OF CREATION

Edwards' typological claims are based on a matrix of relations that defines the order of the world and the processes of reasoning. His emphasis on the communicative character of reality challenges the classical dismissal of speech as subordinate to an independent ontology. In its place he proposes a non-foundationalist account of how signification is possible without having to rely on a metaphysics of subjectivity. Admittedly, the fall into subjectivity (along with its incumbent problems of skepticism) depicts the condition of sinful humanity. But Edwards does not assume that a logic that distances human beings from God, the world, and one another can serve as the model on which to defend assertions of the integrity of creation.

Likewise, though he borrows much of Neoplatonism's vocabulary of emanation and communication, Edwards cannot accept its implicit reduction of creation and its history to mere illusion. To locate the significance or meaning of existence outside of the world means drawing up the same barriers to intelligibility found in peripatetic distinctions of things, ideas, and words, or of matter and form. Only in the attempts to break through these distinctions does Edwards discover the procedures to undercut the difficulties raised by their forced dichotomies.

My focus on Edwards' semiotics attempts to open up a new space for investigation, one that resists the temptation to associate him with either the transcendent symbolism of Neoplatonism or the Aristotelian empiricism of Locke. When scholars have sought a middle ground in portraying Edwards' thought—as in Sang Lee's Leibnizian or process-theology retention of dispositional subjectivity—the logic of Edwards' communicative ontology recedes into the background.[1] The reason for this is that the implicit perspectivalism of a Leibnizian monadology does not account for how subjectivity itself is meaningful only in the context of the discourse in which it is a function.

In referring to the Stoic-Renaissance alternative to the classical (Platonic, Aristotelian, Lockean) mentality, I have invoked Foucault's depiction of it as a system of signification in which things signify as much as do ideas or words. Apart from describing the assumptions of such an episteme, though, I have not made explicit either why we should refer to this logic of signification as Stoic

---

1. See Sang Hyun Lee, *The Philosophical Theology of Jonathan Edwards*, 3–10, 50, 78.

or Renaissance or how Edwards employs such a logic in his account of the natural world; these topics are addressed in this chapter.

Part of the difficulty in reading Edwards' oft-repeated remarks about being's consent to being or matter's not really being matter lies in not taking seriously, or being unfamiliar with, the radically different ontology presumed in what Edwards affectionately calls "the old logic." This logic combines elements from Ramist thought with hermetic, astrological strategies and Renaissance appropriations of practices of Stoic reasoning. Those practices rely on communication as the means by which the "places" of reasoning are established. In such a logic, bodies, minds, matter, space, gravity—all of the classical, even Newtonian terms—have significance only as functions in propositional expressions, that is, as parts of speech.

This is not to say, however, that everything Edwards says in speaking about mind or matter assumes the propriety of Stoic logic. Indeed, as he increasingly confronts the fallen human condition in his later writings, he tends to employ fewer of the concepts in which his youthful ontology is couched. Yet he never fully repudiates the logic of the harmonious "fitness" of things revealed in his Ramist training. The appeal of such a logic, and its contrasts with the newer, Jansenist logic of Port Royal, sets up competing ontological schemes: one in which the elect hear God's speech, and one in which natural human beings hear sounds that only hint at something more profound.

The previous chapter's discussion of typology indicated that Edwards' reasoning procedures employ a different strategy than those used either by Neoplatonists bent on making signs into symbols or by Lockean empiricists intent on showing up type relations as mere tropes of fancy. If types are to avoid either extreme, they must assume some ontology that is at once essentially communicational and yet immanent in created things. Stoic-Ramist logic provides just such a device by defining things in terms of the pronouncements or commonplaces of the teacher.

Even if Edwards himself was unaware of how his strategies appeal to Ramist thought and its implicit Stoicism, that in no way argues against our own understanding of the principles that order his philosophy.[2] Accordingly, chapter 1 began with Foucault's description of the Renaissance episteme before arguing that such a mentality identifies the presuppositions of much of Edwards' thought (including his typology). Because the Renaissance episteme invites a reorientation of how we think through the problematics with which Edwards is confronted, it conditions the possibility for a historiographic reappropriation of Edwards in other than classical (modernist) terms. Instead of merely assuming that the proper way to study Edwards is to treat him as a subject who gets ideas from other subjects and who has his own (internal) ideas which he

2. For more on authorship and how this kind of attribution of ideas avoids anachronism, see Jorge J. E. Gracia, *Philosophy and Its History: Issues in Philosophical Historiography*, 199–203, 297–302, 313; and Michael L. Morgan, "Authorship and the History of Philosophy," *Review of Metaphysics* 42 (1988), 327–55.

communicates through words, we can attempt to discern how it is possible that he and others can think those ideas at all.

My discussion of the semiotic character of the Stoic-Ramist (Renaissance) episteme is not intended to install Rudolph Agricola or Peter Ramus (after Franco Burgersdijck, Adriaan Heereboord, Nicolas Malebranche, Henry More, or John Locke) as yet another candidate for the primary influence on Edwards' metaphysics. For in the Renaissance episteme, individuals like Agricola or Ramus do not manipulate the system of signs with certain intents in mind; rather, they are themselves functions of the sign system in which they appear. Thus, to seek out the personal influences on Edwards' thought is already to betray the modernist prejudice that the appeal to semiotics forestalls. Within a semiotic perspective Agricola and Ramus indicate a discourse or logic that overrides its classical distancing from ontology. In this sense, my turn to Ramist logic is not motivated by an attempt to exhume Edwards' antecedents (despite the appeal that such an inquiry might have for some modernist readers). Instead, my concern lies in discussing the discursive conditions that disclose the intelligibility of his thought.

Nonetheless, this focus on semiotics trades on the not-so-accidental importance of Ramist doctrines within Edwards' philosophical upbringing and in the Puritan experience in general. By itself Ramism is unable to support the claims of the Renaissance episteme, and thus Ramism cannot provide the sole context for understanding Edwards. But if the appeal to Ramist logic is used to unpack the implicit resonances of the Stoic-Renaissance episteme within Edwards' philosophy, it reveals unexpected harmonies among aspects of his thought.

If Ramist logic is understood—as it often is—as simply another way of arranging our ideas, then it will not support the weight I place on it in describing Edwards' philosophy. I contend that Ramist logic is not merely a rhetorical system for arranging human thought, because it situates thought in a matrix of exchange beyond human control. That matrix includes the medical, magical, and astrological assumptions of Renaissance thinkers like Paracelsus, as well as the more noticeably logical doctrines of Agricola and Ramus. Its significance for understanding Edwards lies in its insistence on placing a system of signification or communication squarely at the heart of meaning.

The Stoicism of Ramist Logic

As scholars have often pointed out, elements of Edwards' metaphysics seem to draw on a variety of sources, resonating with general themes developed in scholastic theology, Cartesianism, Cambridge Platonism, Newtonian physics, and Lockean epistemology. From such a smorgasbord of perspectives Edwards extracts anti-materialist doctrines about God's constant creation and purposive

direction of a typologically permeated world.[3] In terms of the classical vocabu-
laries in which these perspectives are fashioned, distinctions about divine
creation versus conservation, materialism versus idealism, teleology versus efficient causality, and necessity versus contingency escape critical analysis, because
the binary (re-presentational) logic in which they are formulated not only validates the propriety of such contrasts; it also defines reasoning itself in terms of
the availability of such contrasts.

When Wallace Anderson says, then, that Edwards refutes metaphysical materialism by appealing to Henry More's notions of matter, space, and time, or that
Edwards' scientific approaches are more like those of Descartes, Gassendi, or
Boyle than those found in scholastic allusions to qualities or entelechies, he
situates the Edwardsian project in a framework that reinforces rather than dissolves such dualisms.[4] By perpetuating this way of posing the questions with
which Edwards is concerned, we set for ourselves the almost impossible task
of trying to force an artificial unity onto his reformulation of doctrines of classical metaphysics. Because those doctrines (about mind and matter, atoms and
the void, fate and freedom) are designed to handle issues often raised in distinctly classical terms, it is no wonder that they appear puzzling and even
contradictory when juxtaposed in what emerges as Edwards' eclecticism.

As I have suggested, an alternative strategy for interpreting Edwards is available, one that acknowledges that he uses classical ideas but does not accept the
ontological presuppositions in which they are formulated. By engaging in such
a practice, Edwards transforms the meaning of such concepts. But more importantly, he points to the possibility of a logic in which the intentionality of
thought characterizes ontological relations in necessarily communicational terms.

Within such a logic, atomism and immaterialism can be made compatible
by redefining the nature of matter and being in general in terms of propositions rather than predications. In predicate logic, everything that can be said
or predicated of a subject (including its relations) is accidental to the subject
with which it is associated in a proposition. A subject itself is intelligible without specific reference to its predicates. Even when a thinker like Leibniz
incorporates predicates into a subject, the same distinction guarantees the survival of the monadic substantiality inherent in the classical ontology of
predicate logic. The cognitive independence of the subject—like the cognitive
independence of the Cartesian cogito or Lockean substance—thus becomes
both a logical requirement and a metaphysical doctrine. Insofar as the metaphysical assumptions of atomism and materialism are expressed in terms of a
predicate logic, they describe atoms or material things as substances to which
predicates are attributed.

3. See, for example, Norman Fiering, "The Rationalist Foundations of Jonathan Edwards's Metaphysics," in *Jonathan Edwards and the American Experience*, ed. Nathan O. Hatch and Harry S.
Stout, 78; and William S. Morris, *The Young Jonathan Edwards: A Reconstruction*, 537–42.
4. Cf. Wallace E. Anderson, ed., *Scientific and Philosophic Writings*, by Jonathan Edwards, 24, 47.

By contrast, where being is defined in terms of propositional logic, no thing can be understood apart from its functional place in a system of discourse. The ontological status of atoms or material things is defined in terms of the order in which they are expressed. That order constitutes the logic of expression, which itself serves as the rhetorical or communicational matrix of ontological possibility. Because expressions or propositions are the smallest intelligible units in such a logic, atoms are thought-expressions, functions of intelligent meaning. For Edwards, such a logic transforms bodies from substances into expressions of divine communication or, to use the Ramist term, "arguments." This portrayal of the elements of being and reasoning in turn opens up the possibility that bodies can be understood as immaterial.

The radical challenge to classical metaphysics implicit in this alternative logic so dominates Edwards' fundamental insights into the nature of reality and his arguments concerning reason, beauty, freedom, and divine purpose that it is difficult to overemphasize it. However, for Edwards the system of signification which such a logic expresses always seems just out of reach of human cognition, making it, in Foucault's words, one cog out of alignment with the system of divine intelligibility. Its attraction lies in its provocation to move to another moment in the ongoing conversation. It is the lure of the other implicit in the very possibility of signification, the requirement that being be understood as intentional.

In place of this logic, fallen humanity turns to the "other logic" of classical, Platonic-Aristotelian predication contained in Locke's way of ideas or the Cartesianism of Antoine Arnauld's *Art of Thinking*. That other logic surfaces in Edwards' discussions of ordinary language and artificial signs. It runs throughout his examinations of epistemological questions. Wherever he wants to avoid the appearance of speaking with certainty, he turns to what for him is that new approach for associating ideas.

As fashionable as Locke or Arnauld might have been, the old logic of Edwards' Ramist education continues to promise him new and strange suggestions for reflective exploration. At the time he was teaching both forms of logic to his Yale undergraduates, he notes that the (typically Ramist) predilection for classification among our ideas suggests a pleasing harmony that only hints at the order that unites all things in beauty or excellence:

> One reason why at first, before I knew other logic, I used to be mightily pleased with the study of the old logic, was because it was very pleasant to see my thoughts, that before lay in my mind jumbled without any distinction, ranged into order and distributed into classes and subdivisions, that I could tell where they all belonged and run up to their general heads. For this logic consisted much in distributions and definitions; and their maxims gave occasion to observe new and strange dependencies of ideas, and a seeming agreement of multitudes of them in the same thing, that I never observed before.[5]

5. Edwards, "The Mind," #17 [1725], *Scientific and Philosophic Writings*, 345. Cf. Morris, *Young Jonathan Edwards*, 404; and Rick Kennedy, "The Alliance between Puritanism and Cartesian Logic at Harvard, 1687–1735," *Journal of the History of Ideas* 51 (1990), 571–72.

The distributions, definitions, and maxims by which these strange dependencies of ideas emerge establish an order or agreement of things that would otherwise go unnoticed. Here Edwards could not be referring to obvious differences in species or natural kinds, but rather must be referring to what he elsewhere calls the analogy, consent, agreeableness, or harmony that holds between things and their "mental perfections," the "order of the world, the designed distribution of God and nature."[6] That order encompasses not only the typological relations of analogy or consent between "the beauty of the skies, trees, fields, flowers, etc. and spiritual excellencies," but also "the analogy there is in the bodies of all animals and in all plants and in the different parts of the inanimate creation."[7] Concerning this latter set of relations, Edwards singles out for special notice the peculiar effects that certain plants have on animal bodies.

To some extent these references to the hidden analogies of things as the foundation of their agreement or "inward conformation" might rely on Locke's theory that the real essences of things could be discerned only at a molecular level. Yet that would not account for Edwards' association of the analogies found in nature with their spiritual counterparts. In order to make the spiritual connection, Edwards has to appeal to a logic that assumes a uniformity and universal extension of harmonic relations, a logic in which things are seen to come together, to convene in the strange dependencies that unite multitudes of ideas in the same thing. What looks at first like an art of reasoning based on a rhetoric of maxims and distinctions thus becomes the epistemological introduction to an ontology of universal relations. By means of such a logic, Edwards unites typological inferences with the agreement of ideas and the mutual conformity of bodies in nature. In effect, nature is translated into terms compatible with the spiritual.

Since this logic covers all aspects of intelligible reality, all relations—including the implicit medical, magical, and astrological agreements of things—presume its presence. Since it constitutes the possibility of meaning in discourse (human and otherwise), it cannot be distinguished, as can Locke's way of ideas or the Port-Royal art of thinking, from ontology. It comprises the logico-metaphysical order that guarantees the non-arbitrary linkages between ideas.[8] It is the logic of the genesis of meaning and existence, the logic of things coming into being. Most importantly from a semiotic stance, because it is the logic of expression, enunciation, and communication, it is the Ur-rhetoric of original signification.

As Miklós Vetö observes, Edwards' position here is comparable to that of Leibniz. Indeed Leibniz's search for a universal language sounds similar to Edwards' project. But Leibniz's early interest in an aboriginal language of

---

6. See Edwards, "The Mind," #47 [1726], 366–67; and Miscellany #108 [1724].
7. See Miscellany #108; and Miscellany #651 [1734], in Jonathan Edwards, *The Philosophy of Jonathan Edwards*, ed. Harvey G. Townsend, 262.
8. See Miklós Vetö, *La Pensée de Jonathan Edwards*, 312.

significance gradually gives way to the logic of the monadology, a logic of predication that validates the propriety of separating word, idea, and thing.[9] It is in terms of this latter logic that Vetö juxtaposes Edwards and Leibniz.

In those same terms, William Morris links Edwards to the Dutch Protestant Suarezians Burgersdijck and Heereboord.[10] His strategy of drawing attention to their shared Ramist heritage inappropriately reads back into Ramist ontology the substance-accident metaphysics that ultimately convinces Morris that Ramist logic undermines the possibility for any metaphysics. Indeed, in the context of the Aristotelian-Cartesian-Lockean logic of predication used by Burgersdijck, Heereboord, and the later Leibniz, the alternative presented by Ramist ontology makes no sense at all and thus (in Morris' reading) cannot support a metaphysics.

As fundamental and pervasive as the Ramist outlook is in the Renaissance episteme, it comes as no surprise, though, that elements of the mentality surface even in supposedly non-Ramist works with which Edwards is familiar. For example, in his discussion of the "Convenience of Things," Burgersdijck notes that analogy may be attributed to all things in general, insofar as any thing can be brought together or convened with anything else in providing an account or rationale for the thing. "Convenience," Burgersdijck writes, "is that by which many, or as many, are united amongst themselves. Real convenience is the convenience of one thing with itself; reason, the convenience of many things in one conception."[11] Insofar as things come to be and are thought in terms of one another, they exist in relation. The relation necessarily implies an other, a cause or reason, without which a thing cannot exist or be thought. The formal necessity of such relations accounts (as Edwards himself often remarks) for why all things that begin to be must have a sufficient reason for their existence.

This coming together of things appears in Edwards' doctrine of excellency as being's consent to being; but exactly what that means can still puzzle students of Edwards—at least until it is interpreted in terms of Ramist logic. In this regard Samuel Johnson, tutor at Yale prior to and (briefly) during Edwards' undergraduate years, provides a clue concerning the essential relatability of all things. In his *Synopsis of Natural Philosophy,* composed sometime around 1714, Johnson notes that "Relativity is an affection of nature in accordance with which nature is fit to be relative or to have relations. And all creatures are without exception related."[12] There is in nature a fitness or propriety in a thing's being related; and in being related, natural things exhibit the affections

9. Cf. Michael Losonsky, "Leibniz's Adamic Language of Thought," *Journal of the History of Philosophy* 30 (1992), 530–39.

10. See Morris, *Young Jonathan Edwards,* 91–92, 112–13, 463, 537, 545. Cf. Lee W. Gibbs, ed., *Technometry,* by William Ames (Philadelphia: University of Pennsylvania Press, 1979), 51–53, 82–84.

11. Franco Burgersdijck, *Monitic Logica* [an abstract of his *Institutio Logicae*] (London: R. Cumberland, 1697), 1:77; also 1:75, 78. Cf. William S. Morris, "The Genius of Jonathan Edwards," in *Reinterpretation in American Church History,* ed. Jerald C. Brauer, 40–41, 49.

12. Cited in *Samuel Johnson, President of King's College: His Career and Writings,* ed. Herbert Schneider and Carol Schneider, 2:35. Cf. Morris, *Young Jonathan Edwards,* 433, 572–73.

or consents whereby all things are linked rationally through the conveniences of specific conceptions.

Since concepts by their very nature exhibit their affects or affections as internal relations to other things, they constitute the "arguments" that guide the proper use of reason. As such, the ability of a thing to have relations and to be related rationally to other things is a feature of the thing. The rationality of the arguments that relate things is a function of the things themselves and not a passive function of their mode of apprehension, because arguments are ontological, and not merely conceptual or rhetorical, relations. In contrast to the predicate logic of the Aristotelian-Lockean mentality, the economy of Ramist logic identifies arguments as the real existents of the world, and it is in terms of their affections that things are intelligible. As the guide for reasoning, each argument establishes (in Perry Miller's words) a "grammar without verbs," an implicit order of things that defines the activity of right reason.[13] This Ramist coalescence of rhetoric, logic, epistemology, and ontology in the device of the argument provides Edwards with the precise mechanism he needs to justify the association of typological argumentation with his analysis of matter, bodies, and being in general.

The seed for such a union had already been sown by a contemporary of Burgersdijck, William Ames. Warmly recommended (by Cotton Mather, for one) to students at Harvard and Yale, Ames reiterates Ramus' claim that the intelligible order that pervades all reality is contained in the arguments (or things) that comprise the world. The account of such an order, he claims, outlines an explicitly non-Neoplatonic "technometry," a strategy for reasoning that makes each argument a type, and each type the means by which the world becomes discursive. As part of the study of being itself, this consideration of typological relations falls properly under physics, insofar as things contain complicitly the *logos* or reason by which meaningful speech is made possible. In fact, the principles of discourse are identical to the relational strategies of understanding and reason, because the mutual affections of a thing define it as a thing immanently and typologically related to other things as part of the network of discursive relations that comprise reason:

> Reason, relation, and the mutual affection of things shine forth around the type from all sides and from its every part, so that by this means the things themselves are conveyed to our understanding, which does not perceive otherwise than under reason and some affections. Hence the principles of discoursing.[14]

---

13. See Perry Miller, *The New England Mind: The Seventeenth Century*, 124, 149. Cf. Morris, *Young Jonathan Edwards*, 68–69.

14. See Gibbs, ed., *Technometry*, 54–56; and Miller, *Seventeenth Century*, 150, 177. Ames was a student of Alexander Richardson, author of the Ramist *Logicians School-Master* (1629, 1657). For more on Richardson, see John C. Adams, "Alexander Richardson's Puritan Theory of Discourse," *Rhetorica* 4 (1986), 255–74, especially 264–66; John C. Adams, "Alexander Richardson's Philosophy of Art and the Sources of the Puritan Social Ethic," *Journal of the History of Ideas* 50 (1989), 233–45; and Stephen R. Yarbrough and John C. Adams, *Delightful Conviction: Jonathan Edwards and the Rhetoric of Conversion*, 48, 69–76.

Because typology and logic deal with the relations of things (i.e., arguments), rather than mere words, their principles of discourse radically revise the classical understanding of physical things. Physics in this view cannot treat a body as an inert object; rather, it must acknowledge the lively affections in terms of which a thing is said to exist and to generate reasoned movement of thought. To the extent that our understanding is activated by and subsequently traces the affections that "shine forth from all sides and from every part" of the thing, we participate in the discourse, speech, *logos,* or logic of things.

This generative reunderstanding of the nature of a thing in terms of an argument resonates in Edwards' peculiar talk of how natural things represent spiritual things "livelily." As if drawing particular attention to the spirited character of even so-called inanimate objects, Edwards (like Ames) displaces physics with physiology, mere rhetorical augmentation with a logico-rhetoric of things. As the physiological expression of the ontological union or harmony of things, the motions of "animal spirits" guarantee the proper union of things to one another in virtue of spirited or lively indications about how ideas of those things are to move.[15] Through their mutual affections, things enliven discourse and implicate logic in an ontology of activity. As Ames notes in his fittingly titled *Theses Physiologiae,* logic functions in the philosophy of things, not in the philosophy of words.[16]

The physiological and medical implications of the analogies of plants and animal bodies trade on the same ontology that establishes the affective relations between celestial bodies and terrestrial creatures. In the context of Edwards' astrological considerations, the essential relations that order and mutually define things permeate nature as an infinitely subtle matter. As the embodiment of the lines of affection or analogies disclosed in the Ramist doctrine of arguments, this subtle matter joins things in nature in precisely the same way that Johnson's relativity or Ames' typological physiology unites things logically.

In Edwards' version, the stars and planets "may act upon sublunary things, as plants, animals, bodies of men, and, indirectly, upon their souls too, by that infinitely subtle matter diffused all round them, which in all probability is so subtle as to permeate the air and any bodies whatsoever."[17] Distributed universally throughout nature, this matter constitutes the logical matrix in which astrological or medical inferences are ontologically grounded. The availability of such a matrix permits Edwards and other thinkers working in the Renaissance episteme not only to consider the possibility of astrological, alchemical,

15. See Edwards, "The Mind," #1 [1723] and #42 [1725], 336, 361. Cf. Morris, *Young Jonathan Edwards,* 429–30.

16. See Edwards' personal copy of William Partridge's handwritten version of Ames' *Theses Physiologiae* [p. 24], Beinecke Library, Yale University.

17. "Things to be Considered an[d] Written fully about" [c. 1721], in *Scientific and Philosophic Writings,* 236; also 252-53 [c. 1723–24]. See also Miscellany #976 [c. 1744], in *Philosophy of Edwards,* 109. On Heereboord's nature mysticism, see Morris, *Young Jonathan Edwards,* 108, 538–39. Cf. Walter Pagel, *Paracelsus: An Introduction to Philosophical Medicine in the Era of the Renaissance,* 2d ed., 65–72.

or magical relations, but also to justify scientific and typological argumentation by appealing to the specific marks of signification found in and on things.

In terms of medicine, such an inquiry assumes that things by their nature must signify other things in order to have any meaning of their own. Because those signs always appear as part of a divine discourse, their communicative network of expressions infuses nature with a distinctively rhetorical character. To say, as Johnson does in 1714, that "things are God's words in print," repeats a commonplace not only in Ramist doctrines, but also in medical texts.[18] Such texts emphasize how the practice of medicine requires that one humbly submit to the order of creation, while recognizing that nature exhibits a system of signs that can be read. Things in nature are intelligible because they communicate, and they can communicate only if they are legible.

The demand that things be legible conflates two tasks in the Ramist project that ultimately permits Edwards' divine semiotics. The first task is to describe how things are legible signs, that is, how the significance of one thing for another can be discerned by those familiar with the often arcane script of nature. Such a script provides the ontological grounding necessary for medical, alchemical, and astrological practices and reasoning. The second task is to explain how the legibility of signs assumes a strategy of rhetorical or communicative exchange. This task reveals the presuppositions of the practical use of signs in reasoning by examining the practices that establish and maintain a system of signs in the first place. The first task is the concern of alchemists and physicians like Paracelsus and his follower Oswald Croll (c. 1560–1609); the second, the concern of Agricola and Ramus.

Chapter 1 alluded to the 1669 English translation of Croll's *Signatures of Internal Things* in regard to Foucault's discussion of the Renaissance episteme. Here I return to Croll in part to draw out more closely the relevance of such views for Edwards. Anyone who has read Edwards' "Images of Divine Things" cannot help but recognize Croll's commonplace references to "the Shadow and Image of the Creatour imprest in the Creatures."[19] Even if Edwards had never seen a copy of Croll's work—including the copy owned by Thomas James (d. 1711) of Easthampton, who studied under Charles Chauncy, tutor at Harvard—he certainly would have been familiar with the Renaissance mentality that could read possible medical remedies in the signatures of things.

Indeed, the key word here is *read*, for Croll, like others, wants to drive home the way in which the signatures of nature provide a script for empowering even the most abject creature in God's rhetoric of excellence:

All Herbs, Flowers, Trees, and other things which proceed out of the Earth, are Books, and Magick Signes, communicated to us, by the immense Mercy of God,

18. See his *Technologia sive Technometria*, in *Samuel Johnson*, 2:67. Cf. Miller, *Seventeenth Century*, 124.

19. See Oswald Croll, *Signatures of Internal Things*, bound with Croll's *Basilica Chymica*, trans. John Hartman (London: John Stukey and Thomas Passenger, 1669–70), preface. For more on Croll, see Allen G. Debus, *The Chemical Philosophy: Paracelsian Science and Medicine in the Sixteenth and Seventeenth Centuries*, 1:117–24.

which Signes are our Medicine. God hath Created nothing in vain, but he has endowed every Creature, though never so abject, with peculiar vertues, according to his Divine Will and Pleasure. For which Cause, they far otherwise understand, who observe Nature in the least and most abject Creatures, to be most excellent, and where it seems to be deficient in Body, to abound in Vertues. . . . Nothing is placed in the Family of Plants either unadvisedly or in vain, but in a rare manner, from their seasonable ordained causes, are produced in exact number, time, and place. And as in things Mute the Gesture is instead of Speech; and other Animals wanting speech, by the Motion of the body declare the Affects of their Sense: So also God to every Plant hath insisted its discoverer, that the Genuine Vertues of Herbs latently abscondited, by their External Signatures, that is, by the similitude of their Form and Figure (as by Index's of their Office, Essence, and Latent Vertues) may by their Aspect be known, discovered, and manifested: yea so, as in the manner aforesaid, by their Signatures they Magically seem to speak to us. For, as Men who in digging find a Treasure, are wont to note the place by some certain Sign: So also GOD Himself hath signated very many things in Nature, which he hath not apparently manifested, by which only Signature we may, though diligent inquisition find them out.[20]

Implicit in Croll's discussion of folk medicine and in other treatments of hermetic astrology is more than simply an extended use of the book-of-nature metaphor. The thematic return to the virtues of things, juxtaposed with the rhetorical vocabulary of affective declarations that "magically seem to speak to us," places the hidden, the deferred, the magical at the center of what drives the possibility of the literacy of nature. To read the signs one has to acknowledge their absolutely ineradicable presence within the divine discourse. Made legible precisely because of their significatory powers, they are not dispensed with when what they signify is identified.

As Edwards will later acknowledge, this historicity of things marks them with the sign of God, not in the sense that God is in history, but in the sense that the meaning of things is to be understood in terms of what they communicate or say of an other. In this economy of signification, each thing signifies because its existence contributes as a necessary component to the excellence of all. In addition, the significance of the whole (nature, history) is defined and perfected in terms of its Other, God. Underlying all of this is an ontology that endorses the inescapable immediacy of signifier-signified units as the irreducible components of existence. Each of these units in its turn comprises nothing less than a speech.

By making the signature a determinate and ineradicable aspect of each unit of meaning, this rhetorical reformulation of reality validates the necessary role of the signature in understanding the text of nature.[21] For both Croll and Edwards, this legibility of creation ultimately enacts the speech of God. That speech instills in things the mutual affections that determine the propriety of their relations and guide all reasoning, including medical diagnoses and treat-

20. *Signatures,* preface. Thomas James' copy of Croll's *Signatures* is in the Beinecke Library.
21. Cf. Pagel, *Paracelsus,* 50–57.

ments. It likewise serves as the transcendental condition for astrological and alchemical speculation, and in that way it legitimates the "diligent inquisitions" of Croll and his mentor Paracelsus.

In choosing discourse as the model on which to challenge the classical, substantialist ontology, though, Paracelsian inquiries point only to the benefits that follow from using this alternative ontology as verification of its propriety. No attempt is made to explain how such an ontology itself is to be established. Instead of justifying strategies for reasoning about nature, thinkers in the Renaissance episteme enact the rhetorical or incantational process by which those strategies are legitimated precisely as parts of a discourse. These thinkers recognize that any attempt to justify the very structure of signatures, types, or affective relations must itself appeal to that same structure. In appealing to astrology and signatures to explain the world, Paracelsus and other thinkers in the hermetic tradition thus do not search for meaning apart from discursive practices in which meaning is embedded. Rather, they celebrate the immanence of figural immediacy and all the prospects of ontological enhancement and disruption implicit in it.

Like Johnson and Ames, Edwards relies for the internal rationale of that alternative ontology on the patterns of reasoning outlined by Ramus and his predecessor Rudolph Agricola.[22] But because Edwards and his contemporaries presuppose those patterns as the essential characteristics of thought itself, they see little need to make explicit reference to them. Edwards' silence turns the best of scholars away from pursuing the Ramist context: witness Perry Miller's *The New England Mind: The Seventeenth Century* where, as Walter Ong observes, Ramism is pervasive; but in Miller's *Jonathan Edwards*, Ramus is not mentioned once.[23]

Together, Agricola (1444–1485), Paracelsus (1493–1541), and Peter Ramus (1515–1572) epitomize the Renaissance episteme. They lay out the conditions for a method of reasoning that competes side by side with the classical (predicate logic) mentality appropriated in Cartesian and Lockean discussions. They participate in a tradition ignored and misinterpreted by the Italian humanists and Edwards' modernist contemporaries. But through thinkers like Richardson and Ames, they establish an intellectual context in terms of which Edwards' doctrines have significance.

Whether Edwards read any of these Renaissance thinkers, or even whether we or Edwards interpret their texts correctly, is not at issue here. If it were, I would certainly attend more closely to their writings in a comparison with

---

22. On Ramus' admiration of Paracelsus, see Henry M. Pachter, *Paracelsus: Magic into Science*, 305. Cf. Morris, *Young Jonathan Edwards*, 423.

23. Cf. Walter J. Ong, *Ramus: Method, and the Decay of Dialogue*, 4; and Perry Miller, *Jonathan Edwards*. In *The New England Mind: The Seventeenth Century* (p. 116), Miller writes: "The fundamental fact concerning the intellectual life of New Englanders is that they ranged themselves definitely under the banner of the Ramists. . . . It is not too much to say that, while Augustine and Calvin have been widely recognized as the sources of Puritanism, upon New England Puritans the logic of Petrus Ramus exerted fully as great an influence as did either of the theologians."

Edwards' works. Instead, I use Agricola or Ramus as markers for an outlook that can help explain how Edwards can reason as he does.

Admittedly, Edwards' contemporaries recognize that Ramists espouse a complete philosophy, not simply another pedagogy, rhetoric, or form of logic unencumbered by ontological commitments. Comparable in stature to Neoplatonism or Aristotelianism, Ramism supplies an epistemology, an ontology, an aesthetics—in short, every aspect of a comprehensive philosophy. But Ramist thought never allows reflective activity to become divorced from the rhetorical genesis of meanings in its essentially Stoic logic of propositions. By assuming the legitimacy of Stoic doctrines (e.g., the *lekton*), Ramists are able to argue that predication (speech) creates things in creating the discourse of which they are functions. Philosophy in such a view is generated literally out of reading that discourse: it is the *ek-lekton* par excellence.

When Samuel Johnson thus characterizes philosophy in terms of three schools—Platonists, Peripatetics, and the Eclectics headed up by Ramus—he does not mean to imply that the Ramists simply combine features of the other two.[24] Rather, in reinforcing Justus Lipsius' identification of Stoics as Eclectics, Johnson brings into prominence the Ramist logic of reading signatures as a generative ontology or epistemic physiology in which meaning comes into being in the rhetoric of logical expression.[25] In pronouncing on the significance of signatures, the eclectic (the *ek-lector*) reinstates the centrality of speech and communication in ontology. Such a move is so thoroughly at odds with the substantialist, predicate logics of both Platonists and Aristotelians that a different category of philosophizing must be created to accommodate it.

Making room for this alternate way of thinking, however, does not mean that Neoplatonic or Peripatetic thought has no role to play in Edwards' philosophy. Indeed, he retains the classical episteme in its Cartesian and Lockean forms in explaining a number of his positions. But at those points where Edwards appears particularly vulnerable to a classical critique (e.g., in his doctrines on divine providence, human freedom, or the communicative *Logos* underlying his typology), he appeals to the argumentation of the Renaissance (Stoic-Ramist) episteme. Again, such appeals do not make Edwards a Stoic philosopher, if by that were meant that he endorses the doctrines of the middle or late Stoa. Instead, he appeals to the logic of propositions developed by the early Stoics (e.g., Zeno of Citium and Chrysippus) and then, for the most part, lost by later members of the school.

---

24. See *Samuel Johnson*, 2: 60–61. Cf. Gibbs, ed., *Technometry*, 73; and Miller, *Seventeenth Century*, 119.

25. Justus Lipsius (1547–1606) refers to the Stoics as Eclectics in his *Manuductio ad Stoicam Philosophiam* (1604), and he addresses the *lekton* issue in his *Physiologia Stoicorum* (1604). Cf. Jason L. Saunders, *Justus Lipsius: The Philosophy of Renaissance Stoicism*, 75, 181; and Philip A. Smith, "Bishop Hall, 'Our English Seneca'," *PMLA* 63 (1948), 1191–99. For a sample of some of the works by Seneca, Lipsius, and Hall at Yale during Edwards' stay, see Louise May Bryant and Mary Patterson, "The List of Books Sent by Jeremiah Dummer . . . ," in *Papers in Honor of Andrew Keogh, Librarian of Yale University*, ed. Yale University Library Staff, 423–92.

Scholars admit that it is notoriously difficult to discover exactly what the early Stoics meant in proposing a logic centered on propositions.[26] But at least part of the rationale for such a position appears in the Stoic insistence on the importance of hypothetical and disjunctive syllogisms in marked contrast to the Aristotelian logic of classes. As both Miller and Ong recognize, that alternative to predicate logic is renewed in the Agricolan-Ramist program underlying New England's fascination with Cicero and Seneca. Even Burgersdijck remarks, in his widely used logic textbook, that Agricola particularly effects the turn of logic away from Aristotle to Cicero, and through Cicero to the Stoic tradition in general.[27]

What the Stoics themselves may have meant by their propositional logic; or whether Agricola and Ramus knew that they were employing a distinctively Stoic form of reasoning; or whether New Englanders like Edwards recognized how the practical, action-oriented, and generative nature of hypothetical and disjunctive thinking affects the doctrines of the middle and later Stoa—all are secondary issues (for present purposes) to the question of how Stoic, Ramist, hermetic, or "eclectic" strategies function in the Renaissance episteme. To the extent that Edwards' thought is developed in terms of that paradigm, it assumes that all reality exhibits an intelligible order in virtue of its rhetorical or communicative character. For Edwards to say, then, that the world is a divine communication is for him to allude to an ontology that undercuts the divorce of rhetoric from metaphysics. The fact that he does not have to justify or explain such a move indicates that it has already been made apparent by the Ramist project.

At the heart of that project are what the Ramists call "arguments," the things that comprise the universe. They are, at one and the same time, the ultimate simples of both sensation and terminology (*simplicia sensa, simplicia nomina*), because the possibility of their discrimination depends on their placement in a discourse by which they are meaningfully related and distinguished. The visual discrimination of things touted in the *theoria* of Plato and Aristotle is here subordinated to the aural ordering of things in assertions.[28] In that ordering, a thing is that which can be expressed meaningfully and recognizably as a commonplace in discourse.

What makes an expression recognizable, though, is not the idea to which it refers; rather, it is its place in the pattern or sequence of (in themselves) unintelligible, and therefore unexperienced, sounds or marks. Even phonemes and morphemes have to be learned as discrete elements within a discourse, so the recognition of syllables already implies a familiarity with a network of figural

---

26. See, for example, Benson Mates, *Stoic Logic*, 2; and Andreas Graeser, "The Stoic Theory of Meaning," in *The Stoics*, ed. John M. Rist, 89. Cf. John Corcoran, "Remarks on Stoic Deduction," in *Ancient Logic and Its Modern Interpretations*, ed. John Corcoran, 171.

27. See Franco Burgersdijck, *Institutionum logicorum libri duo*, preface. Cf. Ong, *Ramus*, 93, 125, 186. See also Miller, *Seventeenth Century*, 136, 244, 261.

28. Cf. Ong, *Ramus*, 66, 107, 195, 308; and Miller, *Seventeenth Century*, 124, 148–50.

differentiations and relations.[29] To say (as the Ramists do) that even a human being is an argument and is composed of arguments (e.g., hands, passions, causes, size, being a father) discloses how each of those terms points to and relies on others for meaning.

Arguments are determinate things because they are the commonplaces (the *topoi* or *loci*) of differentiation within discourse. The order of arguments follows from the order of things. But since the two are the same as expressions of generative discourse, the key to discerning the order of reason lies in learning the rhetorical order of the commonplaces. Insofar as a network of differentiations exhibits the determinate relations embodied by arguments, it establishes the specific order of reasoning or *logos* that characterizes discourse.[30]

If marks were identifiable only as differentiated in virtue of their place in a discursive structure (as in Saussure's semiotics), then signatures could not guarantee the propriety or rationality of any inference based on them. That would require that the structure itself be legitimated or grounded in something other than discourse. However, because the Ramist doctrine of arguments assumes that nothing (not even the smallest particle or atom) can exist apart from its expression in a discourse, no thing can be determinate apart from its coming into being as part of the process of communicative exchange.

As in the case of the interpretant in Peirce's semiotics, a Ramist argument exhibits a certain degree of arbitrariness. Why a particular thing should come into being in certain signifier-signified relations at first appears gratuitous, but the charge of arbitrariness can be raised only from a substantialist perspective, because in the Stoic-Ramist view a thing cannot even be imagined apart from its embodiment precisely in those relations. Being *placed* as related in a specific enunciation brings an entity into being; the entity is that speech, that *lekton*. The *lekton* identifies the ontological coming into being of a thing specifically as its expression in a proposition.[31] Accordingly, God's speech or communication provides the interpretant or *lekton* by which a thing becomes the very thing that it is and nothing else. Its identity depends on its place as an expression in the divine discourse, and its meaning or significance depends on its being recognized in those terms.

When Edwards claims that bodies are specific determinations of God's will and that individuals embody specific tendencies to commit evil acts, his position appeals to a thoroughly Stoic doctrine of providence, mediated by a Ramist ontology of expression. According to that ontology, the very possibility of being or meaning assumes a strategy of pedagogic, communicative, or rhetorical activity. God's providential creation is of necessity an act of teaching, a communication, a pronouncement of judgment on the order of discourse.

---

29. See Ong, *Ramus*, 195, 308.

30. Cf. A. A. Long, *Hellenistic Philosophy: Stoics, Epicureans, Sceptics*, 2d ed., 124–25.

31. See A. A. Long, "Language and Thought in Stoicism," in *Problems in Stoicism*, ed. A. A. Long, 75–113; Michael Frede, *Essays in Ancient Philosophy*, 156, 344–45; Michael Frede, "The Original Notion of Cause," in *Doubt and Dogmatism: Studies in Hellenistic Epistemology*, ed. Malcolm Schofield, Myles Burnyeat, and Jonathan Barnes, 223; and Graeser, "Stoic Theory of Meaning," 89.

Agricola makes precisely this point in claiming that all discourse is directed to teaching (*doctrina*). Ramus repeats the idea: Learning the places—that is, "finding" arguments (*inventio*)—means learning the teachings of discursivity itself.[32] In "pronouncing sentence" on arguments, the teacher reinforces the commonplaces in terms of which subsequent judgment is possible.[33] Before a judgment can be made using arguments, the meaning of such arguments must be determined. Finding or determining that meaning requires that the teacher place the argument into the traditional expressions of a culture. The classicist, linguist, and philologist all recover the oratorical heritage and legacy of a discourse, and in doing so they retrieve the expansive possibilities of the ontology of the Ciceronian (and Stoic) tradition.[34] In fashioning the order of arguments, speech (in the person of the teacher) defines the rationality of being by legislating what is legible, literally lecturing the *lekton.*

Linguistic or communicative signatures establish the foundation for rationality by providing the seeds of the divine *Logos* or wisdom of God's first productive principle (σπερματικὸν λόγον ὄντα τὰ κόσμος).[35] In terms of such signs, the mind passes a judgment (in Edwards' words) "not only exceedingly quick, as soon as one thought can follow another, but absolutely without any reflection at all, and at the same moment without any time intervening. . . . Thus when I hear such and such sounds, or see such letters, I judge that such things are signified, without reasoning."[36] In contrast to Aristotelian discursivity, this logic of signification employs a discourse in which judgment coincides with understanding, and understanding means learning the policies of communicative order.

Developing themes raised by St. Augustine, Edwards suggests that the task of the teacher is to pronounce judgment on arguments, validating the implicit arrangement or assembly of things which, apart from this oral or rhetorical performance, remain disjointed atoms of thought. When Edwards concludes that "knowledge in the teacher is the universal cause of knowledge in the scholar," he highlights the causal integrity of teaching and knowing.[37] Knowl-

---

32. See Ong, *Ramus*, 103–05, 114, 122, 160, 212; and Wilbur Samuel Howell, *Logic and Rhetoric in England, 1500–1700*, 23–24. Cf. R. A. Markus, "St. Augustine on Signs," in *Augustine: A Collection of Critical Essays*, ed. R. A. Markus, 70–71.

33. For references to "arguments," see Jonathan Edwards, "Images of Divine Things," ed. Wallace E. Anderson, in *Typological Writings*, ed. Wallace E. Anderson and Mason I. Lowance, Jr., with David Watters, 56n, 57. Cf. Ong, *Ramus*, 72, 184–87, 203.

34. Edwards' contemporary, Giambattista Vico, associates the judicial and rhetorical character of arguments with Stoic ontology in *On the Most Ancient Wisdom of the Italians*, trans. Lucia M. Palmer, 69–76, 99, 178, 184. See Stephen H. Daniel, "Vico's Historicism and the Ontology of Arguments," *Journal of the History of Philosophy*, forthcoming.

35. In Miscellanies #955 and #956 [both mid-1740s], Edwards extracts passages about these and other Stoic doctrines from Theophilus Gale's *Court of the Gentiles*, 2d ed. In Miscellany #975 [mid-1740s], he refers to Isaac Barrow's approving reference to the Stoic treatment of the unity of God, noting in particular Seneca's depiction of God as the author of things. For comparable Stoic themes in Paracelsus, see Pagel, *Paracelsus*, 84–85.

36. Edwards, "The Mind," #59 [1728], 373.

37. See Edwards' notes [1724–25] in his copy of William Brattle's "Compendium of Logic," cited by Anderson, ed., *Scientific and Philosophic Writings*, 350n.

edge in the teacher is intelligible only when it is recognized by the scholar in arguments. The teacher's doctrines are thus meaningful only insofar as they rehearse a rhetorical history of enunciation filled with aphorisms and committed to the use and interpretation of signs.

That is why knowing is an art learned through an apprenticeship in the study of texts. The texts report the commonplaces of speeches uttered, judgments pronounced, diagnoses and cures explained. Medicine must be "shot through with rhetoric," because the Book of Nature is written in aphorisms and signatures without which it would be absolutely unintelligible.[38] In one performative act, the enunciation of places establishes the syntactic and semantic requirements for signification. Because of that, the scholar can know only what is taught, only what is asserted in the invention of arguments and in the expression of axioms (the declaration of the order of arguments). As the Stoic doctrines of the *lekton* and *axioma* maintain, one can think only what can be said or has been said.

In denying that arguments are either physical things placed into an intellectual context or ideas translated into a physical vocabulary, Ramus retrieves the Stoic grasp of the importance of the legal and rhetorical history of a thing. That history defines a thing as an argument, the rationale of the thing by which it takes on historical significance and in terms of which history itself exhibits its own rationale. Thus, in addition to its differentiation from other contemporaneous (synchronic) events, a thing has meaning insofar as its placement points to what it displaces historically (diachronically). For Edwards, and anyone else in the Ramist tradition, in order for a thing to be, it must be posited or *supposed* in place of something else. That act of supposition identifies the aboriginal moment in which both history and meaning are generated.

As Ames points out, this in turn means that the rational order of things (the *logos* of nature) is implicit in things, because every thing contains the reason or argument by which it is intelligibly related to other things in virtue of its being uttered. Even synteresis—the intuitive grasp of the highest principles, the immediate sense of right and wrong, or recognition of fitness—is simply a logical inference of right reason, the act of reaching a conclusion through knowing the argument.[39] Since the mind, as an argument itself, is inherently part of the rhetorical and legal history of other arguments and axioms, it is able to achieve scientific certainty—even to the point of being able to judge whether the narration of someone's religious conversion is genuine. For insofar as a narration causes a listener to make the same connections as those adopted in the narration, it establishes the possibility for a charitable hearing.[40] By con-

38. See Ong, *Ramus*, 226–28.
39. See Miller, *Seventeenth Century*, 150, 193. On how Ames denies that this way of thinking is Platonic, see ibid., 177. Cf. Ong, *Ramus*, 105, 206, 252.
40. See John C. Adams, "Ramist Concepts of Testimony, Judicial Analogies, and the Puritan Conversion Narrative," *Rhetorica* 9 (1991), 254–67.

trast, since syllogistic reasoning does not include the actual formation of mind as a function of its own constitutive structure, it yields only probability and raises only doubt.

The Ontology of Supposition

To say that the mind is an argument, itself a commonplace among other commonplaces, immediately alerts us to how this view dissolves the substantialist distinction of mind and world through an appeal to the rhetorical strategies that permit distinctions in the first place. Expressed originally and irreducibly as propositions rather than as terms in a proposition, the mind and all its objects function implicitly as moments of intelligible communication. By its very nature, that intelligibility designates the otherness of all reality expressed by the Stoic emphasis on hypothetical or disjunctive reasoning. Always already defined in terms of its intentionality as implying an other or as distinct from an other, every intelligible existent enacts a strategic dismantling of classical predicate logic. In the process, modernist assumptions about the independence of epistemology or metaphysics from rhetoric are overturned by the emergence of a logic that locates minds and other existents as places in the discursive space of being.

Nowhere is such a practice more evident or more misunderstood than in regard to Edwards' repeated attacks on the notion of nothingness and his insistence that everything has a cause. Absolute nothingness, he points out, cannot be conceived, because to conceive it would be to conceive something and thus would involve a contradiction:

> That there should absolutely be nothing at all is utterly impossible. The mind can never, let it stretch its conceptions ever so much, bring itself to conceive of a state of perfect nothing. It puts the mind into mere convulsion and confusion to endeavor to think of such a state, and it contradicts the very nature of the soul to think that it should be; and it is the greatest contradiction, and the aggregate of all contradictions, to say that there should not be. 'Tis true we can't so distinctly shew the contradiction by words because we cannot talk about it without speaking horrid nonsense, and contradicting ourselves at every word, and because 'nothing' is that whereby we distinctly shew other particular contradictions. But here we are run up to our first principle, and have no other to explain the nothingness or not being of nothing by. Indeed, we can mean nothing else by 'nothing' but a state of absolute contradiction.[41]

More often than not this kind of charge is understood to apply only to the *mind's* inability to conceive of nothing. But that epistemological limitation cannot be extended to the claim of ontological impossibility unless we import, ready-made, some form of idealism that defines all reality in terms of mind. Such a move, while convenient, would open Edwards up to all the accusations

41. Edwards, "Of Being" [c. 1721], in *Scientific and Philosophic Writings*, 202.

of skepticism typically directed against Berkeley's immaterialism (even when augmented by the appeal to God's involvement in experience).

In order for Edwards to claim that nothing is not only inconceivable but also impossible, however, he must assume that epistemology does not set the limits for ontology. Even if the distinction of epistemology and metaphysics permits a discussion of nothing as a topic, its being a topic (*topos*) relies on its place or function in a network of discursive practices. There can be a place for nothing insofar as it is supposed (sup-posited) as a place in discourse: "If anyone says, no, there be nothing, he supposes as the same time nothing has a being. And indeed nothing, when we speak properly, or when the word has any meaning, i.e. when we speak of nothing in contradiction [to] some particular being, has truly a being."[42] The being of nothing lies in its disjunction with another being, not with being itself. What makes the other being is its being supposed as other. In other words, something is intelligible if it is communicated, and the only way to communicate something is to appeal to a context in terms of which the thing can be expressed.

Though nothing can come to mean something in other epistemological and metaphysical discussions, in the ontology that identifies the places of communication in terms of propositional functions, nothing is not even the contradiction of being, because for it to function in such a disjunction would mean for it to occupy a place:

> When we go to inquire whether or no there can be absolutely nothing we speak nonsense. In inquiring, the stating of the question is nonsense, because we make a disjunction, where there is none. 'Either being or absolute nothing' is no disjunction, no more than whether a triangle is a triangle or not a triangle. There is no other way, but only for there to be existence; there is no such thing as absolute nothing. There is such a thing as nothing with respect to you and me. There is such a thing as nothing with respect to this globe of earth, and with respect to this created universe. There is another way besides these things having existence. But there is no such thing as nothing with respect to entity or being, absolutely considered. And we don't know what we say, if we say we think it possible in itself that there should not be entity.[43]

Absolute nothing cannot be thought because absolute nothing cannot be said. Even to say "absolute nothing" is to say something and therefore to say exactly what we mistakenly think might be sayable, but in fact is not. What can be said (and therefore thought) is limited to things defined in terms of propositional forms. That means that every intelligible or significant thing constitutes a disjunctive or conditional argument intentionally related to other things. Since absolute nothing is not defined in terms of such relations, it cannot have a place in Edwards' ontology.

Because this pattern of reasoning occurs throughout Edwards' writings, its organizational importance for understanding his argumentative procedures must

42. Miscellany #650 [c. 1734], in *Philosophy of Edwards*, 82.
43. Edwards, "Of Being" [1732 addition], 207.

not be underestimated. Whether it underlies his belief that no thing exists without a cause or that no thing can be understood apart from its contribution to the divine purpose of creation, this logic describes the order of thought and being by which every thing is differentiated and associated with everything else. In short, it displays the structure of discourse itself.

Yet if discourse is the space in which the supposition of disjunctions and hypotheticals occurs, then the logic of such supposition must constitute the logic of the creation of meaning. Such a logic, as Edwards' repeated appeals to the vocabulary of supposition attest, recalls the medieval theory of supposition.[44] From Ramist modifications of elements of that theory, Edwards extracts the doctrine that to suppose something is to accept that thing in place of something else. For terminists like Peter of Spain, the doctrine of supposition had allowed thinkers to use already significant terms as substitutes in propositions in order to avoid problems of quantification in Aristotelian predicate logic. But in Edwards' hands, the separation of words and things assumed in some earlier versions of supposition theory dissolves, and in its place he proposes the view that every act of supposition calls into being a new entity. The supposing of a thing places it into a discourse in which each existent is defined in terms of its disjunction from an other. Insofar as the enunciation of a thing communicates what it is (as a function of discourse), each thing exists in virtue of its rhetorical displacement of other moments of communication.

In his logic of supposition, a supposition is not something we do, as if we were to suppose a proposition ("let us suppose that . . ."); such would be the case only in the classical modern sense of supposition. From the Stoic-Ramist perspective, supposition is the displacement of a term in a proposition, by means of which displacement the term has meaning as posited in place of something else in a proposition, a supposition, a discourse. The space of discourse is always presupposed, because nothing can be supposed without being supposed as part of discourse. The fact that the space of supposition can itself have no disjunct indicates how the logic of supposition supports the necessary existence of God:

> 'Tis absurd to suppose that anything is and there is absolutely no reason why it is. When there are two parts of a disjunction, one of them will not be and not the other, unless there be some reason why one should be rather than the other. . . . A supposition of something is a supposition of the being of God. It don't only presuppose it but it implies it. It implies it not only consequently but immediately. God is the sum of all being and there is no being without his being. All things are in him, and he in all. But there is no such thing supposable as an absolute universal nothing. We talk nonsense when we suppose any such thing. We deceive ourselves when we think we do in our minds suppose it, or when we imagine we suppose it to be possible. What we do when we go to think of absolute nihility (if I may so speak) is only to remove one thing to make way for and suppose another.

44. See Ong. *Ramus*, 66–72; Philotheus Boehner, *Medieval Logic*, 27-51; and Ernest A. Moody, *Studies in Medieval Philosophy, Science and Logic*, 380–86.

> In this case there is no such thing as two parts of a disjunction. When we are come
> to being in general we are come to one single point without a disjunction. There-
> fore . . . God is, because there is nothing else to make a supposition of.[45]

Without placing such a passage in the context of a theory of supposition, Edwards' remarks appear merely to repeat standard homiletic lines (albeit with
an odd fixation on variants of the word *suppose*). Once situated in that context, however, his discussion reveals a logic that requires the existence of the
space of places as the discourse in which supposition is the first principle of
creation.

An act of supposition incorporates a thing into discourse by validating its
argumentative or rational implication of other propositional expressions. Instead of assuming that things are significant prior to their incorporation into
the rhetoric of creation, Edwards' supposition theory defines each thing in
terms of its supposition of something other than itself. In literally supposing a
thing we imply the existence of God as the other always already removed in
suppositing any thing. In terms of this theory one cannot suppose something
without highlighting how supposition itself is an act of supplementarity, an act
that treats subject and predicate terms or classes as necessarily derivative.

The absurdity of thinking of a thing as having no reason or cause thus depends less on what we can imagine than on what we can suppose. As Hume
will show by appealing to the substantialist logic of predication, we can imagine an event without reason or cause—but only if we assume precisely that
logic. By adopting a logic of supposition in which no thing can be supposed
as a thing without assuming its disjunctive relation to another, we recognize
the inherently rational nature of things. Any thing lacking such a rationale
would simply not be expressible or legible; it would be, as Edwards says,
nonsensical.

To adopt the Stoic logic of propositions or supposition in place of the logic
of substantialist predicate logic involves a fundamental change in the way one
thinks. Because the two strategies of reasoning start from radically different
assumptions, they view the policies of inference of their counterparts as misdirected and ill-founded. The typological inferences made by the elect and
supported by the logic of supposition appear, in the predicate logic of fallen
humanity, as illegitimate products of an overactive imagination. In the logic of
the elect, the halting attempts at reason by fallen intelligence falter from their
beginnings, in treating things as atomistically significant prior to their incorporation into expressions, propositions, communication, or (in general) discourse.
In terms of the logic of supposition, acts of imagination (e.g., the attempt to
think nothing) and predicational inferences are nonsense. For fallen, sinful humanity the pronouncements of the saintly are likewise nonsense. No line of
reasoning can lead from one strategy to the other, for both provide the para-

---

45. Miscellany #880 [early 1740s], in *Philosophy of Edwards*, 87. See also Miscellanies #365 [1729]
and #587 [c. 1733], ibid., 80, 81; and Jonathan Edwards, *Freedom of the Will* [1754], ed. Paul
Ramsey, 182.

meters of what it means to reason in the first place. From the standpoint of the logics involved, all one can do is highlight their paradigmatic differences in policies and assumptions.

Edwards suggests, however, that the suppositional and propositional practices of Stoic or Ramist doctrines are more encompassing than those of predication, because they can account for the logic of predication as a distorted derivation of reason. Predicate logic, on the contrary, cannot incorporate the hypothetical or disjunctive features of propositional logic without losing irrevocably the ability of propositional logic to account for the generation of meaning. In order to make aspects of his philosophy intelligible and to give the justification for his lines of argument, Edwards appeals at different times to both strategies of reasoning. Yet since he recognizes how propositions display the process by which predicates come into being and become meaningful, he grants priority to the logic of supposition embodied in propositional expression.

What looks like a simply logical issue thus extends into the central place Edwards accords to the communication or rhetoric of being. In the speech of discourse, things come into being; they have significance or meaning because they are places in a rhetorical network of communicative exchanges. Even things considered as atomistically differentiated from one another (as addressed in predicate logic) are intelligible as atoms of meaning only in terms of a rhetorical system of propositions and expressions. Outside of that system of what can be or is supposed, all is nonsense.

As the transcendental condition for all being and intelligibility, the space of discourse can be nothing other than God. Apart from God no supposition is possible, because supposing or sup-positing something means placing it in the space of all places, namely, God. Insofar as no thing can be supposed as the disjunct to the space of supposition, every supposition immediately implies the existence of that space at the same time as marking the supposition as the displacement of God. All things are in God and God in all things, because the act of supposition or displacement by which a thing comes to be affirms the existence of the space in which it is a place, while differentiating itself in terms of its supplementarity:

> Space is this necessary, eternal, infinite and omnipresent being. We find that we can with ease conceive how all other beings should not be. We can remove them out of our minds, and place some other in the room of them; but space is the very thing we can never remove and conceive of its not being. . . . But I had as good speak plain: I have already said as much as that space is God.[46]

To conceive of God as possibly not existing would be to suppose something else for God. But to suppose anything at all is to posit that thing in some place relative to other things. Even if one supposes the non-existence of all things, the very act of supposing assumes a discourse or space from which the supposition

---

46. Edwards, "Of Being," 203. Cf. Anderson, ibid., 24, 57–58, 74.

removes those things. Insofar as the supposition itself affirms the existence of the space in which the supposition itself is meaningful, it affirms the existence of God.

Space or God can be understood as a being only in a derivative sense, because in the logic of supposition individual things (i.e., Ramist "arguments") always imply the immanent presence of the rhetorical or discursive space in terms of which expressions are uttered. Accordingly, Edwards is reluctant to refer to space as a being at all; to do so (in scholastic terms) would be to collapse *esse* into *ens*, being into a being. Since *esse* (as the "act" of being) can function in classical discourse as a subject of predication relatable to other things as objects, it is better understood propositionally as *essendi*, the ontological exchange of discursivity. Only by translating the discursivity of space into a derivative context in which exteriority is conceivable can Edwards then treat space as a simple idea necessarily connected with other simple (though exterior) ideas.

That context—most often identified as Edwards' idealism—acknowledges the inherent intentionality of mind: Consciousness is always consciousness *of* something. Indeed, the metaphysics implicit in such intentionality at first seems to approximate the relational features of the Ramist or propositional logic that guides Edwards' primary discussion of space. However, by saying that all existence is mental, or by saying that simple ideas are necessarily connected to other simple "exterior" ideas, he supposes a distinction between the mental and the physical which itself can be meaningful only in terms of some prior discursive context:

> Space, as has been already observed, is a necessary being (if it may be called a being); and yet we have also shewn that all existence is mental, that the existence of all exterior things is ideal. Therefore it is a necessary being only as it is a necessary idea—so far as it is a simple idea that is necessarily connected with other simple exterior ideas, and is, as it were, their common substance or subject. It is in the same manner a necessary being, as anything external is a being.[47]

In terms of being considered external to one another, God is as much a being as any other thing is a being; but it is only as a function of mind that God is so identified. To define God in those terms alone would completely reverse the ontology of supposition in which God's expressions or communications comprise the language of being.

Metaphysical idealism thus reveals less about the space of aboriginal discourse than about space understood in terms of the derivative places located in it. In other words, instead of drawing on the rhetorical tradition of places (*topoi*), idealism relies on a Newtonian notion of space as the place of places. But by defining that space in terms of derivative places, it ignores the rhetorical heritage of place in which the things occupying those places are originally defined.

---

47. Edwards, "The Mind" #9 [c. 1724], 341.

For Edwards, the exteriority of things is possible precisely because mind, as a rhetorical place itself, is a supposition of differentiation or exteriority. When he employs derivative concepts such as mental, external, or necessary, he describes the space of discourse from the perspective of concepts that already assume the demarcation of meanings expressed in a logic of supposition. In a logic of predication, as Hume makes clear, simple exterior ideas provide no guide for justified inference. Without an alternative to that logic, Edwards can give no justification for how God is necessarily connected with other simple exterior ideas.[48] With it, he can provide the rationale for even a priori judgments:

> When we therefore see anything begin to be, we intuitively know that there is a cause of it, and not by ratiocination or any kind of argument. This is an innate principle, in that sense that the soul is born with it, a necessary fatal propensity so to conclude on every occasion.[49]

The soul's very coming into being-related-to-a-thing coincides with the thing's coming into being. Fate dictates such a coincidence insofar as fate enacts the order of emerging reason, the order of causality and rationality in which mind occupies a place and in which the things of the material universe come to occupy their places. All of reality comes into being as a function of mind, because mind is the supposition of all other places. Our intuitive knowledge that everything that comes to be has a cause is due to our immanent relation to every thing we know as coming into being. In literally supposing the thing, mind enacts the displacement of space whereby places come to exist. Mind (as a place among places) intuits the *logos* of the universe by finding out "things" (*inveniendi res*). Those things, as the Stoic legal and rhetorical tradition bears witness, make up the matters at hand or topics with which any particular mind is confronted.

The mind's supposition of things identifies them as the material elements of the universe. Insofar as a thing is supposed to occupy a particular place, it therefore exists "nowhere but in the mind," because "that which we call place is an idea too." But mind itself is nothing less than the supposition of place in which the reasons of things are "found out."[50] As the discernment of the places of material things, the activity of mind discloses the logic of "supposable disjunction" implicit in the rhetorical or communicative ontology of matter. The intuitive ability of the mind to know that every thing that comes to be has a cause thus depends on the same ontology in which it is impossible to suppose any particular distribution of matter without supposing a reason for the distribution:

> If nothing else can be supposed but the existence of such matter as we find in some places, then why is it not everywhere alike? If this matter can be supposed not to be in such a part of space, then surely it is in the nature of things supposable that it should not be in other parts of space. . . . Or why is there so much: why is there not less? Surely here is a supposable disjunction: so much or not

48. Cf. Edwards, "The Mind" #42 [1725], and "Subjects to be Handled in the Treatise on the Mind" #53 [1750s?], in *Scientific and Philosophic Writings*, 360, 392–93.
49. Edwards, "The Mind" #54 [1727], 370.
50. See Edwards, "The Mind" #34 [1724] and #51 [1727], 353, 368.

so much, or so much and more. Yea here is room for infinite different parts of
a disjunction or distribution, all equally supposable, viz. infinite different quan-
tities of matter of which there is no more reason in the thing itself that any one
should be rather than any other. Therefore, to suppose that one certain particular of all this infinite number should be and all the rest not be, without any
disposing cause, is infinitely absurd.[51]

The sup-position or placement of any thing is the dis-position or displacement
of its cause. That act of quantifying by disjunction specifies the matter of a
thing and thus designates it as the material object of the supposition. The cause
of the matter is displaced or disposed relative only to the posing of the place
itself, that is, relative only to the materiality or exteriority of the thing. But because "the matter of the thing" is what the thing is *about*, its placement or
supposition requires its disjunction from both the mind that imagines it as exterior to or discernible from its other intentional objects, and the space that
makes exteriority, mentality, or material discrimination possible.

Just as God is the necessary and immanent cause of a being, so all other
beings are the necessary though exterior causes of one another. As Edwards
often notes, this means that the slightest difference in any particle in the universe would occasion a modification in all other particles, since particles are
themselves expressions of relation.[52] Their materiality is the expression of the
exteriority of expression itself, the implicit deferment to an other for meaning.
That supposition of, or deferment to, mind, other things, and God identifies a
thing as intelligible or significant by locating it within communicative exchange.

The ontology of supposition demarcates the matter of a thing as that which
points to the rhetorical heritage in which it is placed and in which place it
stands. In this way, places are found for material things. In finding a place, we
discern the matter at hand, the topic at issue (i.e., the topic as it issues forth
or comes into being). The materiality of things marks their enunciative capacity by provoking the mind to acknowledge its own participation in the same
discursive heritage that draws both mind and matter into being. Insofar as their
coming into being is in any way intelligible, material things are the contents
of expressions apart from which they are meaningless. Even the mind's en-
counter with material things assumes a propositional status, in that its
apprehension of any thing cannot be distinguished aboriginally from its ontological (i.e., rhetorical) disjunction from the thing.

It is not enough, then, to say that Edwards simply assumes that the mind's
insistence on the causal principle is innate. What Edwards shows is why it must
be innate in virtue of the rhetorical character of reason itself. To think of a
thing at all is already to think of it in terms of its displacement of an other (its
cause), because the very structure of thought is suppositional. A thing comes

---

51. Miscellany #880, in *Philosophy of Edwards*, 87. See also Miscellanies #880 and #1154 [1751],
ibid., 100, 181–82.
52. See, for example, Edwards, "The Mind" #40 [1725], 357-58; and Miscellanies #880 and #976,
in *Philosophy of Edwards*, 93–109.

into being along with its idea and the mind that thinks it in the pronouncement and communication of its prospect for rationality. In learning the
language and order of things, the soul thus reiterates the divine speech of creation, in the beginning of which was the *Logos.*

In spite of its concentration on the rhetorical identification of places, this depiction of being as essentially communicative does not commit Edwards to the
view that each utterance disrupts the possibility for determinate knowledge.
As the Stoics and Ramists maintain, the logic of propositions assumes that a
statement is meaningful only if it is communicated. If the utterance is not heard
and understood, the original speech is nothing more than sounds or marks.

The redundancy of a message in and as history signals the consistency of
topical juxtapositions. Each Ramist "argument" rehearses the divine speech by
drawing on the tradition of pronouncements that situates a thing in terms of
identifying it as a matter of interest. The matter of a body—that which makes
it something "substantial"—depends, in Edwards' rhetorical and communicative depiction of nature, on its having been expressed as the substance or
matter of an argument. The history of such expressions constitutes the context
for the ontological emergence of substances. In turn, those substances exist in
virtue of their having been expressed in a historical and providential communication. Apart from that communication, he observes, natural objects have no
substance, no effective standing:

> And indeed, the secret lies here: that which truly is the substance of all bodies is
> the infinitely exact and precise and perfectly stable idea in God's mind, together
> with his stable will that the same shall gradually be communicated to us, and to
> other minds, according to certain fixed and exact established methods and laws:
> or in somewhat different language, the infinitely exact and precise divine idea,
> together with an answerable, perfectly exact, precise and stable will with respect
> to correspondent communications to created minds, and effects on their minds.[53]

There can be no idea of a determinate thing apart from God's will that it function in a precise and communicated way. Its having been communicated to
created minds is of the essence of the determination of the thing, for no thing
is intelligible apart from the discursive network that defines its rationale. In
short, the impulse of being to fulfill its intentionality in an other allows it to be
determinate and rational.

Only in the fallen discourse of classical modernity can we say that God has
ideas, and wills that they be communicated to us, because God is not a substance or subject (even a transcendent subject) who has ideas or who wills that
those ideas are communicated to other subjects. Such talk, for Edwards, invokes a historicized logic of differentiation that is aboriginally unavailable in
the space of discursivity. Indeed, much of what Edwards says about the integrity of the Persons of the Trinity and the unity of divine intellect and will is
intended precisely to undermine such language.

---

53. Edwards, "The Mind" #13 [c. 1726, possibly as late as the 1740s], 344. Cf. Anderson, ibid., 79.

In fallen discourse, though, God can be identified or supposed as a subject relative to other subjects (insofar as God can be considered a being at all). But because that supposition establishes the subjectivity of both relata simultaneously, the supposition of subjectivity cannot itself be a function of subjectivity: No subject can "suppose" the propriety of its own subjectivity. If it could, it would violate the very point Edwards is often at pains to make, namely, that no thing causes its own existence. Even God cannot be considered as the cause of his own existence, because in a logic of supposition the meaning of cause requires a disjunction which only a derivative notion of God can accommodate.

Not surprisingly, then, in Edwards' protracted sentence describing his "secret," the predicational vocabulary of substance, idea, will, and other minds is held together artificially. Unwilling to let his reader think that God's ideas, will, and communicative interaction with his creatures can be considered apart from one another, Edwards tries to say it all in one expression. But, as medieval modernists like Peter of Spain had discovered, using already significant terms legitimates the logic in which those terms have meaning, even when the act of suppositing those terms attempts to enact a different logic of signification.

In the propositional logic of the elect, the enunciation of a thing is its will-to-meaning, its will to be communicated. The precision of the divine idea depends on its intentional relations to other ideas as expressed in the rhetoric of creation. In terms of supposition, this means that insofar as a thing supplants an other—and discloses that other as inherent to its meaning—it reveals how both things enact a logic "of fixed and exact established methods and laws." In supposing a thing, God is thus dis-posed to create it as its cause.

Accordingly, God's will is the impulse toward semantic and syntactic fulfillment, a function of the inherently communicative character of discourse. Because there is nothing other than discourse to which discourse might be discursively related, that space of discursivity (as Edwards recognizes) can be nothing other than God. In addition, because this God/space has no disjunct, God cannot change or will in any way other than he does, for there is nothing other than God into which he could change.

The question of why God creates or why there is history becomes, then, both immediately pressing and seemingly insurmountable. Since significance and intelligibility require a communicative matrix of signs, the historical appearance of the first sign, expression, argument, or created being must be perfectly gratuitous. That is, from the perspective of any creature, the origin of creation must be meaningless. As will be shown in the next chapter, Edwards is perfectly willing to acknowledge this. After all, it is only through the historical and providential communication of the world that intelligibility itself is defined.

Edwards' secret is therefore contained as much in what he says about God's ideas, will, and communication as in how he refuses to allow them to be considered apart from one another. His rhetoric resists the impulse to treat these terms apart from their appearance in a web of expressions, and in this he implies that understanding any one of these elements will entail an understanding of the others. As in the case of the Stoic doctrine of the *Logos* of the universe, any event in the universe enkindles all other events with meaning. Nothing, though, provides a rationale for either the fire of signification itself, the dynamic allusion of a thing to an other expressed by its propositional form, or (for Edwards) God's will.

What was apparent, then, to the early Stoics and spectacularly lost in the flourishes of Parmenides, Plato, and their successors, is central to Edwards' project—namely, the divine spark of life is not some thing at all. Any attempted explanation of it in terms of a logic of predication is thus doomed from the outset.

Corporeality and Mentality as Rhetorical Placement

The unsettlingly Spinozistic sound of Edwards' doctrine of substance disappears the moment we recognize how he redefines substance in terms of communicative exchange. For Spinoza, the definition of substance provides the a priori justification for claiming that substance causes itself. Though his subsequent arguments rely on such a definition, Spinoza nowhere explains how substance itself comes to have that meaning other than through elliptical references to a rhetorical heritage appropriated in its being called into the discussion.

In saying that the substance of bodies is idea, will, and communication all at once, Edwards avoids even the possibility that *natura naturans* and *natura naturata* will be confused. For, in contrast to the Spinozistic adoption of a logic of substantialist predication, Edwards' doctrine of creation depends on a logic of displacement that is absolutely meaningless when applied to the activity of supposition itself.

Since the act of displacement or supposition defines an ultimate unit of intelligibility in terms of its communicative intentionality, the act itself could be intelligible only in terms of an end that God would have in mind in so acting. But because the very meaning of God and mind relies on a discursive practice in which those terms would have a place, the designation of such places cannot be understood as anything other than arbitrary.

Thus when Edwards writes (as late as the mid-1750s) that "all union and all created identity is arbitrary," he again invokes a procedure of reasoning that highlights the aboriginally rhetorical posture of determinate existence.[54] As essentially arbitrary, the individuation and union of natural beings establish the "method and rules" of divine creative activity. In bodies these laws of nature are expressed in terms of "laws of resistance and attraction or adhesion and *vis inertiae*, that are essential to the very being of matter." Laws of the "common operations of the mind" likewise are altogether inexplicable in terms other than what is essential to the being of mind.[55] Yet insofar as matter and

---

54. Edwards, "Notes on Knowledge and Existence," in *Scientific and Philosophic Writings*, 398.
55. Miscellany #1263 [1754], in *Philosophy of Edwards*, 185–88.

mind in themselves have no essences apart from arbitrary instantiations, matter and mind designate merely relational contexts in which to locate individuals.

The possibility of being or meaning, then, relies on an absolutely arbitrary supposition of individuation which, because of the logic of supposition, excludes the possibility that the basic atoms of being or meaning have only external relations. The motions of the atoms that comprise the material universe express the intentionality of materiality, the intelligibility of individuality sup-posited in existence. As inherently propositional, each atom of meaning displays providential guidance as the constant re-creation of the universe in the activity of supposition:

> For instance, all the ideas that ever were or ever shall be to all eternity, in any created mind, are answerable to the existence of such a peculiar atom in the beginning of the creation, of such a determinate figure and size, and have such a motion given it. That is, they are all such as infinite wisdom sees would follow, according to the series of nature, from such an atom so moved. That is, all ideal changes of creatures are just so, as if just such a particular atom had actually all along existed even in some finite mind, and never had been out of that mind, and had in that mind caused these effects which are exactly according to nature, that is, according to the nature of other matter that is actually perceived by the mind. God supposes its existence; that is, he causes all changes to arise as if all these things had actually existed in such a series in some created mind, and as if created minds had comprehended all things perfectly.[56]

No atom can be considered in merely accidental relations to other atoms, because no atom exists in a purely physical sense. Atoms exist "in" finite minds as causes of the material effects perceived by minds. That is, atoms designate cause-effect relations more immediately than they describe entities that might participate in such relations.

Even though this reorientation of the meaning of atoms includes revising how we understand notions of figure, size, motion, and exteriority, we may still (Edwards says) "speak in the old way." To do so, however, means that figure or size must refer to the particular way in which an expression is to be understood relative to other expressions. Instead of endorsing a form of "epistemological atomism" sometimes associated with seventeenth-century Harvard logical theses, this revision transforms the problematic of both classical atomism and modernist epistemology by challenging their characterization of place.

In Edwards' ontology the place of a thing does not depend on its existence; rather, its existence depends on its having a place. Furthermore, that place is not determined by the divine mind as much as it is determined in the divine mind. Since the mind itself embodies the activity of supposition, the serial displacement of places implicit in God's communication properly describes the nature of material existence.

When the furniture in this room, for example, is not perceived by any created mind, its existence relies on its being perceived by the divine mind only indirectly. For what needs to be explained is not how God can perceive ma-

---

56. Edwards, "The Mind" #34, 354. Cf. "Things to be Considered an[d] Written fully about," 241; and Miscellany #880, in *Philosophy of Edwards*, 93.

terial things, but how perception by the divine mind actively constitutes, from moment to moment, the individuating identities of the pieces of furniture. Perception does not depend on prior ontological determination, nor does ontological differentiation rest on epistemological engagement. Rather, as necessary though aboriginally arbitrary places in the ontology of creation, unperceived things exist precisely as suppositions of seriality:

> I answer, there has been in times past such a course and succession of existences that these things must be supposed to make the series complete, according to the divine appointment of the order of things; and there will be innumerable things consequential which will be out of joint—out of their constituted series—without the supposition of these. For upon supposition of these things are infinite numbers of things otherwise than they would be, if these were not by God supposed; yea the whole universe would be otherwise, such an influence have these things by their attraction and otherwise. . . . That is, they must be supposed if the train of ideas be in the order and course settled by the supreme mind. So that we may answer in short, that the existence of these things is in God's supposing of them, in order to the rendering complete the series of things—to speak more strictly, the series of ideas—according to his own settled order and that harmony of things which he has appointed. The supposition of God which we speak of is nothing else but God's acting in the course and series of his exciting ideas, as if they, the things supposed, were in actual idea.[57]

The perception of things does not guarantee their existence; and the absence of their being perceived does not entail their non-existence. Existence is a function of the supposition of things in a series of ideas. Apart from the supposition or displacement implied in its being inherently intentional (i.e., ideational), no thing perceived can be supposed to exist. Because ideas exhibit a necessarily intentional structure that cannot be completely erased even in a logic of predication, they best describe the essentially serial character of existence. However, insofar as ideas are contrasted with material things and are considered in substantialist terms, their intentional structure is often ignored. That same contrast likewise overlooks the inherently intentional character of materiality in general and of material things in particular.

In Edwards' logic of supposition, materiality must refer disjunctively to ideality: In order even to think of something as material, one must be able to contrast it to that which it displaces. But in displacing their counterparts, materiality and ideality introduce their counterparts into meaningful discourse. For Edwards this means that materiality is intelligible only in relational terms (viz., as resistance), and material things must be understood as arbitrary terminations of relations. Materiality in general designates the necessity of there being places in the series of divine ideas in order for there to be a series; ideality in general designates the seriality of those places.

By distinguishing between materiality and material things, or between ideality and ideal or spiritual things, we avoid the temptation of an anachronistic

---

57. Edwards, "The Mind" #40 [1725], 356–57. Cf. Vetö, *La Pensée*, 45.

Hegelian or phenomenological interpretation of Edwards. In saying that both material things and ideas exhibit an intentional structure, we do not imply that they play out a purpose or design intended by a mind that exists as an a priori condition for their discrimination. Mind itself (or ideality in general) comes into being as the impulse of referentiality, the power that drives the movement of ideas in series. Things are serial as expressions of the suppositions of divine mind because mind expresses the seriality of supposition. Existents are intelligible not because a mind (even God's) gives them purpose or meaning after their original inception, but because the presence of mind (including God's) marks their intentionality.

Minds and material objects are thus created in the same aboriginal, suppositional act that establishes the series of divine ideas. Prior to this discrimination of mind, no divine purpose awaits instantiation in the material universe, for no criterion of discrimination (e.g., resistance) is supposited as a displacement of space to identify the place of mind. In placing a point of resistance—that is, in arbitrarily indicating the terminus of a relation simply as an unintelligible terminus ("and that's that, the end of the matter")—God's displacement of mind implicates it in resistance.

Edwards can maintain what appear to be contradictory positions, because apart from the mind there is only resistance, and resistance is a mode of an idea.[58] The resistance of an idea is its power to terminate communication, its ability to forestall further intentional movement. To the extent that an idea is a determinate idea of a particular thing, it so perfectly embodies that thing that it ends all discourse. When Edwards comes to speak of Christ as a perfect idea of God, he will appeal to just this manner of reasoning. To the extent that an idea provokes more communication or thought, the idea expresses the relational character of intentionality. Apart from the lure of intentionality (i.e., mind), there is only resistance, the termination of intelligibility. Yet that resistance itself is intelligible precisely as the limit of what can be communicated; it is the brute fact of the unintelligible power to give determinate form to discourse by supposing it.

Material or solid bodies thus exist as expressions of divine power causing there to be resistance in parts of space. Parts of space themselves are discernible only in terms of the power of resistance chronicled in laws of motion as God's communication:

> We by this also clearly see that creation of the corporeal universe is nothing but the first causing resistance in such parts of space as God thought fit, with a power of being communicated successively from one part of space to another, according to such stated conditions as his infinite wisdom directed; and then the first beginning of this communication, so that ever after it might be continued without deviating from those stated conditions.[59]

58. See Edwards, "The Mind" #27 [1725], 351.
59. Edwards, "Of Atoms" [c. 1720–21], in *Scientific and Philosophic Writings*, 215–16. See idem., "The Mind," #29 and #36 [1725], 352, 355; and Anderson, ibid., 64, 67. Cf. Edwards, *Freedom of the Will*, 387–94.

Solidity or resistance signals the simplicity or logical termination of a unit of meaning. As an essentially relational notion, such a unit of resistance cannot comprise a subject or object in predicational terms, so what is communicated by God in creation must be propositions. Moreover, in order for the propositions to be intelligible as communications, they must imply the intentional presence of other propositions. This implication of an other is the ideality or mentality implicit in each unit of meaning as communicative.

The communication of resistance establishes a syntax (the system of natural laws) in which minds function as indicators of the supposition or displacement of each part of space. Inasmuch as the "being of other things" relies on the inherent intentionality of being expressed as mind, minds or spirits "only are properly substance."[60] As Edwards concludes, however, this means that there is no proper substance but God himself, because "the certain unknown substance which philosophers used to think subsisted by itself" does not exhibit any intentional role in the economy of divine discourse.[61] Without the actual exertion of divine power in the establishment of resistance, no determinate differentiation of minds occurs. Ultimately, the differentiation of discursive practices, as outlined in a logic of supposition, causes both minds and bodies to come into being as rationally ordered.

Edwards' ability to make typological and teleological inferences relies, then, on the same logic of serial supposition that supports his confidence in the necessity of cause-effect relations. Even Hume has to admit, in his celebrated acceptance of an unperceived shade of blue, that the continuity implicit in experience does not always rely on experience. Unlike Hume, though, Edwards can appeal to an ontology of supposition to explain the order of both perception and existence without relying on a logic of predication that ultimately undercuts any phenomenology based on it.

By designating mind as the intentionality of things, Edwards sabotages the modernist separation of mind from nature. Mental activities disclose the order of things themselves, because the same processes of supposition that characterize cause-effect relations in nature regulate acts of judgment about objects of consciousness. In memory, for example, the mind cannot but reaffirm the causal integrity of the series of its ideas insofar as it thinks them at all. Embedded in the common heritage of nature, memory refutes any movement toward solipsistic subjectivity by recognizing the necessity of a union of existence and perception:

> Memory is the identity, in some degree, of ideas that we formerly had in our minds, with a consciousness that we formerly had them, and a supposition that their former being in the mind is the cause of their being in us at present. There is not only the presence of the same ideas that were in our minds formerly, but also an act of judgment that they were there formerly; and that judgment not properly from proof, but from natural necessity arising from a law of nature

60. Edwards, "Of Being," 204, 206.
61. Edwards, "Of Atoms," 215. Cf. David Jacobson, "Jonathan Edwards and the 'American Difference': Pragmatic Reflections on the 'Sense of the Heart'," *Journal of American Studies* 21 (1987), 379.

> which God hath fixed. In memory, in mental principles, habits and inclinations, there is something really abiding in the mind when there are no acts or exercises of them, much in the same manner as there is a chair in this room when no mortal perceives it. . . . So, when we say a person has these or those things laid up in his memory, we mean they would actually be repeated in his mind upon some certain occasions according to the law of nature.[62]

In supposing the former being of an idea, we acknowledge that "there is something really abiding in the mind" in virtue of which the thing exists as causally linked to the idea's "being in us at present." As part of the network of interrelated meanings, the idea's being is tied to the being of the mind; and the meaningful existence of both presumes an order of natural necessity. That order—the concern of the hermetic tradition's *ars memoriae*—identifies the place of the mind in the propositional *topoi* that constitute the world.

Each thing, argument, or atom of meaning in this mnemonic system of exchange exists as a function of power, that is, as the ability to cause an effect in another thing. Its affective ability permeates its relations with other things as necessarily as any perfectly inelastic collision among atoms. What characterizes a thing necessarily characterizes its effects on the other things in terms of which it is propositionally defined. So "if [a man] exists after such a manner there follows the existence of another thing." And if ministers are ordained to teach and "the people are obliged to hear what I teach them," says Edwards, "so great is my pastoral, or ministerial, or teaching power."[63] The power of a person or a minister, like the causal efficacy of any other unit of meaning, inheres in the definition of the thing.

Knowledge of a thing is the memory of its functional heritage, insofar as the definition of the thing is the expression of its place in a rhetoric of communication. As the Stoics would say, to know a thing is to retrieve the thing (*res*), the matter at hand. Because the Ramist model of communicative organization displays topics as already engaged in causal relations, its ontology permits the playing out of history and providence as memorial displacements of power. Such an ontology also provides legitimation for Edwards' claims to certainty in typological inference.

Edwards' treatment of matter does not, therefore, arise in a distinctly physical or metaphysical context, because all contexts begin as rhetorical collections of topics, places, matters. Against those who would resist the juxtaposition of such different meanings of matter, Edwards warns that "no matter is, in the most proper sense, matter."[64] If what is meant by matter, body, or substance is something that exists independently of its discursive relations to other matter, body, or substance, then it is "truly nothing at all." The very existence of material bodies, as intentionally delimited by and united to other bodies and mind in general, designates (even if disjunctively) the characteristics of materiality, corporeality, and mental-

62. Edwards, "The Mind" #69 [mid-1740s], 386-87. Cf. Edwards, Miscellany #126 [1724].
63. Edwards, "The Mind" #29, 352; and Miscellany #40 [1723].
64. Edwards, "Things to be Considered," 235; see also 238.

ity as integral features of the communicative exchange in which it is a function.

Edwards accordingly ridicules Locke's suggestion that God might be able to make matter think, because such a change in matter cannot occur without a radical transformation of the entire universe of discourse in which matter functions. In particular, in thinking that matter and thought have some meaning that can be discussed or changed apart from the matrix of communicative exchange in which they exist, Locke fails to recognize that the place of matter in discourse ("what we call matter") is precisely its displacement of thought.

> For if thought be in the same place as matter is, yet, if there be no manner of communication or dependence between that and anything that is material, that is, any of that collection of properties that we call matter; if none of those properties of solidity, extension, etc., wherein materiality consists, which are matter, or at least whereby matter is matter, have any manner of influence towards the exerting of thought; and if that thought be no way dependent on solidity or mobility, and they no way help the matter, but thought could be as well without those properties: then thought is not properly in matter, though it be in the same place. All the properties that are properly said to be in matter depend on the other properties of matter, so that they cannot be without them. . . . If thought's being so fixed to matter as to be in the same place where matter is, be for thought to be in matter, thought not only can be in matter, but actually is, as much as thought can be in place.[65]

The propositional placement of thought in matter would identify thought in terms of rhetorical practices that would preclude the very opportunity for reasoning itself; for if they occupy the same place in discourse, thought and matter are indistinguishable. In order to maintain the possibility of meaning as disjunction, Edwards rejects the atomistic epistemology implicit in Locke's suggestion. To imagine that such places of discourse can be modified without affecting the entire system of signification reveals how a logic of predication completely misunderstands the structures of intelligibility that define the very conditions of Edwards' doctrine of material bodies.

Because gravitational attractions and the motions of bodies contribute to the network of meanings in which notions of matter or body are embedded, they reveal the impossibility of reducing matter to some individually understandable atom of discourse. Inscribed in terms of one another, the notions of solidity, resistance, gravity, and motion identify their respective meanings as practices of discursive exchange. If they were to be abstracted from their places in such exchange (as happens in a logic of predication), they would become signs rather than functions of signifier-signified relations.

Nonetheless, Edwards is still able to mark the places of those functions as aspects of signification. The solidity of a thing, for example, describes its aboriginal resistance to, and termination of any significance beyond itself: It indicates God's designation of a place as the limit-source of power. As in Peirce's notion of firstness, the solidity of a thing expresses merely what it is, an unintelligible something that might or might not exist.

---

65. Edwards, "The Mind" #21(a) [1725], 345–46.

A material thing thus has to be related disjunctively to an other which it re-sists, but to which it is attracted as part of its essence. Its power is intelligible only in terms of something else against which it is an exercise. As cause of an other, its power identifies its essence as the tendency of the thing to move toward the other as its fulfillment (as in the case of the type-antitype relation). The fulfillment of a thing as a type not only locates the thing in a tradition of commonplaces but also identifies the discourse in which it can function as regulated providentially.

The gravitational attraction of all things to one another specifies the condi-tions for historical embodiment. Like Peircean secondness, gravity depicts "the very bare being of body, without supposing harmonious being."[66] The pure that-ness or existence of things in the universe requires that things exist as intentionally related to one another, tending or inclining to one another as part of their essences. But the gravitational tendency of a material thing marks it simply as a being in contrast to another being, a place disjunctively distinguished from another place. The tendency or inclination of a thing to move to its harmonious fulfillment as significant requires the actual movement, supposition, or displacement of material being by mind. That tendency or inclination is not something necessarily contained in the essential supposition of material beings relative to one another. Gravitationally linked to one another in their essences and attracted to harmonious existence, bodies as bodies suppose their other—mind—as the signified cause of their discursive movement.

Rather than imagining the ability of mind to move bodies as if minds were shadowy bodies, Edwards argues that we should "think of thought or inclina-tion" as the proper way of conceiving mind-body relations and even body-body relations.[67] Such a revision of materiality and corporeality transforms the logic of place by acknowledging that the logic of predication at best describes a trun-cated and distorted view of relations. Thus, difficulties concerning mind-body relations, raised by substantialist accounts thematized in materialism, idealism, and dualism, are dissolved. Edwards proposes instead that minds and bodies occupy logical or rhetorical places. In terms of such a revision, perceptions or ideas can be communicated to us immediately by God while our minds are united with our bodies, because minds and bodies are associated essentially with one another and with the objects of perception or ideation.

What Edwards means by the actual motion of a thing—as opposed to its mere tendency to move—is the communication of its aboriginal resistance to meaning (its solidity) in terms consistent with its attraction to an other as its harmonious fulfillment.[68] Gravity is the tendency of a body to move toward that which com-

66. Edwards, "Things to be Considered," 234; cf. 235, 290. See also Robert W. Jenson, *Ameri-ca's Theologian: A Recommendation of Jonathan Edwards,* 28; and Wallace E. Anderson, "Immaterialism in Jonathan Edwards' Early Philosophical Notes," *Journal of the History of Ideas* 25 (1964), 183–88.

67. Edwards, "The Mind" #2 and #3 [1724], 338–39. Cf. Jenson, *America's Theologian,* 32.

68. See Edwards, "Things to be Considered," 236 [1721], 246 [1723–24]; and Miscellanies #204 [c. 1725] and #787 [c. 1739].

pletes it as something significant in spite of and because of its resistance to meaning. Embodiment itself requires, as part of its meaning as the displacement of mind, the actual provocation of its other (viz., mind). In this way, minds move material bodies by being the very process by which existence becomes significant.

The significance of existents is thus determined as a function of the harmony of motions or, as Edwards prefers, the "consent of being to being, being's consent to entity."[69] Motion based on gravitational attraction affirms the essence of a thing as the harmony with other things in the universe in terms of which it exists. Like Peirce's thirdness, this harmonic communication of being as consent provides existence with the interpretant necessary for the emergence of significance or "excellency." The more the actual movements of bodies and thought agree with the essentially propositional being of things inscribed in the ontology of supposition, the more the activity of supposition is acknowledged and the greater is the excellency of the universe.

In displacing the predicate logic of fallen humanity by the Stoic-Ramist logic of propositions, Edwards does not reject the procedures of reasoning espoused by Locke and the Port Royalists. Indeed, he all the more affirms the necessity of such a logic as the disjunctive prerequisite for drawing out the possibility of signification in typological reasoning. Just as the gravitational tendency to motion finds its typical fulfillment in the discursive consent of beings, so also the tendency to significance exhibited by the logic of predication has as its antitype the logic of divine displacement.

Removed from the discursive environment in which both logics function, neither strategy of reasoning can provide the grounds for its own justification. Neither appeals to a foundation for rationality, only to a network of practices that define the possibility for ontological posturing. What makes the logic of places predominant in Edwards' philosophy is its rhetorical ability to locate the logic of predication functionally in a discursive exchange. Insofar as the practice of supposition displays the procedures by which embodiment, mentality, and communication occur, it reveals not only how Edwards' claims can be considered rational, but also why they are rational.

Instead of merely invoking the metaphor of divine communication to account for creation, Edwards' logic of supposition explains the process of God's diffusing or imparting being. This appropriation of Ramist logic in an ontological context rejects the classical-modernist requirement that logic, rhetoric, and ontology be kept distinct. By undermining the barriers between those domains of rationality, Edwards avoids the mere repetition of the vocabulary of communication that permeates classical, Neoplatonic, or modernist conceptions of subjective intentionality.

---

69. Edwards, "The Mind" #1 [1723] and #62 [mid-1740s], 336, 381. Cf. Stephen R. Yarbrough, "Jonathan Edwards on Rhetorical Authority," *Journal of the History of Ideas* 47 (1986), 405; Paula M. Cooey, *Jonathan Edwards on Nature and Destiny: A Systematic Analysis,* 64; and Michael J. Colacurcio, "The Example of Edwards: Idealist Imagination and the Metaphysics of Sovereignty," in *Puritan Influences in American Literature,* ed. Emory Elliott, 105.

IV

THE TRINITY AND CREATION

The greatest hurdle to understanding the meaning and significance of Edwards' doctrine of the Trinity is the presumption of a classical-modernist, humanistic perspective of intentionality. From that perspective every substance is a subject whose ends or purposes can be predicated of it as part of its personal history. As the starting point for all explanation of existence and action, the subject serves as the terminus for predication through which it is related to other things in virtue of its intentionality. Because discourse itself (in such an account) is about things in relation to one another, it cannot challenge the assumption that the world is populated by substances whose objects and objectives have meaning in terms of their relation to some subject. Like all other substances, God must accordingly be related intentionally to other things, either as the object or objective of their actions or as an underlying subject causing their existence.

For Edwards, such an account inappropriately extends to God the logic of predication that describes the fractured relations of fallen creatures. It simply assumes that mind, person, intention, or purpose can be predicated of God as yet another thing in this discursive constellation, when in fact the discursive exchange of divinity designates the alternative to this way of reasoning. In contrast to the Neoplatonic *via negativa*, Edwards' divine semiotics does not treat God as some kind of super-substantial substance; for the uncritical acceptance of the priority of substance itself rests on the creaturely logic of predication. In its place, Edwards portrays subjects and the world in general in terms of a discourse in which substances, mind, and ends are functions in the exchange of signification.

The question of an end or purpose to the existence of the world thus does not begin with the assumption that intentionality reveals the presence of a person guiding an action, for the very notions of person and action are intelligible only in terms of a prior discourse. As will be argued in chapter 6, subordination of the place of subjects has implications for Edwards' doctrine of human freedom. The present chapter is more concerned with Edwards' recognition that a classical-modernist notion of purpose assumes a concept of person at odds with his defense of a doctrine of the Trinity. Specifically, I will suggest that insofar as Edwards links God's creation of the world to the relations of the persons of the Trinity, he focuses the discussion of God's relation to the world on the transformation of the notion of person. Only by displacing the predicational, substantialist notion of person with a propositional, trinitarian notion does Edwards change the concepts of mind and end in ways that indicate the ontological possibility of redemption.

This chapter situates the attempt to explain why God created the world within a larger project of explaining how the internal relations of the Trinity delineate what it means to act for an end. Classical-modern (humanistic) accounts of creation mistakenly start from the assumption that God is a person, a subject who intends to act in a certain way, thus reading into God the logic of predication. Admittedly, that can be done, but it explains creation only in terms of the creation (the "end" for which God created), not in terms of the act of creation as such. For the latter we must first consider what it means for God to create. In terms of Edwards' treatment of the nature of creation, the question of why God creates is easily misunderstood as a humanistic imposition. Just as God does not choose to become a Trinity, so also God on his own terms does not choose to create the world; choice makes sense only in terms of fallen intelligibility.

In the propositional logic of semiotics, on the other hand, there is no way to consider the subject meaningfully apart from its participation in an activity (e.g., of being related as a trinity, of creating a world). To ask why God creates can miss the point that God is intelligible only in his trinitarian relations or creative acts. Because intelligible being and intention emerge in trinitarian distinction and creation, being and intention can occupy no logical place prior to such emergence.

This emergence, performance, or activity is the speech of communicative exchange by which signification is realized. God does not intend that things, antecedently intelligible to him, become significant in creation, for that would mean that he would have had to intend that they first be meaningful to him and to have had a reason why they have those meanings. God would have had to intend things to be significant or meaningful before the notion of a thing itself would be meaningful.

The issue, therefore, turns not on things, but rather on the concept of divine intentionality: God cannot intend to create something which is, for him, unintelligible. But that does not mean that a thing is intelligible prior to God's intention to create it, because the intelligibility of a thing is defined in terms of intentionality. Intentionality, for Edwards, is the displacement or supposition of an other by what is subsequently defined as a thing.

Both the trinitarian differentiation of persons and the differentiation of God from creation establish being, not in dialectical juxtapositions to an ontically meaningful other or in terms of Hegelian non-being, but in the displacement or supposition of being. Insofar as intelligibility and intention are functions of signifier-signified relations, a semiotic analysis rejects questions about God's intentions in creating the world as category mistakes, because such questions rely on humanistic assumptions about subjectivity inappropriate for the discourse that constitutes the intelligibility of subjectivity in the first place.

By using the derivative vocabulary of humanist subjectivity to describe the relations of the persons of the Trinity, commentators on Edwards invert the order of his presentation and thus undercut his radical transformation of the language in which it is couched. Roland Delattre, for example, claims that the internal structure of the Trinity is based on an analogy of the human self, even though Edwards insists (in Delattre's words) that "the meaning of this analogy is expressed the other way around."[1] Instead of following Edwards' clue that something very different from our ordinary understanding of the integrity of human functions characterizes moral selfhood, this approach legitimates fallen, human subjectivity by transposing it onto the Trinity. By beginning with the self as a subject, it subordinates the communication of the Trinity to a series of relations among the three persons of the Trinity, without questioning how the concept of person itself relies on God's being essentially communicative.

Indeed, the classical-modernist subversion of the exchange of signs in favor of subjectivity disenfranchises communication from its central place in Edwards' doctrines of the Trinity and creation. In place of affirming the aboriginal significance of God as essentially a communicative being, this subversion dismisses Edwards' repeated remarks about reality as a divine communication as mere metaphors for the transmission of significance from one substance (mind or subject) to another. Devoid of ontological content—except if understood again metaphorically in some Neoplatonic way as emanations of being—such expressions of communication depend on minds for their intentional legitimacy. Because minds in turn rely on God's will for their existence, and because God's will in granting being is arbitrary and inscrutable, the "communication" of being cannot ultimately be communication from one mind to another. Therefore, the subordination of semiotic exchange to subjectivity legitimates the continued characterization of communication as a merely metaphorical expression, thereby encouraging more vacuous and circular commentary.

When Paula Cooey writes that, for Edwards, "Divine creativity is the process by which divine being enlarges itself by means of communicating its own fullness," she certainly captures Edwards' mood of expansive profusion. But what does it mean to say that being enlarges itself by communicating fullness? When Robert Jenson says of Edwards' natural philosophy, "The world of bodies is the *between* of their communication," he invokes the imagery of spatial distance overcome by the meeting of minds. But why does Edwards' doctrine of communication require that he treat bodies this way? When Thomas Schafer reports that the doctrine of excellency at the heart of Edwards' concept of being presumes the inherent multiplicity of being, he suggests that "consent to being" is the communication of harmony. But why does Edwards assume that the excellency of being requires multiplicity? And when Delattre approvingly quotes Edwards' circular remark that God's goodness is the dispo-

---

1. Roland A. Delattre, *Beauty and Sensibility in the Thought of Jonathan Edwards: An Essay in Aesthetics and Theological Ethics*, 150. See also Thomas A. Schafer, "The Concept of Being in the Thought of Jonathan Edwards," 141–42, 153.

sition to communicate good, he grants Edwards the latitude of a preacher less concerned with philosophical clarity than with edification.[2] But how is communication always already dispositional? Without answering such questions, we allow the central concept of communication to slip by without seeing how Edwards' use of it thoroughly undermines the classical-modernist dogmas in terms of which it continues to be misunderstood and in terms of which his pronouncements can be dismissed all too easily as rhetorical embellishments.

In the propositional logic of Stoic-Ramist supposition, the semiotic character of communication precludes any attempt to portray communication as simply a medium by which minds share their ideas. Because minds and ideas are themselves defined in the exchange of signifiers and signifieds, they can be explicated as functions of communication. Their significance rests more on their roles or places in strategies of displacement than in serving as the sources of discursive exchange.

This semiotic explication of minds, selves, or persons reinstates the possibility of speaking about each person of the Trinity as a divine function or role (a *persona*, a πρόσωπον) by ignoring the classical-modernist reversal of the place of the subject in communicative exchange. In the classical-modernist understanding of a *persona* (the mask worn or role adopted by stage actors), the role is not essential to the subject or actor. The role has significance in virtue of its being acted out by a subject; but the subject does not depend on the role for its existence. The mask can always be discarded by the foundational self, subject, or "person" behind the mask.

When understood in terms of the substantialist, predicational logic of the Platonic-Aristotelian or Cartesian-Lockean interpretation of subjectivity, this vocabulary of the mask either collapses the notion of person into that of the subject or treats a person as a mere role played by a subject. Applied to the Trinity, the first alternative implies that God is comprised of three substances; the second, that the Father, Son, and Holy Spirit are not essential to God. Unable to explain how such theological difficulties can be avoided, those who rely on the logic of substance and predication ultimately have to cloak the Trinity in mystery.

By assuming that communicative exchange establishes the very possibility for subjectivity, a semiotic analysis retains the notion of person as a role. But here the role is not that acted out by a subject or substance; rather, it is a function of communicative exchange itself. Apart from the play there are no *dramatis personae*, no selves or subjects behind the communicative exchange. Like Clement of Alexandria, Edwards can invoke the concept of *persona* or πρόσωπον in his doctrine of the Trinity, because he eliminates the ploy of appealing to a substance or subject behind the divine drama itself.

In Edwards' account, the persons of the Trinity, like all other persons, have significance in virtue of their displacement of one another in and as the divine

2. See Paula M. Cooey, *Jonathan Edwards on Nature and Destiny: A Systematic Analysis*, 51–56; Robert W. Jenson, *America's Theologian: A Recommendation of Jonathan Edwards*, 32, 94–96; Schafer, "Concept of Being," 111–20; and Delattre, *Beauty and Sensibility*, 134.

discursus. The logic of that process of displacement inscribes a radical change of perspective, a fundamental change in the way of reasoning from the classical-modernist logic of predication that authorizes humanistic subjectivity. In Edwards' logic of supposition, the Trinity is a mystery only insofar as attempts to understand the nature of God insist on a non-communicative notion of persons to describe divine existence. By misinterpreting the essential relations of the persons of the Trinity, a logic of predication misdirects all subsequent attempts to model the human personality on God, by failing to transform our vision of the world.

This refocusing of the discussion of communication to the relations of the Trinity throws talk of persons, mind, intentionality, and God's moral attributes into the strange context of semiotic exchange. It rejects the personalistic prejudices of classical modernism, calling into question the presuppositions that permit easy appeals to metaphors of little ontological significance. Edwards' detour into the Trinity to account for the world upends modernist attempts to explain God in substantialist terms, especially when (as in Hegel) substantial being is defined in terms of the dialectic movement of mind.

This chapter examines Edwards' doctrine of the Trinity as the opening through which to explore his treatment of why God created the world. Such an examination quickly turns on itself, however, because the very notion of giving a reason for creation assumes a logic of personal intentionality that Edwards' discussion of the Trinity transforms. In showing that the end for which God creates the world is not chosen like human ends, Edwards points to a radically different way to define *choice* and *end*—a way I have characterized as propositional versus predicational. This new strategy for understanding the world characterizes the discourse of divinity in terms of God's otherness from creation.

In the terms used in the previous chapter: Any mysteriousness of the Trinity is based on a misunderstanding of the logic of supposition that the Trinity enacts. In classical-modern discourse, when someone supposes something, that act itself has no ontological impact on what is supposed, because the act is a function solely of the person making the supposition. As a simple heuristic device whereby subjectivity legitimates itself by pretending to refashion reality without really meaning it, humanistic supposition questions neither the right of the speaker to make such a supposition nor the structure of substantiality implicit in predicational logic. The language of supposition indicates merely a penchant for thought experiments.

When applied to Edwards, however, this interpretation of supposition fails to account for two noticeable features in his writing. First, very rarely does Edwards speak of anyone, including himself, supposing something. Even when God is said to suppose something, that act is not that of a subject engaged in a thought experiment, for God's supposition of a thing is the thing's creation. Second, the grammar of Edwards' theory of supposition is almost inevitably framed in the passive voice. Expressions such as "it must be supposed" indicate less a stylistic preference than an ontological requirement: Things come to be as a result of the suppositional activity of communicative exchange.

God's distinctive place in the vocabulary of supposition prohibits the extension of personal attributes to him without a radical revision of the notion of person. Such a revision requires Edwards to relocate the discussion about persons into the avowedly othered context of the Trinity. In discerning this new meaning of person, he displays the kind of being capable of participating in the process of redemption. "Putting on the new man" requires a radical change not only in one's personality, but also in what personhood itself is. By clarifying the notion of personhood in the Trinity, Edwards provides the model to be emulated by those aspiring to salvation.

The activity of supposition in the Trinity constitutes the internal logic of God, just as creation explicates that logic externally. The distinction of internal and external, though, itself relies on the activity of supposition. Therefore, the logic to which it appeals frustrates attempts to speak of God or creation other than in terms of the very pronouncements in which they are embedded.

The suppositional logic implicit in such a discursive exchange is as different from the classical-modern logic of predication as God is from the world. That difference, however, does not preclude the possibility of attributing personal characteristics (e.g., goodness) to God. It means only that those characteristics themselves must be redefined according to the strategy of suppositional communication in which Edwards' doctrines of God and creation are developed.

The issues raised here point to policies that Edwards uses in diagnosing the meaning of the Fall of creation and the philosophic requirements for humanity's reconciliation with God. The chapters on original sin and freedom (chapters 5 and 6) will rely on the strategy outlined in this chapter, for the trinitarian model of suppositional reasoning accounts for both the logic of redemption and its availability as an alternative to the deterministic logic of substantialist subjectivity. By showing how the Trinity exemplifies the impulse to signification as communication, Edwards transforms intentionality from something that a mind or being has to what a being is. In this way, supposition becomes the hallmark of communication, and communication the hallmark of being.

The Logic of the Trinity

The vocabulary of supposition appears in Edwards' doctrine of God as often as his references to creation as a divine communication, because communication, for Edwards, is the positing of a thing as meaningful relative to that which it displaces and to which it points as its ground. As a communication, the world signals its having been posited in place of something else; this something else cannot be non-being, for that would mean that non-being is something (a blatant contradiction), and it cannot be God, because that would mean that the world can take the place of God.

The problem of the placement of the world relative to God, however, assumes that God occupies some place other than the world if he is displaced in the supposition of creation. To assume that a being occupies a place (even a logical place) already is to invoke the logic of substantialist predication that Edwards' suppositional logic unravels. In contrast to the logic of predication— a logic that presumes the existence of things in terms of some relative place, even if only in the mind—suppositional logic defines existence in terms of the displacement of the very places that would withdraw a thing from all communicative exchange. In the logic of supposition, a thing exists insofar as it is put "into play," inscribed in and as the supposition of meaning.

In virtue of its presupposition of God, the world has meaning and being. Indeed, the possibility that the world is intelligible at all implies its supposition of something other than itself as the ground for its rationality. God's existence, though, does not presuppose any creative act or design, because God's existence is itself the act of all presupposition. As such, creation is not the means by which God's existence is completed or fulfilled. Rather, the presupposition of the possibility of any fulfillment of meaning is what constitutes the existence of God:

> It is evident that God don't make his existence or being the end of the creation, nor can he be supposed to do so without great absurdity. His being and existence can't be conceived of but as prior to any of God's acts or designs: they must be presupposed as the ground of them.[3]

The explanatory ground of God's acts must be his existence. But that existence is understandable in terms of what can be supposed, so understanding the nature of supposition becomes crucial for understanding God's creativity. As the presupposition of the world, God is the displacement of the world, the world's other.[4] Any act or design of God presupposes an end, object, or focus of that act or design. The end of God's acts cannot be himself, for that would mean that God does not yet exist until his act produces himself as an end. Therefore, his existence must be the presupposition of action, the supposition of end or purpose itself.

In other words, the existence of God is the requirement that all existence be communicative, intentionally disposed to and grounded in that which gives meaning in virtue of being other. To say that the world exists means that it points to its displacement as that which gives it meaning. Accordingly, God is not that which supposes or displaces the world, for that would mean that the world exists independently from God. Rather, God is the supposition of the world, the world's having been supposed or displaced.

To ask who or what does the supposing that constitutes the world, betrays the classical-modernist prejudice that supposition must be an activity of a subject or mind. God's supposition of the world is hardly something God *decides* to do, for God's disposition to create is literally the dis-positioning of himself already implied in the communicative character of his existence. As Edwards

---

3. Jonathan Edwards, *Dissertation concerning the End for which God Created the World* [1753–54], in *Ethical Writings*, ed. Paul Ramsey, 469.
4. Cf. Richard C. De Prospo, *Theism in the Discourse of Jonathan Edwards*, 74.

puts it, that communicative character—theologically expressed as God's glory and fullness—carries over into the existence of each of God's creations as the dispositions that constitute their own intentional existences:

> Merely in this disposition to diffuse himself, or to cause an emanation of his glory and fullness, which is prior to the existence of any other being, and is to be considered as the inciting cause of creation, or giving existence to other beings, God can't so properly be said to make the creature his end, as himself. For the creature is not as yet considered as existing. This disposition or desire in God must be prior to the existence of the creature, even in intention and foresight. For it is a disposition that is the original ground of the existence of the creature; and even of the future intended and foreseen existence of the creature.[5]

Just as the disposition whereby a creature comes to have existence must be explained in terms of the creature's other, so also the disposition whereby God creates must be explained in terms of his own otherness, his end. Even though in God's case the desire for the other points to nothing other than himself, the explanation for why there should be or must be such a desire in the first place cannot be dismissed simply by attributing it to God's glory and fullness. For glory and fullness, as we will see below, merely express the transcendentality implicit in the meaning of God. What is needed is an explanation of the logical dynamic that requires disposition or desire in God.

To say that God *has* a disposition to create beings other than himself, therefore, does not explain why he has such a disposition. To say that it is simply in accordance with his nature is to avoid the issue. Claiming that God's disposition to create is a function of his glory or fullness without explaining how is to gloss over the issue with religious platitudes. Even transforming the problem by suggesting that God *is* (at least in some way) the disposition to create being—creativity itself—fails to explain what a disposition is. The substitution of equivalents, such as inclination or tendency, merely begs the question and makes all the more apparent the circularity of reasoning implicit in such accounts.

The only way out of this predicament is acknowledging how Edwards portrays God's disposition to create as the point at which God and creation are united in communicative exchange. Because God *is* the otherness of supposition that drives the mechanism of endless signification, he is the mark of creation's communicability. Through the logic of supposition, Edwards provides the clue for understanding divine desire as the dis-position of the existence of creation. Insofar as creatures are united to God by virtue of his communicative nature, they embody his desire as the deferred intentionality of semiotic exchange. In this way, God's disposition to create follows not from any inherent potentiality or need on his part, but rather from the nature of being itself.

To ask why there is being at all is thus to ask why being is supposed, which means asking for what Edwards calls the "original ultimate end" of creation.

---

5. Edwards, *Dissertation concerning the End*, 438.

That end is established in the supposition of creation's having an end. Because a logic of propositions assumes that nothing can be meaningful apart from its implication in an other as its fulfillment or end, the supposition of a thing is equivalent to its having an end. The supposition that a thing has an end is redundant, because existence itself requires the implicit displacement or supposition of a thing by its end. By simply raising the question of the end of creation, Edwards reveals how God and creation are linked in a communicative exchange that accommodates the very supposition of such a linkage in virtue of the question's having been asked. Instead of being transcendent pronouncements about the relation of God and creation, Edwards' suppositions themselves enact the same logic that governs the possibility for any and all meaning and existence.

Once beings are supposed, their existence retroactively defines God as an agent whose "consequential ultimate" ends are "agreeable to the agent, or the agent's desire of them." Agreeableness, agency, and desire appear as functions within a nexus of mutually defined concepts that depend on "the subject and occasion being supposed."[6] In virtue of the supposition of subjectivity as always already displaced by its intentional relation to an end, the consequential ends of God's acts and all created beings constitute the structure by which relations between God and creation are "agreeable and amiable in themselves."

By their very nature (i.e., in themselves), subjects are supposed as the disposition of God's desire. Their agreeableness or harmony with God consists in their having an end that transcends any subjectivity limited by a substantialist or predicational ontology. Their deference to God reveals how selves, instead of being necessarily understood as divorced from God and other things, are essentially functions of the communicative exchange, in which even God participates consequentially as a self (or as selves, the persons of the Trinity).

However, the consequent appearance of God as a self or selves can now assume a meaning for self that is developed according to the propositional logic of supposition, not the logic of substantialist predication. Within the logic of supposition, the inherent transcendentality of every self marks agency, desire, and subjectivity as derivative features of the aboriginal exchange constituted by the continual deferral of subjectivity to its other. This activity of supposition identifies all beings in terms of their intelligence, their intentionality, their pointing to or shadowing forth an other or others to which they are tied as agreeable or disagreeable in virtue of what *must* be supposed:

> In like manner we must suppose that God before he created the world had some good in view, as a consequence of the world's existence, that was originally agreeable to him in itself considered, that inclined him to create the world, or bring the universe with various intelligent creatures into existence in such a manner as he created it. But after the world was created, and such and such intelligent creatures actually had existence, in such and such circumstances, then

---

6. Ibid., 413.

a wise, just regulation of them was agreeable to God, in itself considered. . . . But yet there is no necessity of supposing that God's love of doing justly to intelligent beings, and hatred of the contrary, was what originally induced God to create the world, and make intelligent beings; and so to order the occasion of doing either justly or unjustly. The justice of God's nature makes a just regulation agreeable, and the contrary disagreeable, as there is occasion, the subject being supposed and the occasion given: but we must suppose something else that should incline him to create the subjects or order the occasion.[7]

Any end God has in creating the world is mutually implied in the world's existence because, in the logic of supposition, existence necessarily entails an end as its supposition. The world in itself has an end necessarily agreeable to God, because the world in itself originally is the supposition of its fulfillment in its other, namely, God. The supposition of the world's existence is the inclination of God to create the world; this is what Edwards means in saying that God's inclination or disposition to create the world is supposed by the existence of the world. Because the supposition of the world establishes the propriety of the relations of beings to one another and to God (including relations of justice), no justification for the existence of the world can be presupposed.

To attempt to justify creation would be to attempt to justify or give a reason for supposition. Since supposition is the communicative procedure by which the strategy of giving reasons is established, supposition cannot itself be supposed by a standard of justification without immediately being reinstated as the procedure by which justice is first enacted. Though the fitness or harmony of things in creation exhibits the operation of divine justice, there is no obligation to be just that induces God to create. For if it is fit, right, or just for God to create, then the standard for what God must or ought to do is somehow prior to him.

Considering its central place in both Edwards' typology and doctrine of virtue, this concept of fitness deserves special consideration. Admittedly, justice does not require that God create anything at all, for what is fit or just is itself a function of the supposition which is the creation of being. But in terms of his standing relative to created being, God (in virtue of his fullness or goodness) has the disposition to create. Seemingly, it is only right and just that he exercise that disposition, just as it is fitting that God exercise his attributes of power, goodness, or mercy.

Here again, the intrusion of a logic of predication threatens to undermine the doctrine of divine activity that Edwards develops. In that fallen logic, justice is predicated of subjects or substances in relation; whereas in the logic of supposition justice refers to the way in which a thing is understood as the displacement of an other in a strategy of communication. To the ear attuned only to classical-modern patterns of thought, this distorts the meaning of justice by wrenching it from its essentially intersubjective matrix. Edwards, though, thinks

7. Ibid., 412.

that it is crucial to outline a programme that unites God and creation, without positing that programme as yet a third thing by which the issue of God's justice in creating and ordering the world is to be adjudicated. In proposing this "third being" precisely as no being at all—that is, in supposing this third person while denying that it can be a person—Edwards moves the question of justice or fitness away from the propriety of substances to the activity of supposition:

> When we are considering with ourselves, what would be most fit and proper for God to have a chief respect to, in his proceedings in general, with regard to the universality of things, it may help us to judge of the matter with the greater ease and satisfaction to consider what we can suppose would be judged and determined by some third being of perfect wisdom and rectitude, neither the Creator nor one of the creatures, that should be perfectly indifferent and disinterested. Or if we make the supposition that wisdom itself, or infinitely wise justice and rectitude were a distinct disinterested person, whose office it was to determine how things shall be most fitly and properly ordered in the whole system, or kingdom of existence, including king and subjects, God and his creatures . . . now such a judge in adjusting the proper measures and kinds of regard that every part of existence is to have, would weigh things in an even balance.[8]

The perfect indifference and disinterest of this third person excludes it from any relation of intentionality that might identify it as meaningful. As nothing more or less than the logic of supposition itself, it provides Edwards the means for alluding to the process through which his own discourse comes to have meaning. That process of supposition, like the communicative discourse of God's creation, inscribes the order or fitness of things in virtue of nothing other than the inscription itself. This is how it can maintain the perfect rectitude that is the hallmark of supposition itself:

> Thus I have gone upon the supposition of a third person, neither Creator nor creature, but a disinterested person stepping in to judge of the concerns of both, and state what is most fit and proper between them. The thing supposed is impossible; but the case is nevertheless just the same as to what is most fit and suitable in itself. For it is most certainly proper for God to act according to the greatest *fitness*, in his proceedings; and he knows what the greatest *fitness* is, as much as if perfect rectitude were a distinct person to direct him. As therefore there is no third being beside God and the created system, nor can be, so there is no need of any, seeing God himself is possessed of that perfect discernment and rectitude which have been supposed. . . . And as there must be some supreme judge of fitness and propriety in the universality of things, as otherwise there could be no order nor regularity, it therefore belongs to God whose are all things, who is perfectly fit for this office, and who alone is so, to state all things according to the most perfect fitness and rectitude, as much as if perfect rectitude were a distinct person.[9]

8. Ibid., 422–23. Cf. Miscellany #1208 [1752–53], in *The Philosophy of Jonathan Edwards*, ed. Harvey G. Townsend, 140–41.

9. Edwards, *Dissertation concerning the End*, 425. Cf. Miscellany #1208, in *Philosophy of Edwards*, 143–44.

To suppose this third being (as with Peirce's thirdness) is to suppose fitness, including what is fit relative to God. The supposition of God's infinite discernment identifies fitness as the mark of divine significance; but this comes only as a result of displacing the impossible and the unintelligible with the supposition of God's propriety. The possibility of God's existence thus depends on the possibility of propriety or rectitude revealed in and as supposition.

As the supposition of fitness itself, the third being is Edwards' device for describing "how things should proceed most fitly, according to the nature of things . . . as much as if the whole system were animated and actuated by one common soul that were possessed of such perfect wisdom and rectitude."[10] The immanent impulse to meaning and intelligibility (expressed as the third being) drives all of reality toward the achievement of communicative significance or fitness. Powered by the very nature of existence as inherently intentional, and guided only by the *prospect* of propriety and not by its initial assumption, the supposition of communicability plays out the dynamic by which existence itself exhibits fitness, harmony, or (in Edwards' preferred term) excellence.

Within this dynamic, the third being designates the first instance of personality in the Trinity, insofar as the supreme arbitration of fitness requires an initial delineation of subjectivity, in terms of which all subsequent propriety is defined. In order for a thing to be fit, harmonious, or proper, it must first be some determinable thing. But, as I have already indicated, no thing is intelligible apart from its supposition of an other to which it is intentionally related (Peircean secondness). The adjudication and determination of the fitness of the thing with its other is the function of the third being or interpretant. This third characteristic stipulates how determinate being necessarily exhibits the fulfillment of the communication of a thing.

In this way, a self or person embodies the completion of a communicative exchange between signifier and signified, between supposite and that which is supposed or sup-posited. According to Edwards, the emergence of the first *person* of the Trinity as the possibility for fitness identifies "what is most proper to take place in all that is acted or comes to pass with relation to God and the creature."

> But it is not necessary that this office should belong to each person of the Trinity. 'Tis most proper that he that is the first person, from whom the other two are, should be the person that should have this office to determine rectitude and propriety for the three persons and for all creatures.[11]

Edwards' circumspect reference to "all that is acted" reinforces his reluctance to posit subjects prior to their appearance as functions in action. Even in regard to the Son and Holy Spirit, the propriety of their personalities depends on there being a first person in terms of which rectitude, propriety, or fitness

10. Miscellany #1208, in *Philosophy of Edwards*, 143. Cf. Edwards, *Dissertation concerning the End*, 424–25; and Ramsey, ibid., 47.
11. Miscellany #1208, in *Philosophy of Edwards*, 149.

is expressed. Consequently, the fitness of all that is enacted by God announces the inherently communicative character of fitness itself.

Here, the passive voice of what is "acted by God" displaces the subjectivity of God by drawing attention to the more fundamental issue of the propriety of subjectivity itself. As the first person, the Father discloses how the fitness or propriety of personhood is a function of something's having been enacted. This enactment, though, does not require the existence of an agent prior to the act. Accordingly, the issue of the fitness of God's acts, including his creation of the world, turns on an ontology—namely, that of supposition—that excludes the possibility of any intelligible communication about the being of God apart from an explication of reasoning or intellection.

However, because such an explication displays the syntax of intentionality by which discourse is enacted as differentiation, it is not a function of human reasoning or intellection. The distinction of human and divine relies on the derivation of a divine personality within a more encompassing strategy of communicative exchange. That exchange constitutes the divine semiotics in terms of which human reasoning about God as a subject of predication can occur.

The propriety of the moves of such reasoning therefore does not depend on the model of the human mind for legitimacy or explanatory power, for propriety is the inherent intentionality of existence. What is fit or proper, even for God, is always the fitness *for* the fulfillment of communication in an intelligent being. As Edwards' so-called idealism makes clear, all true or completed being is intelligent being. Insofar as what he means by intelligence is the intentionality of all being to be communicable, he concludes that only intelligent beings (i.e., persons) participate in the exchange of significance that defines existence.

If the existence of God can make sense only in terms of the intentionality of persons, and if nothing can ultimately be supposed other than God, then the activity of supposition itself must be expressed in terms of persons (viz., the Trinity). Furthermore, in order for creatures to exist, they must be persons and must be able to be understood in relation to a personal God. But since God does not need creatures in order to exist, any personal relations necessary for the existence of God must characterize the nature of God himself. By refocusing the activity of supposition onto the internal nature of God, Edwards sketches out the ontological conditions for a revised sense of personhood. In doing so, he reveals what is necessary for regeneration in interpersonal relations between creatures and God.

Aware that this revision of the meaning of person entails a challenge to the logic of predication that inevitably produces confusion about the Trinity, Edwards resists referring prematurely to the internal relations of God in terms of persons. At the same time he affirms that any subsequent characterization will employ a strategy already exhibited by reasoning in general:

> I think that it is within the reach of naked reason to perceive certainly that there are three distinct in God, each of which is the same [God], three that must be

distinct; and that there are not nor can be any more distinct, really and truly distinct, but three, either distinct persons or properties or anything else; and that of these three, one is (more properly than anything else) begotten of the first, and that the third proceeds alike from both, and that the first neither is begotten nor proceeds. . . . I think it really evident from the light of reason, that there are these three distinct in God. If God has an idea of himself, there is really a duplicity, because [if] there is no duplicity, it will follow that Jehovah thinks of himself no more than a stone. And if God loves himself and delights in himself, there is really a triplicity, three that cannot be confounded, each of which are the Deity substantially.[12]

Accessible even to uninspired reason, the logic of the Trinity must be displayed before we can determine exactly what is meant by referring to the persons, properties, or any other distinctions in the Trinity. This logic sets out the conditions for propriety in intra-trinitarian relations, beginning with the act of displacement or supposition of God the Father by his idea (the Son) and resolved meaningfully in a relation between the two (the Holy Spirit).

In accord with the requirements of propriety in reason itself, Edwards lists the Son first, insofar as the Son is the signifier or idea that displaces the signified (the Father). He then refers to the significance of such displacement (the Holy Spirit). And lastly, he identifies that which is signified in the supposition (the Father). This does not mean, however, that the Son or Holy Spirit are persons ontologically prior to the Father. Instead, it indicates how priority and propriety (for example, in how the Son is begotten) characterize the resulting discourse of substantiality and not the semiotic strategy whereby the duplicity or triplicity of divine personalities draws attention to functions of the logic of supposition.

Because the Father is that which is supposed by the Son, the Father is said to beget the Son. In contrast to accounts employing efficient or final causality, Edwards' appeal to begetting does not assume that the cause of the Son's existence is itself a substance intelligible independently of its effect. The cause or reason (*Logos*) of God—that is, the supposition of the Father by the Son— identifies the Father as the object of the supposition. Here the object exists as a function or person only in terms of its displacement, so the begetting of the Son by the Father does not assume that the Father exists prior to the Son or that the Father can be conceived apart from the Son; rather, the Son is literally the image of the Father, God in displacement.

As opposed to human generation, in which the son is *in* the image of the father, the Son of God *is* the image of the Father. That slight grammatical variation reveals how the internal relations of the Trinity exhibit a different logic than that which characterizes the fallen, human condition. In the logic of supposition, the image is the supposition by which that which is supposed comes into intelligible existence. Apart from the supposition that the Son enacts and that

---

12. Miscellany #94 [1723–24], ibid., 253, 257. Cf. Jonathan Edwards, *An Unpublished Essay of Edwards on the Trinity*, ed. George P. Fisher, 111–13.

the Holy Spirit validates, the Father does not exist. Or rather, the Father exists
as the possibility for having an image or supposition (the Son) with which it
is associated (by and as the Holy Spirit). After all, to say that the Son is the
supposition of the Father can be taken to mean either that the fact of the Father's
being supposed is the Son (and not an act done by an independently existing
person called the Son), or that the Son comes into being in the unusual way of
being "begotten" as an idea of the Father (but which is not entertained by any
mind or person called the Father).

It might be argued, though, that even for human beings a father, as a father,
does not exist until he has a child. The logic of predication permits our saying
that a substantial person exists even in the absence of the person's being related or predicated of another. The logic of predication presumes the original
intelligibility of the distinction between substances and their predicates, even
if it does not explain the dynamics of the presumption itself. Such a logic thus
grounds intelligibility or rationality in an irretrievable and gratuitous assumption of a distinction that fails to acknowledge the communicative exchange by
which distinctions are made in the first place.

In the suppositional logic of the Trinity, on the other hand, rationality is displayed as communicative displacement. In begetting the Son, the Father does
not will the Son into existence, "for that proceeding was natural and *necessary*,
and not arbitrary."[13] The generation of the persons of the Trinity is not an
action done by the Father, for acting is a characteristic of persons, and the
Father is a person only in virtue of his being supposed. However, it would be
misleading to say that the Son supposes the Father (as if supposition were an
act of a person); rather, the Son *is* the supposition of the Father.

Because the supposition of anything specifies exactly what the supposed
thing is in virtue of the supposition itself, the Son is the absolutely perfect idea
of God. "An absolutely perfect idea of a thing," Edwards explains, "is the very
thing, for it wants nothing that is in the thing, substance nor nothing else."
Any ontology that assumes that ideas must be distinct from the things of which
they are ideas ignores how a thing itself is begotten in virtue of its being an
idea *of* precisely that of which it is an image:

> So that by God's reflecting on himself the Deity is begotten, there is a substantial
> image of God begotten. I am satisfied that though this word 'begotten' had never
> been used in Scripture, it would have been used in this case: there is no other
> word that so properly expresses it. . . . Again, that which is the express and per-
> fect image of God, is God's idea of his own essence. There is nothing else can be
> an express and fully perfect image of God but God's idea. Ideas are images of
> things; and there are no other images of things, in the most proper sense, but
> ideas, because other things are only called images, as they beget an idea in us of
> the thing of which they are the image; so that all other images of things are but

---

13. Edwards, "The Excellency of Christ," in *The Works of President Edwards*, ed. Samuel Austin,
7:278. On Heereboord's appeal to the idea of supposition in discussing the Trinity, see William S.
Morris, *The Young Jonathan Edwards: A Reconstruction*, 110–11, 502–503.

images in a secondary sense. But we know that the Son of God is the express and perfect image of God, and his image in the primary and most proper sense.[14]

To think at all means to employ images or ideas, because images or ideas display the necessarily intentional character of thought and (more significantly) being. Insofar as the supposition of being begets the idea of being, the supposition of God is the begetting of the idea of God. Because the idea of God delimits exactly what God is as that which has been displaced and identified in the idea, it not only constitutes a perfect image of God, but also exemplifies what is properly an image or idea.

In its primary or most proper sense, an image (as will be discussed in the final chapter) is not some psychological affection hidden away in personal or subjective consciousness. Rather, it is the signifier aspect of a semiotic relation. The possibility of God's existence depends on there being an idea of God, begotten as the prospect of meaning. This supposition of God in the othering of the Father as an image permits the subsequent designation of God as a source of activity and power (i.e., as a substantial being). Any image of that substantial being therefore draws on the more primary image of God (the Son), insofar as it is through the original idea of God that God becomes accessible. This, Edwards suggests, is what is meant by Christ's comment that no one comes to the Father except through the Son.[15]

Unless the Father (God as displaced in supposition) is understood in relation to the idea that displaces him (viz., the Son), the two remain merely distinct, not differentiated. In relating these two functions of the Godhead (signifier and signified) to one another, the Holy Spirit exhibits the immanent significance of the Trinity. As Edwards notes, "The Holy Spirit is the act of God between the Father and the Son infinitely delighting in each other."[16] This internal activity, delight, or love identifies God as the model of signification, the resolution of supposition. Everything that exists has meaning in terms of what it displaces only if there is some recognition of that connection. Likewise, being itself is fulfilled (delighted) in the mutual complementarity of signifier and signified. The Holy Spirit is the unity of differential signification by means of which not only God's existence, but all existence, becomes meaningful.

The communicative or semiotic relations of the persons of the Trinity establish standards for reasoning in relations between God and his creation and between creatures themselves. By situating his discussion of the dynamics of intelligibility in the transcendental context of the Trinity, Edwards calls for a radical realignment of our thinking in developing "a sense of the heart." That shift substitutes the logic of supposition for the logic of predication.

14. Miscellany #94, in *Philosophy of Edwards*, 253–54. Cf. Edwards, *Essay on the Trinity*, 84–86; and Schafer, "Concept of Being," 156–64.
15. See Miscellany #777 [1738–39].
16. Miscellany #94, in *Philosophy of Edwards*, 256. Cf. Edwards, *Essay on the Trinity*, 77–78, 110.

Restricted to a vocabulary and a semantics driven by a predicational syntax, however, Edwards struggles to describe his doctrine of the Trinity in ways that can avoid the disputes of his contemporaries. Instead of developing a new vocabulary for expressing his doctrines—as Peirce and Whitehead do—Edwards forces the terminology of classical modernity to conform to the principles of the Stoic-Ramist logic of supposition. He glosses over the contortions that result from such a maneuver by appealing to metaphors (e.g., personal attributes) that mask the disruptions of classical syntax required by those principles.

Through these diversionary practices Edwards suggests answers to questions about the Trinity and creation by undermining premises that falsely set up such problems in the first place. Ignoring how his metaphorical discussion of the Trinity employs an ontology that takes metaphor seriously as displacement risks overlooking the subversive character of his tactics.

Why God Creates

Just as Edwards' doctrine of the Trinity requires a reformulation of personhood, so his ontology of supposition revises classical-modern notions of causality. In particular, the question of why God creates the world is changed radically once we recognize that, in such an ontology, God and the world are no longer understandable as things or substances about which acts or properties are predicated. In particular, God's creation of the world is not understood as an action done by an agent whose existence is intelligible apart from the action itself. Instead of being something predicated of a substance or agent, creation is seen as part of the process by which the existence of God becomes significant or intelligible.

This revised understanding of creation acknowledges the inherently intentional character of being by referring to both God and creation as essentially communicative. Here, the requirements for meaning preclude the fragmentation of existence implicit in substantialist predication. God and world exist in a communicative relation, because apart from the dynamic of displacement or intentionality (i.e., the communicative exchange of signifier and signified), intelligibility itself is undefined.

It makes no sense, then, to ask why God creates, without specifying the conditions for determining how answers to the question are meaningful or significant. Any assumed significance of the question reflects on the significance of the terms within it (viz., God, world, creation). And since the significance of those terms consists in their intentional relations to or displacement of one another, the rationale for creation must likewise be understood in terms of such a juxtaposition.

Just as the Son is the displacement or idea of the Father, and whose association with the Father is the Holy Spirit, so the world is the supposition of God authorized in the communication of creation. That is, just as the Father and Son become intelligible in terms of one another in virtue of their association in the Holy Spirit, so God and the world become intelligible in terms of one another in virtue of creation as the communicative resolution of their juxtaposition.

Edwards' logic of the Trinity thus redirects the question of why God creates from having to discover the intentions of the divine mind to reconsidering the nature of intentionality and mind. As I will argue later, this same reorientation of the way the issue is raised allows Edwards to fashion a theory of action that undercuts freedom-determinism problems by dissolving the assumptions about agency that occasion such difficulties. In the ontology of supposition, the intentionality of mind cannot be dissociated from its ends or objects, because the fulfillment of the end is the rationale by which the very existence of the agent is made intelligible.

The relation between the Son (as signifier) and the Father (as signified), internally associated with one another in the Holy Spirit, constitutes the model for meaning or significance. The Trinity's own meaningfulness as a unity lies in its subsequent displacement by the world. Just as the persons of the Trinity are meaningful in virtue of their involvement in the semiosis of supposition, so also the Godhead itself (as a unity) can be meaningful only as the dis-place of the world. The recognition of that displacement as something that has meaning is the recognition of the world as the creation of God.

Accordingly, the end or purpose of creation is the fulfillment or resolution of God's intentionality. Divine intentionality, in turn, is the prospect of the world's having a meaning. For the world to have meaning, it must be understood as a communication, for its significance lies only in its pointing beyond itself to an other. It literally communicates (or becomes one with) its other in being the supposition or dis-position of God.

If supposition is understood as an activity of some already determinate being, then to say that the world is a supposition of God would mean that the existence of the world excludes God from the place that the world inhabits. For if supposition refers exclusively to an action undertaken by God, then his creation of the world produces a separate (and in some sense independent) substance. If it is an action undertaken by the world (as if the world constitutes a substance or person that can suppose God), then the creation of the world is likewise the creation of God, in which case God and world are assimilated pantheistically. But if the supposition of God does not presuppose a being who does the supposing, then a number of things follow: God can be understood as the ground or rationale of all significance; the world can be understood as that which signifies or images God; and creation can be understood as the interpretation of the relation between God and world by which the two are made intelligible in terms of one another.

Creation, in this latter formulation, mirrors the intra-trinitarian relation between the Son and the Father, insofar as the world images God.[17] But in the

---

17. Cf. Edwards, Miscellany #1004 [c. 1745]; and Jenson, *America's Theologian*, 41–47.

Trinity the image or idea of God is internally related to the thing of which it is an idea as a signifier is to its signified. Insofar as the world and things in the world are not recognized as intentionally related to one another, their significance in providential history will be overlooked or misunderstood.

In order to reinstate this redemptive potential at the heart of being, Edwards traces the diffusive and communicative character of divine creativity to what he calls God's glory. By describing God's glory *ad intra* in terms of the Trinity, he warns us that any discussion of God's attributes must respect the fact that ultimately God is not a *subject* of attribution at all. For to predicate glory as an attribute of God would be to think that God as a subject is intelligible apart from his glory. In supplanting predication with supposition, however, Edwards provides the means for explaining how God's glory is presupposed even as prior to any disposition or inclination to manifest itself:

> Surely God's glory that is to be manifested, must be considered as something prior to his disposition or design to manifest it. God's inclining or designing or exerting himself to show his glory, surely is not that very glory which he shows; the glory must be something else beside the manifestation of it.[18]

As the dynamic of displacement presupposed *ad intra* (i.e., in the relations of the Trinity) as well as *ad extra* (i.e., in the creation of the world), God's glory identifies the immanent intentionality of being. In order to claim that "God's external glory is only the emanation of God's internal glory," Edwards recognizes that he has to explain emanation in terms of glory or fullness.[19] But in order to stop the explanatory regress, he appeals to a logic in which glory or fullness provides for its own intelligibility as inherently diffusive and always already othered.

That intelligibility cannot be grounded in a disposition, inclination, or *habitus*, for such a move simply buries the search for an explanation in claims about the ineffable nature of God. To his credit, Edwards acknowledges that to say that God has a disposition to create does not explain why he has such a disposition. To explain Edwards' notion of glory (as some recent commentators have done) in terms of an attribute of fullness or an inclination to emanate being likewise merely shuffles terms without explaining what those substitutions mean or why they are necessary.[20] The fact that Edwards provides no ultimate ground for God's glory does not mean that he thinks that God's glory cannot be explained. Rather, such substitutions constitute the nature of explanation itself and exhibit, in the suppositional exchange of signifiers and signifieds, exactly what it would mean to explain a concept.

---

18. Miscellany #445 [c. 1729], in *Philosophy of Edwards*, 131. Cf. Edwards, *Essay on the Trinity*, 89.

19. Edwards, *Dissertation concerning the End*, 527, 529.

20. See Sang Hyun Lee, *The Philosophical Theology of Jonathan Edwards*, 196–210 (especially 209); Cooey, *Jonathan Edwards*, 54–56; and Janice Knight, "Learning the Language of God: Jonathan Edwards and the Typology of Nature," *William and Mary Quarterly*, 3d ser., 48 (1991), 546–47.

Within such a framework, God's glory is the explanation or rationale for creation, because it identifies the inherently intentional, diffusive, and communicative nature of meaning. God's glory provides a standard on which significance is constituted and without which no explanation is meaningful. In turn, any explanation of God's glory trades on the propriety of the notion of explanation—a propriety that itself is defined only in the communicative exchange designated in and as God's glory. In short, the structure of significance highlighted in the concept of glory inscribes glory as that which provides the explanation for all else.

For Edwards, the internal glory of God as the Trinity explains the external glory of creation, insofar as creation can be understood as an emanation of God. Whereas Neoplatonic emanationism does not explain or justify the notion of emanation other than by appealing merely to metaphorical substitutes, Edwards' use of the term within the context of his doctrine of communication explains how propensity, diffusion, glory, and emanation are intelligible in terms of the immanent intentionality of God:

> This propensity in God to diffuse himself may be considered as a propensity to himself diffused, or to his own glory existing in its emanation. A respect to himself, or an infinite propensity to, and delight in his own glory, is that which causes him to incline to its being abundantly diffused, and to delight in the emanation of it. . . . So God looks on the communication of himself, and the emanation of the infinite glory and good that are in himself to belong to the fullness and completeness of himself, as though he were not in his most complete and glorious state without it. . . . It is a regard to himself that disposes him to diffuse and communicate himself. It is such a delight in his own internal fullness and glory, that disposes him to an abundant effusion and emanation of that glory. . . . The exercises of his communicative disposition are absolutely from within himself, not finding anything, or any object to excite them or draw them forth: but all that is good and worthy in the object, and the very *being* of the object, proceeding from the overflowing of his fullness.[21]

In order for God to be fulfilled or completed, he must communicate himself. But such a communication cannot be directed to something other than God, for that would mean that God needs some other being in order to be complete. At least, that is what is implied if God is intelligible apart from his communication. If, on the other hand, God's propensity to diffuse himself designates the inherent intentionality of meaningful being, then fulfillment of meaning comprises the very being of the objects of such communication in completing the significance of God.

In this way the glory of God explains why God has a diffusive inclination to communicate. But the explanation itself relies on a notion of fulfillment in communication that already assumes that meaning or significance is inherently dispositional, emanational, or diffusive. Even though God is not complete without the exertion and communication of his glory, the rationale for God's glory

---

21. Edwards, *Dissertation concerning the End*, 439–40, 452. Cf. Schafer, "Concept of Being," 282–93.

lies in nothing other than God himself. For the significance of the being of God
(or the being of anything else, for that matter) rests in its supposition of another:

> But here as much as possible to avoid confusion, I observe that there is some im-
> propriety in saying that a disposition in God to communicate himself *to the*
> *creature*, moved him to create the world. For though the diffusive disposition in
> the nature of God, that moved him to create the world, doubtless inclines him to
> communicate himself to the creature when the creature exists; yet this can't be
> all: because an inclination in God to communicate himself to an object, seems to
> presuppose the existence of the object, at least in idea. But the diffusive dispo-
> sition that excited God to give creatures existence was rather a communicative
> disposition in general, or a disposition in the fullness of the divinity to flow out
> and diffuse itself. . . . Therefore to speak more strictly according to truth, we may
> suppose *that a disposition in God, as an original property of his nature, to an*
> *emanation of his own infinite fullness, was what excited him to create the world;*
> *and so that the emanation itself was aimed at by him as a last end of the creation.*[22]

Because the supposition of the other does not presume the prior existence of
the other part from the supposition, God's communicative disposition to exercise his glory is directed toward the world only in terms of himself: The world
becomes significant only as God's other. Without that other, God cannot be intelligible or significant (i.e., fulfilled in a proposition).

In saying that the glory of God provides the rationale for creation, Edwards
thus outlines the procedure for explaining what that claim means and how it
is justified. We need not conclude, then, as Paul Ramsey does, that emanation
as a communication can be read either "biblically" (as if God is a person who
decides to create) or Neoplatonically (as if the world somehow "proceeds"
from God). As I have suggested, Edwards' strategy suspends both biblical-
personalist and fuzzy Neoplatonic accounts of emanation by identifying being
communicationally as always already intentional. Limited, however, by a syntax
that prevents him from explaining how the inherent intentionality of God's activity is his glory, Edwards has to rely on metaphors to make his point:

> Language seems to be defective and to want a proper general word to express
> the supreme end of the creation, and of all God's works, including both these
> branches of it, viz. God's glorifying himself or causing his glory and perfection
> to shine forth, and his communicating himself or communicating his fullness and
> happiness. The one supreme end of all things is the infinite good as it were
> flowing out, or the infinite fountain of light, it as it were shining forth. We need
> some other words more properly and fully to express what I mean.[23]

The classical-modern language of final causality fails here because, according
to the logic of predication, the end or purpose of a thing is not the thing itself.
From that perspective, a logic that would define an end specifically in terms
of the generation of being would seem to confuse origin and end. But in the

---

22. Edwards, *Dissertation concerning the End*, 434–35. Cf. Miscellany #104 [c. 1724].
23. Miscellany #1066 [c. 1745], in *Philosophy of Edwards*, 139. Cf. Ramsey, ed., *Ethical Writings*,
433n, 516n.

logic of communicational supposition, the significance of a being is its point-ing to its other as the end or fulfillment in terms of which it is meaningful. The end or significance of creation lies, then, in God's displacement of himself, his "flowing out" of himself in and as the generation of meaning.

This way of reasoning reemphasizes just how important metaphors are as metaphors. In contrast to the collapsed similes with which they are often con-fused in classical-modern accounts, Edwards' metaphors draw attention to the internal dynamic by which their integrity is maintained because of, and not in spite of, their pointing to what grounds their meaning. As my discussion of Edwards' typology indicated, all things point beyond themselves for their sig-nificance, just as all metaphors tease out remnants of overdetermined meaning from the linguistic constraints of literalist reduction.[24] As the provocation of sig-nificance implicit in all being, the glory of God is that characteristic of meaning expressed in the tendency of a thing to find its completion in an other. Edwards' doctrine of God's glory includes metaphoricity as a central methodological device for highlighting the constant transcendence or overflowing of meaningful being.

Because the two moments of this creative activity (God's causing his glory to shine forth and his communicating this fullness) depict the process by which being emerges, they follow the same logic as intra-trinitarian relations. As the explication of what diffusion, flowing out, or shining forth means, they indi-cate how the procedure for understanding why God creates requires "a twofold manner of egress, or going forth, viz. manifestation and communication."

> These two ways of the divine good beaming forth are agreeable to the two ways of the divine essence flowing out, or proceeding from eternity within the God-head, in the person of the Son and Holy Spirit: the one, in an expression of his glory, in the idea or knowledge of it; the other, the flowing out of the essence in love and joy. It is condecent that correspondent to these proceedings of the divinity *ad intra*, God should also flow forth *ad extra*.[25]

The agreement or condecency of both creation's procession and the relations of the Trinity emphasizes how the logic of supposition that guides the dis-tinction of the persons of the Trinity also guides the distinction of the world from God. The world is significant as the supposed creation of God just as the Godhead is significant as the supposed or sup-posited idea of meaning itself. As the end of creation, the fulfillment of meaning in communication manifests the glory of God only in the recognition or enjoyment of the union between signifier and signified, supposite and supposited. In this way the internal pro-cession of the Trinity and the external procession of God's creation of the world exhibit the same logic and ontology.

Instead of treating communication simply as an activity in which God engages, this semiotic extension of communicative exchange becomes the

---

24. For more on this notion of the metaphoric, see Stephen H. Daniel, *Myth and Modern Phi-losophy*, 11–35.

25. See Miscellanies #1142 and #1151 [both 1751], in *Ethical Writings*, 517n, 530n. Cf. Miscel-lany #259 [c. 1728], in *Philosophy of Edwards*, 259–60.

means by which Edwards defines the divine disposition to create as effective or successful exertion. Without the fulfillment of effort in an interpretation, the juxtaposition of agents, persons, or objects effects no being and communicates no meaning. Ultimately, the rationale of effective communication incorporates all other features in Edwards' account, so that the activities of God *ad intra* and *ad extra* agree in their pragmatic orientation:

> Both these dispositions of exerting himself and communicating himself may be reduced to one, viz. a disposition effectually to exert himself, or to exert himself in order to an effect. That effect is the communication of himself *ad extra*, which is what is called his glory. This communication is of two sorts: the communication that consists in understanding or idea, which is summed up in the knowledge of God; and the other is in the will consisting in love and joy, which may be summed up in the love and enjoyment of God. Thus, that which proceeds from God *ad extra* is agreeable to the twofold subsistences which proceed from him *ad intra*, which is the Son and the Holy Spirit—the Son being the idea of God, or the knowledge of God, and the Holy Spirit which is the love of God and joy in God.[26]

God's disposition to exert himself effectively expresses the trinitarian relation of signification: As that which is signified by the Son, the Father is the disposition or supposition of the Son, and the Holy Spirit is the validation of that signifier-signified relation as an effective exertion (i.e., as a completed communication). As the communicative structure of all being and meaning, the Trinity displays how significance or meaning itself contains a reconciliation to alterity implicit in the Stoic-Ramist requirement that the smallest unit of meaning be a proposition.

By contrast, in the logic of classical-modern predication, the *disposition* to communicate is prior to the actual communication. Its designation as logically prior is an attempt to insulate it from probing questions about how such a disposition itself comes into being. In order to avoid begging the question or simply defining it away by assuming that dispositions are prior to their fulfillment, some commentators have suggested that Edwards proposes another attribute of God (e.g., goodness or fullness) to account for God's disposition to create.[27] God's creation of the world, they claim, is a moral, not a metaphysical event. That tactic merely buries the explanation of why God creates in the obvious circularity of equating God's goodness or fullness with his inclination to communicate goodness or fullness in creation.

This kind of confusion is understandable, considering how even in using these terms Edwards draws attention to their inadequacy for explaining God's creation of the world. For example, in Miscellany #87 Edwards points out how treating goodness as a predicate of God cannot be reconciled with treating it as part of the intentionality-meaning of God (i.e., as the signifier component of a semiotic relation):

---

26. Miscellany #1218 [1751–52], in *Philosophy of Edwards*, 152.
27. See Delattre, *Beauty and Sensibility*, 134; Schafer, "Concept of Being," 120, 275–79; Ramsey, ed., *Ethical Writings*, 527n; and Miklós Vetö, *La Pensée de Jonathan Edwards*, 60–62.

'Tis not proper to ask what moved God to exert his goodness; for this is the notion of goodness, an *inclination* to show goodness. Therefore such a question would be no more proper than this, viz. what inclines God to exert his inclination to exert goodness? which is nonsense, for it is an asking and answering of a question in the same words.[28]

As God's inherent inclination to effective communication, goodness cannot be merely an attribute of God, but must refer to the intelligibility or rationality of being itself. In short, goodness is the inclination of being to be meaningful. To seek a reason for why God is inclined to exert his goodness is to ask for the rationale of rationality itself. Because such a rationale is implicit in the asking of the question (otherwise, the question itself is nonsense), the very possibility of an explanation for God's creative activity is intelligible only in terms of the discursive exchange in which the question appears.

From this semiotic perspective, an inclination or disposition has meaning in terms of its fulfillment in its other, in juxtaposition to which it is aboriginally defined, and in association with which it has meaning. God's disposition to create—that is, his goodness—is the dis-position or supposition of the world, which itself becomes meaningful in virtue of being recognized in terms of its other. Because God's inclination to create is not a property of some substantial being, but rather is a function of the nature of significance or meaning itself, God does not have to *do* anything in order to communicate being. Communicable, intelligible being already contains within itself all that is needed to account for the exertion of creative activity.

In this way, every creature has significance insofar as it fulfills (or "glories in") communication. But what a creature communicates is that to which it points as its fulfillment in intentionality, namely, God. As the communication of God, creation exhibits goodness because the intentionality of communication, as God's disposition, *is* goodness. As Edwards writes, "God's disposition to communicate good, or to cause his own infinite fullness to flow forth, is not the less properly called God's goodness, because the good that he communicates, is something of himself."[29] Goodness or fullness flows forth not because of something other than itself, but because an other is always already implied (as the inherent intentionality of communicable meaning) in the meaningfulness of goodness.

For Edwards, God's creative activity is thus understandable in terms of formal causality, rather than the efficient causality that treats God and creation as if they were two things intelligibly independent of one another. The divine disposition to create is the divine disposition to communicate. But communication, understood in terms of formal relations instead of efficacy, already includes the notion of disposition as the intentionality of signification. Like the signified that is identified only by being displaced by the signifier, the *disposition* to

28. Miscellany #87 [c. 1723], in *Philosophy of Edwards*, 128. Cf. Schafer, "Concept of Being," 271; and Ramsey, ed., *Ethical Writings*, 434n.
29. Edwards, *Dissertation concerning the End*, 460.

communicate goodness can be characterized only in terms of its being related to what it communicates.

This is not to say that God's disposition to communicate must be understood in terms of creation, but rather that both God's disposition and creation are merely abstractions from the signifier-signified relation that comprises goodness or fullness (i.e., communicative significance in general). God's goodness is the fulfillment of significance in virtue of the prospect of reconciliation, that is, in virtue of the prospect of completed communication. Insofar as a creature shadows forth its own otherness, it communicates the glory of God, but it is able to do that only because the glory of God is the prospect of meaningfulness, and meaning (goodness, fullness) necessarily entails an other:

> God and the creature, in this affair of the emanation of the divine fullness, are not properly set in opposition; or made the opposite parts of a disjunction. Nor ought God's glory and the creature's good to be spoken of as if they were properly and entirely distinct. . . . This supposeth that God's having respect to his glory and the communication of good to his creatures, are things altogether different: that God's communicating his fullness for himself, and his doing it for them, are things standing in a proper disjunction and opposition. Whereas if we were capable of having more full and perfect views of God and divine things, which are so much above us, 'tis probable it would appear very clear to us, that the matter is quite otherwise: and that these things, instead of appearing entirely distinct, are implied one in the other. That God in seeking his glory, therein seeks the good of his creatures: because the emanation of his glory (which he seeks and delights in, as he delights in himself and his own eternal glory) implies the communicated excellency and happiness of his creature. And that in communicating his fullness for them, he does it for himself: because their good, which he seeks, is so much in union and communion with himself. God is their good. Their excellency and happiness is nothing but the emanation and expression of God's glory: God in seeking their glory and happiness, seeks himself: and in seeking himself, i.e. himself diffused and expressed (which he delights in, as he delights in his own beauty and fullness), he seeks their glory and happiness.[30]

The reconciliation of the other to that which it displaces constitutes excellency, the consent of being to being. In order even for God to be intelligible (i.e., excellent), he must be understood in terms of the same logic of alterity or supposition that underlies the dynamic of communicative being. God is the good of his creatures, because they are intelligible in terms of their intentionality of an other.

By the same token, God's very being is fulfilled (i.e., made meaningful) in the communication of goodness (i.e., in the fulfillment of himself as a communication). In this regard, the communication of goodness is made possible because of the goodness or intelligibility of communication. Goodness is its own justification because goodness *is* justification, and justification necessarily implies the mutual involvement or communication of a signifier and its other.

---

30. Ibid., 458–59; see also 440–41.

Edwards' well-known claim that "God is a communicative being" can then be understood in two complementary ways, neither of which commits him to a logic of substantialist predication.[31] First, by saying that God is a being who communicates, Edwards situates God in a discourse that itself legitimates his existence as the other of creation, the rationale for the possibility of meaning in creation. Second, Edwards' remark also suggests that God is the communicative or intentional character of every being, the inclination of all being toward fulfillment; insofar as a being communicates, it expresses God, it is God's glory. In either interpretation, communication circumscribes being by insisting that being presumes goodness, and goodness is the validation of the supposition of the other as intelligibility.

This line of thought can explain, at least in part, why Ramsey, in contrast to Townsend and Schafer, would replace "goodness" with "fullness" in his transcription of Edwards' Miscellany #87. He justifies such a substitution by noting that in Edwards' later works the biblical resonance of fullness and glory tends to overshadow the more philosophically loaded concept of goodness. Regardless of whether this legitimizes an apparent contortion of the text, it demonstrates how even Edwards' undisputed references to goodness dismantle the Neoplatonic notion of the Good in favor of one less burdened by the predication of attributes in substantialist logic. Both goodness and fullness refer to God's immanent communicability, which is to say that both presume the displacement of alterity in any significant exchange.

In the logic of supposition, being has significance as a completed or interpreted communication. Every communication assumes a relation between that which is said and that which is meant, between a signifier and a signified. The disposition to communicate is the displacement of the signified by a signifier, and thus the designation of the signified as that which is other. The signifier itself identifies the signified as an absence to which the signifier points. Unless the signifier is interpreted in terms of its relation to the other as displacement itself, the signifier is unintelligible, lost, fallen. Goodness is the validation of the signifier in terms of its being interpreted as the supposition of the signified.

This redefinition of goodness as the prospect of meaning inherent in significant communication requires that the question of what moves God to create be rephrased in terms of an analysis of the necessarily communicative character of goodness. "It still appears to me exceeding plain," Edwards explains, ". . . that the very being of God's goodness necessarily supposes [its communication]."[32] By its very nature, the being of goodness is communicative because the nature of all being consists in the supposition of its other in and as communication. It makes no difference whether or not the other exists prior to the communication, because in a certain sense the other is constituted by the communication:

---

31. See Miscellany #332 [c. 1728–29], in *Philosophy of Edwards*, 130; see also Miscellany #96 [1723–24].
32. Miscellany #243 [1727], in *Philosophy of Edwards*, 129. Cf. Miscellany #445, ibid., 130–31.

But now goodness, or an inclination to communicate good, has merely *possible* being as much [for] its proper object, as actual or designed being. A disposition to communicate good, will move a being to make the occasion for the communication; and indeed, giving being is one part of the communication. If God be in himself disposed to communicate himself, he is therein disposed to make the creatures to communicate himself to; because he can't do what he is in himself disposed to, without it. God's goodness is not an inclination to communicate himself as occasion shall offer, or a disposition conditionally to communicate himself, but absolutely.[33]

The requirements of communicativity determine how communicants are to be related and even created. God's disposition to communicate himself is constrained at least in respect to this requirement of intentionality. To say that God's goodness guides his acting on a disposition to create means, therefore, that the possibility of significance is what lures creation into existence.

Ultimately, Edwards addresses the question of how creation achieves significance in the same way that he explains the internal relations of the persons of the Trinity. As the inclination toward meaning internal to God, the Son points to an other (the Father) as the intentionality or idea of the other. Similarly, the world is the product of the disposition of God to communicate precisely by its being the dis-position of God, the mark of the absence of that without which the mark is unintelligible. However, the rationale or internal intelligibility of the Trinity is not identical to that of God's external relation to creation. For the world is the supposition of God, not the supposition of only the Father; and creation signifies the divinely grounded intelligibility of the world, whereas the Holy Spirit displays the meaning of being itself as the resolution of idea and ideatum, supposite and supposited.

Edwards' shorthand way of handling this distinction pivots on his doctrine of Christ. As will be argued in my concluding remarks, his doctrine of Christ brings together his communicative ontology with his soteriology. Here I want to note how Edwards' divine semiotics explains the way in which God's activity *ad intra* and *ad extra* is highlighted in the distinction between the Son and Christ.

In the Trinity the Son points to completion in an other as that which makes significance possible. The Son is thus intentionality *in* significance. But the displacement or supposition of significance itself constitutes the world as the other to significance. The idea of significance is not the same as significance itself, but is rather that which communicates the otherness of significance. Christ is this inclination toward God in creation; he is the signifier or intentionality *of* significance.

The immanent intentionality of the world (expressed in the person of Christ) is not intelligible unless it is fulfilled in terms that indicate its transcendentality, meaning that Christ has a natural inclination toward, and is incomplete without, the Church.[34] In terms of the logic of supposition, the Church is the

---

33. Miscellany #445, ibid., 132; see also Miscellany #1218 [1751–52], ibid., 149–50.
34. Miscellany #104.

world supposed as creation, the world made significant as a supposition or signification of God. Only when it is understood in terms of how it points to that which it displaces does the world become significant. Redemption (the retrieval of significance) does not result from the world's becoming one with God; instead, it specifies a recognition of how creation is the supposition or disposition of God.

As the disposition to communicate, the Son/Christ points to the general possibility of completed (i.e., significant) communication. Insofar as the creation of the world is a communication, its immediate cause is not the Father or the Godhead (the Trinity taken as a unity), but rather is the Son's communication of himself in presenting an image of himself:

> But yet the Son has also an inclination to communicate himself, in an image of his person that may partake of his happiness: and this was the end of the creation, even the communication of the happiness of the Son of God; and this was the only motive hereto, even the Son's inclination to this.[35]

Just as the Son is the intentionality of God and Christ is the intentionality of the world, so the Church (Christ in the world) is the image of the Son. In this sense Christ is the Word or *Logos* of God (but note: not the Word of the Father). The Father is the other to whom the Son defers; God is the other to whom Christ defers. Through the world Christ signifies significance itself, always deferring to and differing from that which idea displaces. That is why, according to Edwards, Christ communicates himself only to spirits or minds, for they (unlike bodies) are inherently and immediately intentional: Ideation is always ideation *of.* That character of intentionality or inclination in communication drives the search for meaning in history, the fulfillment of which would constitute the communication of divine happiness.

In becoming more Christ-like, creatures overthrow the original sin of defining themselves substantially rather than suppositionally. Like Christ, they recognize that their significance lies not in themselves, but in an other. They discover that the self is intelligible only in terms of its place in discursive exchange. In discovering the connections that regulate the agreements and harmonies implicit within signification, the saints are transformed from being subjects (to whom objects of knowledge are accidentally related) to necessary moments in the process of emerging intelligibility. As I have suggested, this sense of the heart is the displacement of the classical-modern logic of predication with the Stoic-Ramist logic of propositions.

35. Ibid. Cf. Miscellanies #108 and #766 [1738–39].

V

THE ONTOLOGY OF ORIGINAL SIN

Though often treated merely as a topic for theological polemics, Edwards' doctrine of original sin provides yet one more entrance into his philosophy of communicative significance. For it is in the doctrine of original sin that Edwards finds the theological equivalent for the displacement of the Stoic-Ramist logic of supposition by the classical-modern logic of predication. Rather than explaining why the original sin occurs, his doctrine highlights formal discrepancies between prelapsarian and postlapsarian discourses. By thematizing those discrepancies, he is able to identify original sin as the fall into individual subjectivity and the loss of guaranteed significance in discursive exchange.

Edwards' discussion of original sin appeals to both divine and human discursive practices without collapsing one into the other. Indeed, the initial appearance of sin signifies something that cannot be explained by anything other than itself. No theory of agency, freedom, or moral responsibility characteristic of subsequent human action can explain why Adam sins; nor can original sin be attributed to an act of God, because the fall itself defines a new meaning for what constitutes an action. In juxaposing two absolutely incompatible mentalities, Edwards discerns what is truly original about original sin: It is the point at which aboriginal signification is lost and in its place is substituted the divided, fallen condition of representation.

In Edwards' philosophy, original sin marks the boundary between the discourse of the Trinity and the natural discourse of human beings. It provides the framework for his doctrines of human freedom and virtue and outlines the conditions for the retrieval of intelligibility through grace. It reveals how the juxtaposition of incommensurable mentalities or epistemes itself does not have to appeal to some metanarrative in terms of which each mentality is allowed to maintain its individual integrity.

Even though Edwards' arguments are themselves limited by the strictures of a fallen discourse, they nevertheless are formulated to avoid contradictions commonly attributed to him by his critics. To describe original sin, Edwards does not rely on ways of speaking about Adam that would otherwise characterize human subjectivity. Instead, he portrays Adam not as simply another individual human being, but as the prospect that humanity might become individuated, isolated from God and one another in the arrest of the semiotic movement of creation.

Original sin designates this rupture of signification, this displacement of an ontology of typology with a metaphysics of subjectivity. By highlighting the moment of such a displacement, Edwards' doctrine of original sin depicts the classical-modern treatment of human freedom, moral agency, and virtue as already dominated by the centrality of the self. Because the Stoic-Ramist alternative to that treatment thoroughly changes the meaning of notions of freedom, agency, and virtue, "there is [as Edwards notes] no hope of putting an end to the controversy about original sin" unless we first understand how the meaning of sin is likewise altered in that matrix.[1]

Accordingly, Edwards' doctrine of original sin provides both a diagnosis of sin and an indication of what it meant by grace transforming the sinner into the saint. Insofar as sin refers to the disruption of God's communication, it signals the loss of significance, the frustration of the semiotic movement of creation formalized in the fallen predicational ontology of classical-modern metaphysics and epistemology. Grace retrieves for the saint the prelapsarian sense of how existence is tó be understood as essentially communicative—that is, as consistent with principles of meaning in propositional (Stoic-Ramist) ontology.

Far from being an account of the first of all subsequent sins, Edwards' discussion of original sin reveals how sin is the expression of a theory of meaning that links depravity with individuality; the insistence on the legitimacy of individual subjectivity constitutes the prideful rejection of the divine impulse to semiotic exchange. That rejection establishes a counter-discourse (or more properly, a counter to discourse). Since the metaphysics and epistemology of such a counter-discourse do not originally embody the belief that existence is essentially propositional or communicative, they treat meaning or significance as something merely added onto being or knowledge.

When Edwards refers to "putting on the new man" or appeals to a sense of the heart, he therefore relies on a discourse that goes beyond simple religious platitudes, insofar as those same terms provide the context for explaining the philosophic significance of sin. For him, the meaning of meaning is at stake; only a doctrine of original sin that acknowledges that fact could account for the inherently depraved condition of humanity.

This chapter addresses the ontological characteristics of original sin rather than its epistemological consequences (which are considered in chapter 7). Here, the focus is on the two major topics Edwards identifies in his doctrine: the depravity of human nature and the liability of all human beings for Adam's sin.[2] The first topic treats the Fall of humanity as a fall into semiotic isolation, a loss of significance that designates subjects as lacking any inherent meaning. In the context of this topic, the original sin is not something that Adam once did and for which all subsequent human beings are held responsible. Rather,

---

1. See Jonathan Edwards, *Original Sin,* ed. Clyde A. Holbrook, 22–23, 376. Cf. Robert W. Jenson, *America's Theologian: A Recommendation of Jonathan Edwards,* 143.
2. See Edwards, *Original Sin,* 107.

the origination of sinning itself is understood to continue unabated in the very metaphysical definition of humans as individual subjects.

The second topic considers the sin of Adam from the perspective of fallen human consciousness. It portrays original sin as the particular act of an individual by which free choice is curtailed and guilt is imputed to all other human beings. From this perspective, the doctrine of original sin appears to violate moral requirements: first, that individuals must be free in order justly to be held responsible for their actions and, second, that they cannot justly be held responsible for the acts of another. If people are naturally inclined to sin as a result of Adam's sin (the argument goes), then human depravity, in general, and our particular liability for that depravity seem to run counter to the requirements of justice.

Typically Edwards' treatment of this second topic (viz., our liability for Adam's sin) has been interpreted in terms of two alternatives. On the one hand, the realist (Augustinian, Calvinist) view holds that Adam and his posterity, as members of the same species, share the same human nature. In virtue of that continuity, features of Adam's acts also characterize the acts of all subsequent human beings.[3] In this view, the sheer humanity of Adam guarantees his fall, insofar as human beings are created naturally sinful. But that rules out the possibility that Adam could have freely chosen not to sin, because he could not have chosen to be other than human.

The nominalist or federalist view, on the other hand, holds that God links Adam to other human beings as part of a covenant appointing him as the federal head or representative of his posterity. The transfer of the guilt of Adam's sin is a result of a union God ordains in recognizing Adam as a human being.[4] This approach, though, deprives all subsequent human beings the opportunity to have a say in how they are to be represented or to disavow their complicity in Adam's sin.

The ease with which objections can be raised against either alternative suggests that there is a problem with how the issue of Adam's agency is formulated. As one would expect, Edwards traces the difficulties posed by such objections to confused notions of freedom and moral agency, and in place of those notions (as the next chapter will show) he provides his own positions. This chapter focuses on the ontology that makes the discussion of those positions possible.

According to Edwards the perspective of the "natural man" fails to provide a metaphysics of morality necessary to defend his theory of original sin against charges of injustice. He acknowledges that his doctrine requires a reexamination of the philosophic or metaphysical presuppositions that have traditionally informed the discussion of original sin.[5] His doctrine reveals not only how the

3. See Miklós Vetö, *La Pensée de Jonathan Edwards*, 55–56, 108–10, 117; and John E. Smith, *Jonathan Edwards: Puritan, Preacher, Philosopher*, 22.
4. See C. Samuel Storms, *Tragedy in Eden: Original Sin in the Theology of Jonathan Edwards*, 226–35.
5. See Edwards, *Original Sin*, 409.

original sin sets up the problem of human moral agency, but also how original sin designates the very conceptual procedures by which it is examined.

The reflexive impact of Edwards' strategy demonstrates why realist or federalist accounts ultimately must fail to provide a rationale for human depravity. Whereas such accounts assume the propriety of treating Adam and his posterity as individual subjects, Edwards identifies original sin precisely as the frustration of significance expressed as the ontological impropriety of subjectivity.

In Edwards' philosophy of original sin, depravity and its imputation are united in such a way that Adam's posterity shares in his sin not merely *because* God imputes sin to them but because "it is *truly* and *properly* theirs."[6] But what is proper to sinful humanity is not to be understood in terms of any essence or nature by which they are human, for in that regard Adam's humanity in no way distinguishes him as an individual. What makes Adam and all other human beings the proper objects of God's imputation of sin is their own propriety, the individuality that disrupts the semiotic impulse to situate significance in an other. Insofar as all human beings are individuals, they are properly sinful, for sin designates the impropriety of propriety itself. By reformulating the question of the ontology of sin, Edwards indicates how the nature of human individuality itself entails the loss of divine significance that constitutes sin. In this way Edwards can argue that, insofar as we share with Adam the ontological isolation of individuality, we share in his sin. To characterize the imputation of sin as the imputation of subjectivity thus redirects the question of Adam's sin away from a consideration of how he as an individual could have made an evil choice for which we are now held responsible to a consideration of how the choice of evil is itself always the choice for insular individuality.

Edwards sets up the problem this way: If nothing can be sinful unless it is freely chosen, then the free choice to sin must itself be sinful; otherwise nothing could account for the choice to sin. "And we must go back till we come to the very *first* volition, the prime or original act of choice."[7] Not accidentally, the choice to sin appears in the original act of choice, because any movement of thought that even considers the possibility of an alternative to the semiotic unity of divine discourse disrupts the possibility for meaning. Even to be "free" to consider the possibility that two alternative courses of action could both be meaningful or significant is to sin. That is why the very thought of acting contrary to the divinely constituted order of things is itself sinful, and why the condition of being able to imagine alternatively significant options (and thus to choose) is itself depraved.

By appealing to the Renaissance, Stoic-Ramist account of signification, however, Edwards is able to introduce the non-substantialist, non-subjectivist

---

6. Ibid., 408.

7. Ibid., 377. Cf. Stephen R. Yarbrough, "The Beginning of Time: Jonathan Edwards' *Original Sin*," in *Early American Literature and Culture: Essays Honoring Harrison Meserole,* ed. Kathryn Zabelle Derounian, 155, 159–61.

relations of the Trinity into the discussion of original sin. In the Trinity, the distinction of persons is hardly an endorsement of their propriety or individuality, but is rather an indication of how personhood entails a determinate reference to an other. The possibility that referentiality in the Trinity could be used to differentiate the divine persons as different subjects is precluded by how the figure of Christ, the new Adam, functions in the propositional understanding of meaning. As a person in the Trinity, the Son enacts the ontology of the divine discourse, even while as an individual, Jesus exhibits the ambiguities of human nature. Christ's choice to retrieve the unity of divine significance by atoning for human subjectivity reinstates the integrity of creation by pointing to the need for semiotic fulfillment (in the Holy Spirit). In this way, the prelapsarian order of creation can be reinstated in the new Adam's act of reconciling God and humanity.

The Fall

Dispositions can be understood in two different ways. According to the logic of predication, a disposition is some trait, inclination, habit, or characteristic predicated of an individual subject or self. Its meaning or significance is independent of the subject of which it is predicated, and it can be predicated of different subjects without affecting its own meaning or significance or that of the subjects of which it is predicated. In such a view, to say that human beings have a disposition to sin means that human beings have that characteristic (inherited from Adam), though there need not be anything inherently sinful about human nature.

In the logic of propositions, a disposition is not some trait of a self; rather, it is that moment in a discursive exchange that defines the self in a proposition as a place (a *topos*) that dis-places an other in the semiotic network in which it resides. In this logic, the subject and predicate of a proposition have no meaning apart from the proposition, and the proposition has no meaning apart from its function in a discourse. A disposition is a dis-position, a position whose meaning consists in pointing beyond itself to an other. To say that human beings have a disposition to sin, in this logic, means that human beings embody the denial of signification or meaning by attempting to affirm their own significance apart from a semiotic matrix.

This second way of treating dispositions requires that we consider Edwards' remarks about supposition not as referring to an activity performed by an individual mind, but as expressing the ontological procedure by which meaning is generated in communicative exchange. Just as the Son is the supposition or displacement of the Father, and the world is the supposition of God, so a person (e.g., the Son, or Adam) is the supposition or prospect of the significance of an individual. The individuality of a person signals his or her isolation from the communicative matrix in which that person has meaning. A person per se is not an individual, but is rather the displacement of the prospect that an individual has meaning independently of the activity of supposition. In short, a person is a sign of the dis-placement of individuality, a sign of the impropriety of the proper (i.e., "one's own").

Such a recondite description challenges typical strategies for addressing Edwards' discussion of original sin by refusing to treat the disposition to sin as a characteristic predicated of prelapsarian humanity or attributed to some act or failure of God.[8] No such attribution is possible (except in the discourse of fallen humanity), because neither Adam before the Fall nor God are individual selves or subjects.

Before the Fall, Adam is the supposition of God, made in the image of God as that intentionality or consciousness by which the world has the prospect for fulfillment and significance as God's creation. After the Fall into the semiotic isolation of human individuality, the new Adam (Christ) becomes the supposition of God, the prospect of the world's semiotic completion. Through Christ God is meaningfully accessible to fallen human individuals; that is, God becomes a person with whom human beings share the prospect of communication. But as is indicated in the communicative relations of the person of the Trinity, the prospect of personal relations with God relies on the semiotic character of being itself.

Therefore, a personal relationship with God would entail a rejection of the notion that God is a self or an individual, for such a notion describes only fallen human beings. In contrast to human relations based on an ontology of individuality, the relationship of Christ to God demonstrates how the very existence of Christ makes sense only insofar as he is understood as a signifier of God.[9] To have a personal relation with God thus requires that one become like Christ, intelligible only in terms of a propositional or communicative ontology. In such an ontology, being related to another (or "consenting to another") entails a radical transformation of the notion of self. As a result of Christ's overcoming of original sin, relations no longer need to be understood as predicable of individuals, and consent should not be considered as something that an individual conscious mind does.

Christ's retrieval of the prelapsarian relation of God and his creation makes sense only by understanding how Christ embodies the very ontology that the notion of sin itself displaces. Because the explanation of sin relies on a discursive strategy different from that of the prelapsarian relation of God and Adam, the reinstatement of that relation by the new Adam can only be understood as a retrieval of the semiotic condition lost in the Fall. The fall from that semiotic condition cannot be explained in terms of the condition itself, for nothing about the prelapsarian integrity of being can account for the loss of that integrity.

This way of setting up the problem indicates how, for Edwards, there can be no efficient cause for the Fall in the first place. At least no efficient-cause explanation

---

8. Cf. James Hoopes, *Consciousness in New England: From Puritanism and Ideas to Psychoanalysis and Semiotic*, 90, 205, 231; and Storms, *Tragedy in Eden*, 215.

9. Cf. Jenson, *America's Theologian*, 33–34, 121–22.

for the Fall can properly address the issue of the origin of sin. Insofar as sin is
precisely the fall from intelligibility, to seek an intelligible explanation for sin is
thus to misunderstand the problem. In the absence of such an efficient-cause
explanation—that is, one that would provide some internal or external cause of
sin (e.g., a natural sinful inclination, or Satan)—Edwards resorts to a formal-
cause explanation, one that presents the origin of sin simply as the implicit,
ever-present possibility of the disruption of communicative significance.

To defend this approach, Edwards denies that God could cause the original
sin, because for God to do so would be contrary to the inherent goodness, significance, or intelligibility of the space of discourse Edwards identifies as God.
Edwards also eliminates the possibility that Adam himself could somehow have
caused this fall from significance. Because the original sin has no precedent,
Adam's inclination to sin could not have been the product of his prior sinful
actions.[10] Besides, according to the doctrine of original righteousness (which
Edwards endorses), Adam was created inclined to act rightly. As part of his
very nature, Adam's inclination to moral rectitude cannot be used to explain
his choice to sin, unless some formal feature of that explanation accounts for
his having acted contrary to this inclination.

To provide a formal-cause explanation of original sin, Edwards appeals to
the ontology of supposition. In that ontology, the notion of disposition does
not refer to some private inclination of an individual; rather, it refers to the discursive matrix of thought, choice, and action united in intentionality. It signals
the dis-position of meaning, the way in which being consists in its continual
self-effacement.

When Edwards writes about dispositions, he thus assumes an ontology at
odds with the metaphysics of subjectivity. In the pride-based metaphysics of
subjectivity, the prelapsarian (Stoic-Ramist) meaning of disposition as inherent
intentionality is misappropriated in the domain of predication. In that misap-
propriation, subject and predicate are assumed to be meaningful apart from
their appearances in propositional relations. This contortion of the meaning of
disposition entails a loss of the prelapsarian sense of significance contained in
the notion of disposition; it accordingly designates the ontological condition
of sin itself. The very concept of Adam's having a disposition to sin thus rests
on a contradiction; for a disposition to sin would be an indication that the inherently other-oriented intentionality of meaning is limited to the prideful
isolation of the self from an other.

Whereas the classical-modern mentality appeals to the dispositions of an isolated Cartesian self to explain human thought and action, the Stoic-Ramist
ontology of semiotic significance defines the metaphysical status of a person
in terms that do not presume an aboriginal distinction between agent and act.
Before the Fall, thoughts, choices, and actions suppose one another—that is,
they point to one another as conditions for their mutual intelligibility. In this

---

10. See Edwards, *Original Sin,* 229–34. Cf. Storms, *Tragedy in Eden,* 219–21.

way there is no distinction between what Adam is, thinks, or does. His dispo-sitions situate him in a typological order of things that specifies right actions by defining his relation to what is fitting or appropriate for human existence.

Without these dispositions human nature lacks the intentionality by which thought, will, and act have meaning. Apart from its disposition, no choice could have any significance, for as Edwards observes, a choice has significance only if it is consistent with the dispositional rationale of the order of existence. Since that rationale specifies how a choice can have meaning or effect, any choice in-consistent with that in virtue of which it is intelligible—that is, any choice lacking virtue—would be unintelligible, and could be considered a choice only in a derivative sense.

A choice is thus intelligible specifically as a particular choice in virtue of nothing less than its moral character. That moral character, in turn, is a func-tion of the disposition of the choice, which is another way of saying that the power or virtue of the choice consists in its intentionality or ability to point to its fulfillment beyond itself in an other which it supposes and of which it is the disposition:

> The act of choosing that which is good, is no further virtuous than it proceeds from a good principle, or virtuous disposition of mind. Which supposes, that a virtuous disposition of mind may be before a virtuous act of choice; and that therefore it is not necessary that there should first be thought, reflection and choice, before there can be any virtuous disposition. If the choice be first, before the existence of a good disposition of heart, what signifies that choice? There can, according to our natural notions, be no virtue in a choice which proceeds from no virtuous principle, but from mere self-love, ambition, or some animal appetite. . . . Human nature must be created with some dispositions; a dispo-sition to relish some things as good and amiable, and to be averse to other things as odious and disagreeable. Otherwise, it must be without any such thing as inclination or will. It must be perfectly indifferent, without preference, without choice or aversion towards anything, as agreeable or disagreeable. But if it had any concreated dispositions at all, they must be either right or wrong, either agreeable or disagreeable to the nature of things.[11]

The significance of a choice depends on its place in the order of things. That place is determined as a disposition or function of intentionality. The virtue or moral power of a place lies in its significance for that with which it is agreeable or disagreeable. Mere self-love is blind to the need to consider the dis-position or dis-placement to which a thing alludes as that which inscribes its significance.

Prior to the Fall, Adam is simply the conscious (mental) disposition of the world to fulfill the intentionality of the divine communication. Such a role does not require that Adam be an individual human being, for as Edwards notes, the biblical texts speak of God's making man, not *a* man.[12] As the sign of the inten-tionality of significance, prelapsarian humanity thus need not be individuated,

---

11. Edwards, *Original Sin,* 224, 231.
12. Ibid., 234.

for (as it subsequently becomes all too evident) individuality merely registers the rupture and failure of communicated meaning.

Edwards, therefore, changes the question of *why* Adam sinned into an inquiry about the semiotic or ontological requirements for understanding *how* Adam could have sinned. This revision of the problematic of original sin relies on Edwards' assumption that sin is unintelligible within the context of moral righteousness. Such an assumption does not amount to a refusal to explain the origin of sin as much as it reveals how the search for an efficient cause of the original sin makes sense only in an already fallen discourse.

To claim that Adam would not have sinned had he not been tempted by Satan (and thus to blame Satan for original sin) merely pushes the question of the Fall one step back. It raises two further questions: why would Satan choose to sin in the first place, and why would Adam choose what was contrary to his virtuous disposition? Insofar as the answer to either question relies on recognizing how Satan personifies the act of individuality that aborts the disposition to virtue, the two questions ultimately become one. That, however, does not prevent Edwards from showing the fruitlessness of trying to provide an efficient cause of the origin of sin.

To the first question, for example, Edwards responds rather cryptically: The fall of the devil, he says, is due to "some extraordinary manifestation of God's sovereignty."[13] Just what such a manifestation might entail disappears in its characterization as extraordinary. As outside of what is meaningful even according to divine discursive practices, the aboriginal sin of Satan designates only the failure of designation.

Edwards' answer to the second question follows suit. To say that Adam was free to act contrary to his virtuous disposition makes no sense in Edwards' doctrine of will, for (as the next chapter will show) that would require that the intentionality by which the will is defined would be contradictory. Therefore, the key to understanding Edwards' concept of original sin is not simply the offhand claim that Adam misused his free will.

More importantly, talk of Adam's simply deciding to sin fails to emphasize how the very notion of a choice between meaningfully alternative actions already embodies the metaphysical prerequisite for sin. In Edwards' account Adam does not decide to sin, nor can Adam think of the significance of any act that would constitute sin. Such a decision or action would be unintelligible by itself, since nothing considered solely by itself has any meaning or significance except in a metaphysics of sin (as opposed to an ontology of virtue). Unlike everything else in the prelapsarian world, sin has no significance, no meaning. The choice to sin would be a choice for which there is no rationale; or, more properly, sin is the choice of a world in which there is no rationale, only the self-reflexive affirmation of the choice or act itself.

It is no wonder, then, that in supposing this ontological characterization of

13. Miscellany #290 [1726], cited in William S. Morris, *The Young Jonathan Edwards: A Reconstruction*, 521–22.

sin, Edwards consistently avoids giving any satisfactory explanation for why Adam sins. Often, after speaking about the prelapsarian condition of humanity, Edwards turns to the description of fallen existence simply with a brief mention of "when man fell" or "once Adam lost his holiness." [14] Hardly clarified by the familiar homiletic references to the wiles of Satan or the weakness of Eve, Edwards' account provides no clue as to why Adam should turn away from the "positive good principles" of his virtuous dispositions. As he makes clear, the original human condition cannot be used to explain the Fall:

> The case with man was plainly this: when God made man at first, he implanted in him two kinds of principles. There was an *inferior* kind, which may be called *natural,* being the principles of mere human nature; such as self-love, with those natural appetites and passions, which belong to the nature of man, in which his love to his own liberty, honor and pleasure, were exercised: these when alone, and left to themselves, are what the Scriptures sometimes call *flesh.* Besides these, there were *superior* principles, that were spiritual, holy and divine, summarily comprehended in divine love; wherein consisted the spiritual image of God, and man's righteousness and true holiness; which are called in Scripture the *divine nature.* These principles may, in some sense, be called *supernatural,* being (however concreated or connate, yet) such as are above those principles that are essentially implied in, or necessarily resulting from, and inseparably connected with, *mere human nature;* and being such as immediately depend on man's union and communion with God, or divine communications and influences of God's spirit: which though withdrawn, and man's nature foresaken of these principles, human nature would be human nature still; man's nature as such, being entire without those divine principles, which the Scripture sometimes calls *spirit,* in contradistinction to *flesh.* These superior principles were given to possess the throne, and maintain an absolute dominion in the heart: the other, to be wholly subordinate and subservient. And while things continued thus, all things were in excellent order, peace and beautiful harmony, and in their proper and perfect state. These divine principles thus reigning, were the dignity, life, happiness, and glory of man's nature. When man sinned, and broke God's Covenant, and fell under his curse, these superior principles left his heart: for indeed God then left him; that communion with God, on which these principles depended, entirely ceased. . . . The inferior principles of self-love and natural appetite, which were given only to serve, being alone, and left to themselves, of course became reigning principles; having no superior principles to regulate or control them, they became absolute masters of the heart. [15]

The divine principles inseparably connected with mere human nature situate humanity in the divine matrix of communicative significance. Once withdrawn from that matrix, human nature becomes intelligible only in terms of the artificial relations predicated of isolated, human individuals. In such a fallen state,

14. See, for example, Edwards, *Original Sin,* 279, 381, 385; and *Charity and Its Fruits* [1738], in Jonathan Edwards, *Ethical Writings,* ed. Paul Ramsey, 252–54. Cf. Miscellany #437 [1729], in *The Philosophy of Jonathan Edwards,* ed. Harvey G. Townsend, 159–60.

15. Edwards, *Original Sin,* 381–82. See also Miscellany #436 [1729], in *Philosophy of Edwards,* 157–58. Cf. Vetö, *La Pensée,* 179.

human beings no longer resonate in the harmonic order of things, because God withholds the "special divine influence to impart and maintain those good principles, leaving the common natural principles of self-love, natural appetite, etc."[16] Yet as much as God's validation of this situation explains why Adam's posterity labors under this condition, it cannot provide the rationale for the Fall in the first place.

Indeed, in laying out the contrast between the principles of the spirit and those of the flesh, Edwards alludes to the fact that the inferiority of natural appetites and passions consists simply in their lack of communicative influence on anything else in creation. This lack of significance is expressed graphically in the self-absorbed materiality of individual bodies. The principles of the flesh designate the resistance to significance that sin embodies. The simple existence of bodies (or the flesh in general) marks the loss of the semiotic integrity of creation implicit in the prospect of communicative fulfillment. Accordingly, the prominence of the flesh in accounts of original sin designates the formal possibility of the termination of significance.

By equating the ontology of sin with the ontology of bodies, this semiotic account of original sin explains the existence of bodies in a distinctly non-Neoplatonic way. Instead of including bodily existence in the emanation of substantial being, Edwards' scheme defines being in terms of propositional or significatory displacement. Within such a scheme, a substance is the termination of a relation and, as such, it functions precisely as a body.

The fall from the matrix of intentionality permits a reconsideration of the subject as an individual in terms now regulated by a metaphysics of substantialist predication. Because that metaphysics assumes the propriety of individuality characteristic of bodily existence, it treats spiritual or divinely communicative significance as an extrinsic relation of an individual. In classical-modern metaphysics, the spiritual significance of existence expressed in the intentionality of mind is made to conform to the model of bodies. The irony of such an appropriation is that, according to the ontology of prelapsarian humanity, the individuation characteristic of bodies is precisely that which makes them in principle unintelligible apart from the arbitrary artifice of God's ordering of things in the world according to laws of nature.

The question of how individual bodies come to exist in the world is therefore the same question as how Adam could have sinned, for sin designates the formal condition of individuality made possible through bodily existence. In claiming that Adam was not originally an individual nor originally susceptible to an individual's death, Edwards implies that Adam had no body. Adam's sin is intelligible only in virtue of the possibility that he can see himself as an individual body (naked, an object of possible shame), for sin is nothing other than the assumption that meaning or significance terminates in the self.

16. Edwards, *Original Sin,* 381.

In contrast, insofar as the meaning of a person (e.g., Christ) consists essentially in supposing an other, no person can be understood as an individual body, for bodily existence signals the loss of the communicative significance thematized by the ontology of supposition. As Edwards points out in distinguishing Christ from Adam after the Fall, the supposition of an individual body assumes the propriety of the body and what it supposes:

> I believe that Jesus Christ not only is exactly in the image of [God], but in the most proper sense *is* the image of God. Now however exactly one being, suppose one human body, [is] like another; yet, I think, one is not in the most proper sense the image of the other, but more properly *in* the image of the other. Adam did not beget a son that was his image properly, but in his image: but the idea of a thing is, in the most proper sense of all, its image; and God's idea, the most perfect image.[17]

Because an idea (e.g., Christ) is already the supposition of an other (God) in virtue of its intentionality—an idea is always an idea *of*—there can be no such thing as an autonomously meaningful idea. Like prelapsarian Adam, Christ supposes or signifies God as His idea. In that regard, Christ's body is properly considered only in a spiritual sense, only in terms of its transfiguration in and as the Church. The supposition of the distinction of Adam's and his son's bodies, however, introduces the possibility of another form of image, a form in which a body serves as the image of another body. As Edwards notes, though, because this does not connote the proper meaning of image (as idea), the imagery provided by bodies only hints at the spiritual ontology that unites Adam and his posterity in spite of their fall into individual (bodily) subjectivity.

Just as spiritual supposition characterizes prelapsarian ontology, so supposing predicates of bodies characterizes the Fall. Because the Stoic-Ramist ontology of supposition identifies a thing only in terms of its intentional relations, anything that lacks characteristics of intentionality (e.g., a body) simply cannot be imagined apart from its dis-place as a limit concept. This boundary of signification is necessary for defining the determinateness or specificity of the divine communication.

At the same time, the sheer existence of the "natural and necessary inclination to ourselves" raises the prospect of the loss of communicative significance. The natural and necessary condition for human significance requires that there be something dis-posed, something supernatural which is supposed as its other. Even though natural and supernatural, and signifier and signified, are different, they cannot be thought apart from one another. It is the misdirected prospect that one might be thought without the other, the prospect of considering the natural as merely embodied and as terminating thought rather than serving as the conduit of its fulfillment, that constitutes the original sin:

> There is nothing new put into the nature that we call sin, but only the same self-love that necessarily belongs to the nature, working and influencing, without

17. Miscellany #151 [1724].

regulation from that superior principle that primitively belongs to our nature, and that is necessary in order to the harmonious exercise of it.[18]

The differentiation of signifier and signified expresses natural and necessary moments in the divine impulse toward semiosis. When these natural components are interpreted as a harmonious, "supernatural" communication, they are made intelligible in virtue of the sign they together comprise. Sin becomes intelligible only when the signifier can be considered no longer merely as a moment in the communication but as a self-subsistent sign.[19] In Edwards' account of original sin, that shift from one semiotic strategy to another coincides with the possibility of thinking in terms of bodies.

There is nothing that can explain this adoption of another episteme; all that Edwards can do is diagnose the situation. To try to provide a dialectical account of the original sin—as if the Fall is the supposition of supposition—cannot succeed because that would imply that the Fall has a significance (when it, in fact, entails precisely the loss of significance). In addition, to invoke the eschatological doctrine of the *felix culpa* or "happy fault" is to smuggle in a meaning for meaninglessness, by appealing to a fallen logic of predication in which any predicate can be linked in some way or other (even if by contrast or negation) to a subject.

By posing his doctrine of sin in terms of a logic of supposition, Edwards incorporates his discussion of bodies and natural dispositions into the broader explanation of how subjectivity constitutes the loss of spiritual significance. That isolation of the bodily from the matrix of communication (i.e., God) introduces the possibility of Adam's natural death by raising the prospect of eternal death (i.e., permanent exclusion from the economy of being). Sin signals both the possibility of individual existence (along with the possibility of the death of the body) and the prospect of individual non-existence (the loss of significance).

Adam's existence as an individual is thus equivalent to the possibility of his death, and the possibility of his death coincides with his embodiment. But, as Edwards notes, even though the embodiment (or "flesh") natural to human beings alienates Adam from God and all other humans, the possibility for transcending that isolation likewise characterizes human nature from its inception:

> To prevent all cavils, the reader is desired particularly to observe, in what sense I here use the words, 'natural' and 'supernatural': not as epithets of distinction between that which is concreated or connate, and that which is extraordinarily introduced afterwards, besides the first state of things, or the order established originally, beginning when man's nature began; but as distinguishing between what belongs *to*, or flows *from*, that nature which man has, merely *as* man, and those things which are *above* this, by which one is denominated, not only a *man*, but a truly *virtuous, holy* and *spiritual* man; which, though they began, in Adam, as soon as humanity began, and are necessary to the perfection and well

18. Miscellany #301 [1726], in *Philosophy of Edwards*, 243.
19. Cf. Stephen R. Yarbrough and John C. Adams, *Delightful Conviction: Jonathan Edwards and the Rhetoric of Conversion*, 36, 80.

being of the human nature, yet are not essential to the constitution of it, or necessary to its being: inasmuch as one may have everything needful to his being *man* exclusively of them.[20]

Humanity is innately supernatural, connately significant, born to be perfected. The frustration of such an impulse designates "man as he is in himself, in his natural state." Isolated from God and one another, human beings literally *embody* sin, originating a new nature, a new discourse in which the truncation of significance is considered natural, necessary, and therefore nothing of which we should be ashamed.[21]

From the perspective of that fallen consciousness, the referential content of experience (what experience is experience *of*) is thought to be independent of consciousness itself, and the appearance of anything in consciousness is considered fortuitous, arbitrary, accidental. This notion of consciousness reduces the mental to the purely subjective, thus precluding the prospect of an innate human spirituality. Insofar as the mental cannot legitimate its relation to its objects, it stands as a testimony to the loss of signification and as the invitation to skepticism.

Of greater concern to Edwards, though, is that in this fallen consciousness the mental is erroneously substituted for the spiritual. That substitution begins with the assumption that to be human necessarily means being an embodied individual. In attempting to overcome the isolation of individuality by developing interpersonal relations, well-meaning, though misdirected, believers bestow on God substantialist properties (including having a mind). However, just as discursive features of mind become isolated semiotically from those of the body, so the divine begins to appear more remote from human experience. In the end, fallen consciousness terminates in alienation, as the concern for a spiritual other is dismissed as an accidental feature of human existence.

Though commentators have often pointed out that Edwards links original sin to bodily existence and self-love, they have generally failed to show how that relationship depends on an ontology of sin.[22] By describing the Fall as the isolation of the self (defined as a body), Edwards shows how the interpretive confusion about his account of original sin itself relies on the fallen notion that sin is something that an individual self does, rather than being the embodiment of what an individual self is.

As the formal expression of a subjectivistic and isolated way of reasoning, the classical-modern mentality provides an explanation of Adam's choice to sin in the only terms in which it defines rationality (namely, subjective intentionality). It comes as no surprise, then, that in terms of such a mentality, the reason for Adam's sin is his pride. But when the question is raised as to why

20. Edwards, *Original Sin*, 381n–382n.
21. Ibid., 279, 375, 383. Cf. Yarbrough, "Beginning of Time," 149–50.
22. See Paula M. Cooey, *Jonathan Edwards on Nature and Destiny*, 91–92; and Thomas A. Schafer, "The Concept of Being in the Thought of Jonathan Edwards," 240–42, 247n. By contrast, see Yarbrough, "Beginning of Time," 156–59.

Adam pridefully chooses to misuse his free will or why God would create Adam with such a penchant, the only answer provided is one couched in the inscrutability of the divine mind. In circumventing this obvious evasion, Edwards refocuses the question onto the issue of subjectivity itself. By so doing he is able to formulate a theory of rationality in which subjectivity is merely a function of discursive exchange rather than its organizing principle.

The Imputation of Subjectivity

The liability of all human beings for Adam's sin can be justified only to the extent that moral requirements concerning freedom and responsibility are respected. Those requirements are generally thought to include the beliefs that individuals cannot justly be held responsible for actions that they are constrained to do, and that an individual cannot justly be held responsible for actions of another. In spite of Edwards' acceptance of such prerequisites for morality, it is not unusual to hear his critics charge him with inconsistency on this point because of his doctrine of original sin. If Adam's sin is the cause of the general human inclination to depravity, then the imputation of moral responsibility and guilt to posterity appears to violate these principles of justice.

How Edwards anticipates and answers such objections about freedom and morality in terms of the Stoic-Ramist ontology of supposition is the concern of the next chapter. Here, however, it is necessary to highlight how the attempt to read Edwards in terms of a postlapsarian ontology inevitably fails to make sense of his position. In tracing our inclination to sin to the Fall, Edwards not only draws attention to the ontological character of sin, but also throws into question what is meant by inclination and, especially, what it means to be a subject so inclined. In this regard the question of how Adam's sin is justly imputed to all other human beings becomes a question of how Adam is related ontologically to his posterity.

Adam's sin is not the act of an individual, but the act by which individuality itself comes into being. In saying, then, that the inclination to sin is "truly and properly" imputed to all human beings, Edwards suggests that, insofar as their significance is "proper" to themselves (*propria*), humans are individuated in the Fall. In this way, the Fall marks the termination of significance in and as discrete entities. Related to one another by purely arbitrary laws of nature, these entities embody the metaphysics of substance characteristic of postlapsarian discourse. Such a Cartesian-Lockean discourse assumes that it is proper to begin with distinct individuals—for example, simple natures or ideas—and then to link those individuals with one another through laws of nature or association.

The problem with this approach, however, is that it fails to account for individuality itself, which is precisely what Edwards' discussion of the Fall tries to do. Even to describe entities as patterns or laws of relations (as Sang Lee has proposed) is to borrow terminology (e.g., *habitus*) from the very substantialist, Aristotelian discourse that the Edwardsian analysis of original sin overthrows.[23] In saying that "a thing *is* only as it is related to other things," Lee captures the spirit of intentionality that Edwards attributes to the saint's perception of things. But this way of speaking, as the case of Leibniz amply demonstrates, is burdened by the nagging grammatical, predicational insistence that relations always are relations *of* something. To interpret Edwards as espousing a relational ontology certainly reveals the problem with which Edwards and those who study him struggle, namely, how to express the propositional discourse of the saint in terms of the predicational discourse of the sinner. But the old wineskins of substance-accident talk cannot accommodate the new wine of the Stoic-Ramist ontology. Rather than attempting to show how the two views can be understood in terms of another, Edwards is ultimately satisfied with accepting their incommensurability.

This does not mean that he ignores the attempt to describe the order of nature in terms of the fallen discourse of individuality; but he does acknowledge that, once the intrinsic integrity of creation has been disrupted by the fall into individuality, only God's artificial establishment of continuity in nature keeps alive the possibility that any thing can have significance in virtue of anything else. Just as consciousness does not reveal any inherent order among a person's ideas or memories and "depends wholly on a divine establishment" for its continuity, so the relation of Adam to his posterity is likewise understandable in terms that already accept the fragmentation of meaning designated as the Fall.

After the Fall, things in the world exhibit no order apart from what God establishes through the laws of nature. By enacting those laws, God ensures that at least some semblance of significance (as artificial and accidental as it may be) is substituted for disruptive individuality. Otherwise, Edwards remarks, even the identity of a person or the identification of human beings with one another would be threatened:

> For, that habits, either good or bad, should continue after being once established, or that habits should be settled and have existence, in consequence of repeated acts, can be owing only to a *course of nature*, and those *laws of nature* which God has established. That the posterity of Adam should be born without holiness, and so with a depraved nature, comes to pass as much by the *established course of nature*, as the continuance of a corrupt disposition in a particular person, after he once has it; or as much as Adam's continuing unholy and corrupt, after he had once lost his holiness. For Adam's posterity are from him, and as it were in him, and belonging to him, according to a course of nature.[24]

Unlike Adam, all subsequent human beings are *born*, not created; they are particular persons intelligible only in terms of a corrupted notion of disposition. In fact, they are the corruption of the very dis-position that aboriginally defines

---

23. See Sang Hyun Lee, *The Philosophical Theology of Jonathan Edwards,* 49–50, 78. Cf. Jenson, *America's Theologian,* 47–48.
24. Edwards, *Original Sin,* 385; cf. 398, 401. Cf. Jenson, *America's Theologian,* 35.

personhood in the Trinity. Their disposition to sin consists in their particularity, the individuality which not only links them to Adamic subjectivity through a course of nature, but also (by the same course of nature) keeps alive the prospect of their redemption through the holy dis-position of the new Adam.

In order to explain not only how it is possible for Adam to be united to his posterity, but also why a union is necessary, Edwards thus appeals to the same logic that he uses in explaining the unity of the Trinity. It is a disservice to Edwards simply to note, then, that God lays the guilt of Adam's sin on the rest of humanity by means of arbitrarily designating Adam as the father of the race, even if such a designation is informed by infinite reason and goodness.[25] What must be explained is how this arbitrary designation provides the criteria for reason and goodness.

While it may be arbitrary to think of all human beings as sharing Adam's sin when seen from the perspective of fallen rationality, it is far from arbitrary when understood in terms of the justification Edwards gives for referring to such a designation as arbitrary. By highlighting the arbitrariness of uniting Adam and his posterity, Edwards draws attention to how the appeal to a substantialist notion of a self regulated by laws of nature fails to provide an adequate context for resolving the issue in any rational way:

> Of the two kinds of divine operation, viz. that which is arbitrary and that which is limited by fixed laws, the former, viz. arbitrary, is the first and foundation of the other, and that which all divine operation must finally be resolved into, and which all events and divine effects whatsoever primarily depend upon. Even the fixing of the method and rules of the other kind of operation is an instance of arbitrary operation. When I speak of arbitrary operation, I don't mean arbitrary in opposition to an operation directed by wisdom, but in opposition to an operation confined to, and limited by, those fixed establishments and laws commonly called laws of nature. The one of these I shall therefore, for want of better phrases, call *a natural operation,* the other *an arbitrary operation.* The latter of these, as I observed, is first and supreme, and to which the other is wholly subject and absolutely dependent, and without which there could be no divine operation at all, and no effect ever produced, and nothing besides God could ever exist. Arbitrary operation is that to which is owing the existence of the subject of natural operation—the manner, measure, and all the circumstances of their existence. 'Tis arbitrary operation that fixes, determines, and limits the laws of natural operation.[26]

Individual subjects are intelligible according to the method and rules of natural reason. But insofar as the laws of natural reason assume individualized subjectivity, they do not provide a justification for natural operations or for why there should be any individual things at all. From the standpoint of natural reason, the existence of individuals is purely arbitrary. Likewise, there is no ra-

25. Cf. David Weddle, "Jonathan Edwards on Men and Trees, and the Problem of Solidarity," *Harvard Theological Review* 67 (1974), 164, 174; Jenson, *America's Theologian,* 149–50; and Storms, *Tragedy in Eden,* 236–42, 255–57.

26. Miscellany #1263, in *Philosophy of Edwards,* 185–86.

tional justification for how individual human beings are associated with one another (or, for that matter, with Adam), because the association itself constitutes a pattern of regularity that inscribes a law of nature.

That there are individuals, and laws of nature regulating their interactions, is something that cannot be explained according to natural reason, and in this sense, the explanation is arbitrary. But in saying that arbitrary operations provide a rationale for natural operations, Edwards is not claiming that arbitrary operations are intelligible in natural terms. God's creation of individuals cannot be explained in terms of acts by an individual subject (in this case, God), for such an account would presume the very individuality for which the explanation is intended to account.

From the standpoint of natural operations, "nothing besides God could ever exist," because no account could be given for differentiating God from anything else. Natural operations can be made intelligible only by means of treating them as the effects of another individual; but in regard to divine creativity, this would require fallen cognition to portray God as if he also is an individual subject, the self-absorbed terminus of signification identified by substantialist philosophers from Aristotle to Hegel as self-thinking thought.

By contrast, in prelapsarian discourse there is nothing besides God before the Fall, since Adam and the rest of the world are dispositionally identified in terms of God. Only when intelligibility is limited to regular patterns of associating discrete individuals does it become necessary to refer to the cause of such regularity as arbitrary.

In explaining how Adam and his posterity share original sin, Edwards is not constrained by the substantialist logic of predication that characterizes laws of natural operation and that presumes the ontological propriety of individual subjectivity. Just as no laws of natural operation explain individuality itself, no natural operation can explain how individuals are united to one another. This is why Edwards claims that "all union and all created existence is arbitrary."[27] Through God's arbitrary union of one individual to another, the unintelligibility of individual existence is supplanted by the rationality of natural laws, constituting the possibility of retrieving meaning in nature, in spite of the isolation embodied in individual subjectivity:

> In this sense, the continuance of the very being of the world and all its parts, as well as the manner of continued being, depends entirely on an arbitrary constitution. . . . Thus it appears, if we consider matters strictly, there is no such thing as any identity or oneness in created objects, existing at different times, but what depends on *God's sovereign constitution*. And so it appears, that the objection we are upon, made against a supposed divine constitution, whereby Adam and his posterity are viewed and treated as one, in the manner and for the purposes supposed, as if it were not consistent with the truth, because no constitution can make those to be one, which are not one; I say, it appears that this objection is

27. Edwards, "Notes on Knowledge and Existence" [mid-1750s], in Jonathan Edwards, *Scientific and Philosophic Writings*, ed. Wallace E. Anderson, 398.

built on a false hypothesis: for it appears, that a *divine constitution* is the thing which *makes truth*, in affairs of this nature.[28]

The objection that Adam's posterity does not share in his sin is based on two mistaken notions: that Adam is an individual, and that truth is defined in terms of predications made of individuals. To be sure, sin displays Adam's individuality, insofar as sin is nothing less than the denial of meaning or significance beyond one's self. But in treating Adam and his posterity as one, God reinstates the possibility for truth by associating all natural human beings to one another in virtue of the very character that threatens to undermine signification, namely, their individuality. United to one another by their refusal to recognize the inherent intentionality of everything in creation, human beings "truly and properly" embody the inclination to sin, insofar as they are individuals. It is their insistence that they be considered as individuals which unites them according to the laws of nature that comprise truth "in affairs of this nature." Even though their very nature as individuals makes them all sinners, they are thus still intelligible and can embody truth through divine coordination.

This ontology of original sin reveals how Edwards can reject, in one fell swoop, both the Lockean political notion that individuals have a natural right to their own lives, liberties, and properties, and Locke's ontological claim that personal identity is grounded in memory and in the consistency of the content of consciousness. By assuming that human beings have a natural right to pursue their own self-interests, Locke ignores the possibility that the very existence of individuals in nature might indicate an ontological, epistemological, and moral failure. To cloak individuality in the mantle of natural law (as Locke does) is to disregard the need to engage in an assessment of individuality itself. In his critique, Edwards indicates how the Lockean (and for that matter, the Cartesian) discussion of the self does not provide the radical examination necessary to legitimate the elevation of the self implicit in the moral and political project of modern liberalism.[29]

As with the unity of Adam and his posterity, the personal identity of any individual over time consists not in memory or in the content of consciousness, but rather in the way that God orders otherwise discontinuous experience according to laws of nature. In the absence of God's arbitrary imposition of continuity, there would be no way to guarantee that an individual memory or idea is in any way related to any other. The Cartesian-Lockean fragmentation of consciousness requires the artifice of divine intercession, because, in the ontology of fallen subjectivity, objects of consciousness do not have any inherent relation or intentional connection with one another.

Rather than saying that identity depends on a person's memory or on how ideas appear to be associated in the mind, Edwards reverses the question of what accounts for personal identity. In his account there can be no identity

28. Edwards, *Original Sin*, 404.
29. For an extended treatment of Edwards' social and political thought, see Gerald R. McDermott, *One Holy and Happy Society: The Public Theology of Jonathan Edwards*.

or continuity of mind apart from God's arbitrary association, because even the mind's own procedures for associating ideas depends on God:

> From these things it will clearly follow, that identity of consciousness depends wholly on a law of nature; and so, on the sovereign will and agency of God; and therefore, that personal identity, and so the derivation of the pollution and guilt of past sins in the same person, depends on an arbitrary divine constitution. . . . It appears, particularly, from what has been said, that all oneness, by virtue whereof pollution and guilt from past wickedness are derived, depends entirely on a divine establishment. . . . 'Tis this, that must account for the continuance of any such thing, anywhere, as *consciousness* of acts that are past; and for the continuance of all *habits*, either good or bad: and on this depends everything that can belong to *personal identity.*[30]

Since identity of consciousness depends wholly on a law of nature, personal identity is defined less in terms of the ideas that the mind entertains than in terms of the patterns of ideas the mind enacts. The sameness of a person is thus not due to some metaphysical substance underlying a person's ideas, but rather to the sameness of pattern in how those ideas are organized. Insofar as things in the world seem to be related to one another only accidentally or are conceivable in terms other than they appear, they replicate the isolated subjectivity of the fallen human condition. Even to think of things in these terms is to sin, insofar as sin is the rejection of the premise that existence has an inherent and typological integrity.

The criterion to which Locke appeals for personal identity (viz., memory) merely adds support to the fragmentation of nature by allowing individuals who do not remember having committed a sin (including Adam's sin) to think that they are guiltless. For Edwards (like Hume), the very notion of a consciousness that is able to have ideas or memories requires a transcendental justification unavailable to anyone who starts only with the contents of experience. By uncritically assuming the transcendental unity of perception, Locke fails to provide a justification for the identity of consciousness.[31]

Considering the possibility that fallen human consciousness could easily have overlooked its own limitations, Edwards suggests that personal identity can be better understood as a divine activity. By itself, fallen subjectivity can provide as little guarantee for discerning the unity of the self as it can for explaining how all human beings are united with Adam. By appealing to the divine semiotics of the Book of Nature, Scripture, and providential history, Edwards identifies the discourse in terms of which personal identity is defined. He concludes that, because the identification of individuality requires the consideration of the person in a community, and since no community can be

---

30. Edwards, *Original Sin*, 399; see also 397–98, and Holbrook, ed., ibid., 55. Cf. Edwards, "The Mind" #72 [after 1748], in *Scientific and Philosophic Writings*, 385–86; and Yarbrough, "Beginning of Time," 157.

31. Cf. David Lyttle, "Jonathan Edwards on Personal Identity," *Early American Literature* 7 (1972–73), 165; and Clyde A. Holbrook, "Jonathan Edwards on Self-Identity and Original Sin," *The Eighteenth Century: Theory and Interpretation* 25 (1984), 55–56.

identified without acknowledging its historical character, the significance and integrity of any individual must be tied to the significance of history.

The significance of any natural being thus depends on its membership in a history that either affirms itself without warrant as its own justification (as in the Adamic heritage) or that points beyond itself to a fulfillment of creation as redemption (as in the legacy of Christ).[32] Because a self does not have a history independent of the significance it embodies, it relies for its intelligibility on the dis-placement of its own temporal embodiment. Therefore, in order for a historical being to have significance as a historical individual, its historicity and individuality must be displaced or supposed in the continual supplementation of history by the "scheme" of providential intervention. Thus, the history of individuals is intelligible as a history in spite of, rather than because of, their individuality:

> God don't fully obtain his design in any one particular state that the world has been in at one time, but in the various successive states that the world is in, in different ages, connected in a scheme. 'Tis evident that he don't fully obtain his end, his design, in any particular state that the world has ever been in; for if so, we would have no change. But God is continually causing revolutions.[33]

The supposition of time itself constitutes the radical scheme by which different ages are linked in virtue of their very discontinuity. As with the insularity and autonomy that divide human individuals from one another and that unite all humans with Adam, the fragmented nature of history is held together only by means of the juxtapositions or dis-positions of times considered no longer as times at all, but as places within the discursive scheme of providence.

Moreover, as places of discursive exchange, persons are themselves signs; they are the places of shared communication, commonplaces. United to Adam like branches of a tree, different only in place but not in time, their characterization as individuals does not rely on their temporal differentiation, for temporal differentiation itself is a function of communal exchange.[34]

This shift in describing discrete subjects in terms of place instead of time relieves Edwards of the classical-modern burden of showing how moral autonomy is possible in spite of temporal determination. The modern emphasis on the inherent temporality of individuals uncritically accepts the notion that time is a continuum in term of which individuals are related. Yet if time is always simultaneous with itself, then there must be something other than time that accounts for the appearance of individuals in time.

32. See Miscellany #1071 [1751]. Cf. Weddle, "Edwards on Men and Trees," 175; Ramsey, ed., *Dissertation concerning the End for which God Created the World,* by Jonathan Edwards, in *Ethical Writings,* 531n; Jenson, *America's Theologian,* 41–42; and Cooey, *Jonathan Edwards,* 33–34, 160.
33. Miscellany #547 [1731–32], in *Philosophy of Edwards,* 135. Cf. Richard C. De Prospo, *Theism in the Discourse of Jonathan Edwards,* 140–41; and Sacvan Bercovitch, *The American Jeremiad,* 98.
34. See Edwards, *Original Sin,* 391n–392n, 405n–406n; Jenson, *America's Theologian,* 35; and Hoopes, *Consciousness in New England,* 80. Cf. Yarbrough, "Beginning of Time," 156; and Yarbrough and Adams, *Delightful Conviction,* 20, 48–49.

That alternative rationale cannot be another continuum (e.g., Newtonian space), for the very same objections about the introduction of individuation could be raised thereof. Instead, what Edwards proposes is a rationale that treats individuation in terms of the disruption or displacement of continuity. Such a rationale reappropriates the figure of Adam in a positive light, by showing how the loss of significance through the Fall is correctible through the retrieval of our prelapsarian place in relation to God in the new Adam, Christ.

Edwards' revision of the problematic of original sin has significant implications for other topics in his philosophy—in particular, his treatments of freedom and virtue. If a person is a place of divine communication (as Edwards' remarks on the spiritual or supernatural understanding of human nature imply), then human choices and actions must likewise be understood as signs. Such an understanding would require recasting the classical-modern problematic of freedom and virtue in the same terms that Edwards uses in describing the ontology of the Trinity.

To the extent that human nature (like all other terms) is recognized as a function within the matrix of divine discourse, its original fall from significance serves as a mark of the frustration of intelligible, valuable, purposive (and thus free) action. But if original sin precludes the possibility of free and purposive action for fallen human beings, then Edwards' attempt to salvage moral value seems doomed from the start.

However, just as he does in regard to the issues raised by original sin, Edwards responds to the challenge posed by determinism by refuting the subjectivistic principles that underlie the classical-modern mentality on which determinism depends. As he shows in his doctrine of original sin, that mentality can be displaced by the alternative rationality suggested by the ontology of supposition. How Edwards pursues that discussion of freedom and virtue is the topic to which I now turn.

VI

FREEDOM AND MORAL AGENCY

The strategies for addressing the issue of free will have become so entrenched that any approach like Edwards', which challenges the fundamentally modernist presuppositions underlying the discussion, is either dismissed as beside the point or (worse) forced into one of the competing positions. His doctrine is typically identified as soft determinism or compatibilism, because he appears to claim that, even though our wills are determined, our actions (insofar as they are the result of our choices) are free. Thus Edwards is portrayed as rejecting, on the one hand, the hard determinist line that human beings have no freedom in action or choice, and on the other hand, the indeterminist view that free choices, like free acts, are chance, uncaused events.

A fourth option, the libertarian, person, or agency theory, is seldom invoked in discussions of Edwards, even though he alludes to something like it before dismissing it as unintelligible when applied to any being other than God.[1] According to agency theory, choices and acts constitute the self rather than being caused by a self; to ask what causes someone to choose or act in particular ways is to search for the ends the person has in mind in virtue of doing such acts or making such choices. For Edwards, this merely begs the question of why any self rather than another is constituted in virtue of particular choices or actions. Since no being except God contains the rationale for its own existence, any explanation of why choices or acts occur at all requires that there be something to ground them. For the agency theorist to reply that no ground is needed for intelligibility other than that provided in virtue of after-the-fact choices or acts is to miss the point Edwards raises: namely, why is any particular choice or act made in the first place? In dismissing the need for an explanatory ground for choice or action, agency theory is ultimately reduced to indeterminism.

The question of free will turns, then, on how to provide a rationale for human choices and actions without allowing the fact of there being an explanation to overwhelm any possibility of freedom. By denying that such a rationale is compatible with freedom, the indeterminist concludes that freedom of the will is possible only if choices are chance events, undetermined finally

---

1. See Jonathan Edwards, *Freedom of the Will,* ed. Paul Ramsey, 177–78; and Ramsey, ibid., 24–27.

by anything. In Edwards' terms this is the liberty of indifference espoused by the Arminians, the freedom to decide based on nothing decisive. Edwards ridicules this position as eminently unintelligible.

For Edwards, the Charybdis to the Scylla of indifference is the denial of all freedom. If human beings are not free to act as they choose, then their actions have no moral character, for morality presumes the ability to act in alternate ways.[2] Moreover, without the ability to do what they want, human beings cannot justly be expected to respond to exhortations or commands, nor can they legitimately be placed under moral obligations. Freedom of action must not only be possible, but also necessary; and it must at the same time be compatible with divine foreknowledge and predestination. Explaining how all these doctrines can be brought together requires Edwards to provide a critique of the classical-modern notion of will. In so doing, he turns the free-will debate away from its fixation on an ontology of fallen subjectivity.

Edwards' treatment of will draws on ideas developed in his theory of original sin. His analysis of will incorporates with these ideas Calvinist doctrines of divine foreknowledge and predestination.[3] As I have suggested in previous chapters, Edwards' discussions are guided by an ontology that provides the context for his criticisms of a Aristotelian-Lockean mentality that confuses issues like freedom of the will. In his view, the classical-modern mentality imports the vocabulary of action into the discourse of will by treating the will as some thing apart from its intentional objects. This attempt to understand "acts of will" creates the conditions for what we now identify as the freedom-determinism debate.

By contrast, Edwards discusses the will in terms of the same strategy he employs in discussing typological relations, creation, and the Trinity. According to that strategy, every real thing is intelligible in virtue of its supposition of or disposition to another thing. This ontology of supposition or disposition is highlighted all the more in the discussion of free will, because it embodies a direct attack against the autonomy of the individual subject (the hallmark of the modernist notion of freedom).

Edwards' discussion of free will thus raises not only the issues of moral agency and virtue (the concern of this chapter), but also gives rise to the more general question of the nature of the reality revealed by his alternative ontology. That more general question (to be examined in chapter 7) extends beyond the consideration of how individuals relate to the rest of reality through their choices and actions. It also addresses Edwards' emphasis on how the intentionality of existence consists in relations of beauty or excellence. When those relations of agreement or "consent" refer to something that someone *does* (as they do in acts or choices), they indicate the discursive context for the debate about human

---

2. Cf. Edward Williams, comments on Jonathan Edwards, "Miscellaneous Observations Concerning the Divine Decrees in General, and Election in Particular," in *The Works of Jonathan Edwards*, ed. Edward Hickman, 2:531n.

3. Cf. C. Samuel Storms, *Tragedy in Eden: Original Sin in the Theology of Jonathan Edwards*, 165; and Ramsey, ed., *Freedom of the Will*, 70.

freedom. When they refer to the way that something *is*, such relations identify the conditions of intelligibility for existence itself, and therefore raise issues concerning the transcendental conditions for knowledge and the essentially aesthetic character of being.

Intentionality of Will as Philosophical Necessity

Edwards' discussion of freedom has two parts. The first part reveals the inadequacy of treating the will as if it were a subject about which one predicates acts. To pursue that line of thought, he claims, ends up either denying that human beings are free in any way, or that the indifference predicated of will in order to ensure its freedom undercuts any motivation to act. The second part explains how the inherent intentionality of will makes the question of its freedom moot. If the identification of the will depends on determining its rationale as expressed in action, then to isolate will from its engagements in actions is to import the very substantialist ontology that the Stoic-Ramist preference for propositional discourse overthrows.

To counteract the attempt to remove the discussion of will from discursive practice, Edwards insists on maintaining that "sense of things which is found everywhere in the common people, who are furthest from having their thoughts perverted from their natural channel, by metaphysical and philosophical subtleties."

> The common people, in their notion of a faulty or praiseworthy deed or work done by anyone, do suppose that the man does it in the exercise of *liberty*. But then their notion of liberty is only a person's having opportunity of doing as he pleases. They have no notion of liberty consisting in the will's first acting, and so causing its own acts; and determining, and so causing its own determinations; or choosing, and so causing its own choice. Such a notion of liberty is what none have, but those that have darkened their own minds with confused metaphysical speculation, and abstruse and ambiguous terms. If a man is not restrained from acting as his will determines, or constrained to act otherwise; then he has liberty, according to common notions of liberty. . . . Nor have men commonly any notion of freedom consisting in indifference. For if so, then it would be agreeable to their notion, that the greater indifference men act with, the more freedom they act with; whereas the reverse is true.[4]

All morally significant actions are done freely, that is, as a result of choice. Such choice indicates how the person doing the action is far from indifferent in acting, for the act itself becomes this or that kind of act specifically in virtue of its being a result of this or that choice. If no choice informs the act, or if the choice is so indifferent as to provide no determination of the character of the act, then the act cannot be said to have a moral character.

---

4. Edwards, *Freedom of the Will*, 357–59.

Only when we introduce the confused metaphysical speculations of those who search for the rationale of choices considered apart from acts, do we depart from the common-sense context in which Edwards develops his argument. Because choices cannot be considered intelligible apart from the actions they inform, they cannot be the object of an investigation that seeks their determining causes. From the standpoint of the predicational logic implicit in substantialist metaphysics, this appears to be merely an ungrounded assumption with which Edwards begins. Edwards turns such suspicions back on themselves by pointing out how the treatment of the will as a subject of predication confounds ordinary discourse by portraying the will as the cause of its choices. Only one thoroughly committed to a metaphysics of substances and accidents or a logic of subjects and predicates would think that the discussion of free will must begin by assuming that the will is intelligible apart from what is predicated of it. Only in such a view would it make sense to ask what determines the will or to propose that the will is free only insofar as it determines itself.

Edwards acknowledges that it is possible to speak of the will as if it were an independent subject; indeed, the whole Arminian or indeterminist project is based on just such a practice. The point that Edwards wants to make, though, is that using this metaphysics of substantialist, fallen subjectivity, the only conclusion one can draw from the discussion is either that any determination of the will undermines the possibility of free acts or that moral attribution of praise or blame cannot be justified due to the absolute indifference of the will in any act.

It is not, then, a question of whether Edwards is able to think or speak with those who adopt the metaphysics of classical modernity, for much of his endeavor is directed at showing how, even on its own terms, such a discursive strategy undercuts the very possibility of moral autonomy that supposedly drives the effort to defend the claim that the will is free. By temporarily adopting the premises of that metaphysics, Edwards shows how fallen reason is ultimately forced into paradoxical doctrines of divine foreknowledge and predestination.

If he had had no alternative strategy in terms of which the paradoxical character of those doctrines could be recognized, Edwards' account would have ended there. But his ontology of supposition provides him with precisely the means to explain how such well-intentioned doctrines provide answers to questions that are themselves based on the wrong-headed assumptions of classical-modern metaphysics. Such doctrines provide an intellectual answer to a theological problem; but they do not provide for a heart-felt conviction of the truths they contain, because their truths are accidental to the subjects or topics they address.

Edwards' critique of the notion of a free, self-determining will cannot therefore be fully explicated in terms of the problematic which his alternative ontology supplants. Neither does it rely on the strategies of that alternative to disclose exactly where the discourse of subjectivity breaks down. The very notion of moral agency developed in this discourse requires the subject to be autonomous (i.e., isolated from others in the self-constituting activity of the cogito). The emphasis on moral autonomy undercuts the moral propriety of communal persuasion and education and accordingly suggests that true freedom is possible only to the extent that individuals are able to act apart from any determining influences. In short, freedom becomes possible as freedom from community.[5]

As Edwards points out, this notion of insular self-determination so misunderstands the idea of a determining propensity, that the search for an undetermined choice as the prerequisite for moral agency ultimately makes action itself impossible:

> For that act which is performed without inclination, without motive, without end, must be performed without any concern of the will. To suppose an act of the will without these, implies a contradiction. If the soul in its act has no motive or end; then in that act (as was observed before) it seeks nothing, goes after nothing, exerts no inclination to anything; and this implies, that in that act it desires nothing, and chooses nothing; so that there is no act of choice in the case: and that is as much as to say, there is no act of will in the case.[6]

In the absence of some inclination or previous disposition that determines the will to make a particular choice, no choice will be made. Contrary to what the advocate of free will maintains, the presence of such an inclination or disposition does not disqualify an action based on it from being free. A person's propensity or disposition to do a particular act is precisely what explains the person's choice to do that act. Because the act is intelligible only in terms of the choice made to do it, and because the choice is intelligible only in terms of the inclination of the will to act in that particular way, an "exercise of bias" is not merely permissible, but necessary, for moral attribution. The choice itself designates the disposition of the will operating in the act. Otherwise, nothing can be identified as providing a rationale for the act; its occurrence would be due to mere chance.[7]

For Edwards, contingency or chance explains nothing about how the will determines itself; rather, it marks the failure to provide any explanation at all precisely in regard to those issues of most practical interest to human beings. Our natural or common sense teaches us, Edwards says, that an action based on indifference lacks all moral value because such an action is informed or guided by no intention or aim. Insofar as it lacks any rationale, its pure contingency or chance character "is so far from being essential to the morality or merit of those actions, that it would destroy it; and . . . the dependence of our actions on such causes, as inward inclinations, incitements and ends, is essential to the being of it."[8] Instead of providing independence from the causal

5. See Robert W. Jenson, *America's Theologian: A Recommendation of Jonathan Edwards,* 143, 166–67.

6. Edwards, *Freedom of the Will,* 333.

7. Ibid., 326–27.

8. Edwards, "Remarks on the *Essays on the Principles of Morality and Natural Religion* [by Henry Home, Lord Kames]," letter to John Erskine, 25 July 1757, in *Freedom of the Will,* 459. See also Edwards, *Freedom of the Will,* 321.

determinacy that threatens the moral worth of actions, the prospect of contingency reduces all actions (which are by their very nature intentional) to events lacking intentionality and moral significance.

This contrast between intentional acts and contingent, disconnected events reinscribes the contrast to which I have often drawn attention, namely, that between the ontology of propositions and the metaphysics of predication. In the propositional ontology of supposition, all reality (including human action) exhibits a spiritual or ideal character; no thing can be thought apart from its necessary connections to other things. In its terms, a choice is the intentionality of will in an action, and an action is what is intended by the will.

In contrast, in the substantialist metaphysics of subjectivity individual objects are intelligible as independent substances or subjects, and they are related to one another only by means of chance or contingency. Because a choice is conceivable as independent from the action it informs, it is understandable as merely another isolated event. To relate it causally to other events destroys the freedom of the will, so whatever freedom the will has must be due to its own self-determination, which originates as a function of its essential indifference or contingency.

In rejecting such a view, Edwards limits his discussion of freedom to actions, ignoring the question of the cause of the choices informing those actions. He does so precisely because, from within the propositional ontology of disposition or supposition, it makes no sense to treat choices as if they are things caused by anything else. This is not simply a tactic of bracketing a topic from consideration in order to focus the discussion (as Paul Ramsey suggests).[9] Rather, it is an essential feature of Edwards' doctrine that an act and the choice that marks it as intentional are not ontologically separate events. To consider them as separate would fail to recognize how their significance depends on their mutual appearance in and as a historical proposition.

This approach, Edwards claims, is consistent with ordinary speech and common sense, for in neither does the cause of one's choices ever present the kinds of quandaries in which metaphysical speculation revels. To say that someone is free means nothing more than that the person is not restrained from or compelled to a particular action. This is not to say that free acts are uncaused or undetermined, only that treatment of choices as if they were acts appropriates a vocabulary ill-suited for the discussion of freedom:

> But one thing more I would observe concerning what is vulgarly called liberty; namely, that power and opportunity for one to do and conduct as he will, or according to his choice, is all that is meant by it; without taking into the meaning of the word, anything of the cause or original of that choice; or at all considering how the person came to have such a volition; whether it was caused by some external motive, or internal habitual bias; whether it was determined by some internal antecedent volition, or whether it happened without a cause; whether it was necessarily connected with something foregoing, or not

9. See Ramsey, ed., *Freedom of the Will*, 11, 15–16.

connected. Let the person come by his volition or choice how he will, yet, if he is able, and there is nothing in the way to hinder his pursuing and executing his will, the man is fully and perfectly free, according to the primary and common notion of freedom.[10]

Because the question of freedom is limited to the opportunity to act according to one's choice, the freedom to choose one thing rather than another is simply the freedom to act on one's choices. The modernist insistence that liberty and freedom be treated separately—because liberty is a political issue and freedom (especially freedom of the will) is a metaphysical or epistemological issue—therefore mistakenly assumes the propriety of distinguishing the political from the metaphysical. By equating freedom with liberty, Edwards rejects the modernist attempt to smuggle in talk of internal versus external motives, habits, or volitions, for such talk merely enacts the substantialist metaphysics that isolates subjects from one another and removes them from public, historical activity.

The modernist depiction of the autonomy of the will or subject as a disembodied, unhistorical spirit threatens to pervert the very meaning of spirituality that Edwards identifies with reality. For if the choices of the will are not seen as the intentionality of actions, then the essential spirituality of nature and history will be overlooked. That, in turn, would preclude the possibility for discerning the eschatological character of history.

Edwards is aware that within any eschatology or doctrine of divine providence is the prospect that all human actions are determined by fate and thus cannot be considered as free. Edwards responds to the challenge posed by such a prospect by reminding us that, even if all of our acts are determined by fate, they can still be considered free if they are what we choose to do. "Nothing that I maintain," he claims, "supposes that men are at all hindered by any fatal necessity, from doing, and even willing and choosing as they please, with full freedom."[11] To exist at all human beings must be engaged in the world by means of relations of intentionality; that is, they must act in order to be. In this way they are determined by fate to act in some way or other. Only if they are able to do what they choose to do are they free.

To reject this idea by noting how it retrieves central features of the Stoic doctrine of fate fails to appreciate how (as Edwards observes) Stoic fatalism employs an ontology much more consistent with Christianity than any other philosophy (including Platonism and Aristotelianism). Their doctrines and practices set the Stoics apart as "the greatest, wisest and most virtuous of all the heathen philosophers."[12] The ontology to which they appeal relies on a logic of propositions (reinstated by the Ramists as the logic of supposition) that cannot consider the intentionality of an act apart from the act itself. That is how the fatalism that is characteristic of acts is associated with choices of the will. Insofar as the will is misunderstood as engaged in acts of its own, the as-

10. Edwards, *Freedom of the Will,* 164; see also 163, and Ramsey, ibid., 37.
11. Edwards, "Remarks on *Essays,*" in *Freedom of the Will,* 457.
12. Edwards, *Freedom of the Will,* 372. Cf. Miscellany #1162 [1751].

sociation of external actions and internal acts of will becomes, in substantial-ist metaphysics, a predication of contingency.

For Edwards, though, the will is necessarily bound up with action. Insofar as an action could not have been otherwise in a course of events, neither could the will that informs it. If someone is compelled to act or restrained from acting in accord with his or her will, then the will that informs the act is that of an-other agent; in short, it is someone else's act.

This possibility of the opposition of an other is central to Edwards' account of necessity, because it is central to the logic of supposition. As I pointed out in chapter 3, according to that logic, existence consists in the displacement of something else. Without the opposition of that other, there is no sense or meaning that can be attributed to the thing at all. To say that something is necessary supposes an opposition to our will. More formally, the necessity of a thing is the supposition of an opposition to will:

> The word 'necessary,' as used in common speech, is a relative term; and relates to some supposed opposition made to the existence of the thing spoken of, which is overcome, or proves in vain to hinder or alter it. That is necessary, in the original and proper sense of the word, which is, or will be, notwithstanding all supposable opposition. . . . Things are said to be what must be, or neces-sarily are, *as to us,* when they are, or will be, though we desire or endeavor the contrary, or try to prevent or remove their existence: but such opposition of ours always either consists in, or implies opposition of our wills.[13]

If the opposition to an action is overcome when we endeavor to prevent or remove it, we can be said to have acted freely; if not, our action is compelled or restrained through the force of natural causes (what Edwards calls "natural necessity"). To say that an action is done necessarily would mean that there must be an opposition to the act's occurrence that is no opposition at all. If there is no opposition, then not only is the act not necessary, but it is also un-intelligible and is in fact no act at all. The supposition of opposition identifies the essential intentionality of an act, and it is in terms of such an identification that the act has determinate existence.

In the case of a necessary act, the opposition to the will would be the oppo-sition to any opposition, the negation of will by the will itself—a condition amounting to a "moral necessity," the overcoming of all possibility of being overcome. Edwards dismisses this form of necessity as absolutely incoherent: "For 'tis absurd, to suppose the same individual will to oppose itself, in its pre-sent act; or the present choice to be opposite to, and resisting present choice. And therefore the very case supposed never admits of any trial, whether an opposing or resisting will can overcome this necessity."[14] As the negation of the prospect of supposition, moral necessity undermines the very possibility of intelligibility:

---

13. Edwards, *Freedom of the Will*, 149–50.
14. Ibid., 159; also 156–57; and "Remarks on *Essays,*" ibid., 456, 460.

It follows from what has been observed, that when these terms 'necessary,' 'impossible,' 'irresistible,' 'unable,' etc. are used in cases where no opposition, or insufficient will or endeavor, is supposed, or can be supposed, but the very nature of the supposed case itself excludes and denies any such opposition, will or endeavor; these terms are then not used in their proper signification, but quite beside their use in common speech. The reason is manifest; namely, that in such cases, we can't use the words with reference to a supposable opposition, will or endeavor. . . . It appears from what has been said, that these terms 'necessary,' 'impossible,' etc. are often used by philosophers and metaphysicians in a sense quite diverse from their common use and original signification: for they.apply them to many cases in which no opposition is supposed or supposable.[15]

When terms originally adopted to describe obstacles to external actions are internalized, a question arises as to what obstacle must be supposed in order to determine whether the will is free or constrained in its acts. The issue is not whether the will can enact its choices, but whether the will can overcome itself. If one cannot choose to act contrary to one's own will, the argument goes, then it makes no sense to think of the will as something that exists. But in order to act contrary to one's will, one would have to will to do so, and that would involve the will's acting contrary to itself, a contradiction. Therefore, one must suppose something other than the will as its obstacle in order to be able to identify the will as something that exists.

The question of the necessity of the will is thus generated by means of an improper extension of the logic of supposition. This category mistake depends on a strategy that ignores the factual, historical character of human endeavors, but retains the framework of suppositional opposition. What results is the so-called problem of free will, a problem created by the attempt to use the logic of supposition in the modernist discourse of subjectivity.

In other words, the problem of free will arises when the will is treated as if it were a thing, a subject intelligible apart from its appearance in particular propositions. Fortunately, ordinary speech resists predicational logic's appropriation of the vocabulary of historical action by means of insisting on the ontological primacy of propositional expression.

The proper resolution of the free will problem lies in recognizing how, for Edwards, the episteme of the Stoic-Ramist ontology redefines freedom in terms of the certainty or "philosophical necessity" expressed in propositions (i.e., Ramist "arguments"). Within that mentality, certainty is a function of propositional expression: The utterance identifies the things related in the proposition as intelligible in virtue of their appearance in the proposition. In this way certainty is not simply an epistemological function (as presented in the classical modern mentality). Rather, it describes the ontological condition of determinateness that results from a thing's identification in the rhetoric of history. In that common or natural rhetoric of expression, the freedom to act (liberty) is

15. Edwards, *Freedom of the Will*, 151; see also 376. Cf. Ramsey, ibid., 38–39.

not inconsistent with necessity, for it is by means of the act that the will becomes determinate, identifiable, necessarily certain:

> I speak not now of the certainty of knowledge, but the certainty that is in things
> themselves, which is the foundation of the certainty of the knowledge of them; or
> that wherein lies the ground of the infallibility of the proposition which affirms
> them. . . . Philosophical necessity is really nothing else than the full and fixed con-
> nection between the things signified by the subject and predicate of a proposition,
> which affirms something to be true. When there is such a connection, then the
> thing affirmed in the proposition is necessary, in a philosophical sense; whether
> any opposition, or contrary effort be supposed, or supposable in the case, or no.
> When the subject and predicate of the proposition, which affirms the existence of
> anything, either substance, quality, act or circumstance, have a full and certain
> connection, then the existence or being of that thing is said to be necessary in a
> metaphysical sense. And in this sense . . . necessity is not inconsistent with liberty.[16]

Because philosophical necessity is itself the supposition of opposition in propositional expression, it presumes no prior supposable opposition; it is the means
by which opposition is first supposed. The freedom or liberty to suppose an
opposition in and as an expressive act is consistent with philosophical necessity, because such necessity is nothing other than the determination of the
connections between subjects and predicates.

The introduction of a thing into the expressive discourse of history in terms
of a supposable opposition makes the thing certain, that is, necessarily related
to other things in virtue of its appearance in a proposition. The proposition is
the foundation for the intelligibility of subjects and predicates. A logic of predication that does not account for how its terms come to have meaning ignores
the rhetorical heritage of the *topoi* that constitute the vocabulary of discursive
exchange. It is thus handicapped from the beginning by being committed to
a policy that treats all non-definitional statements as expressions of accidental
or contingent associations of subjects and predicates. In its terms the logic of
propositions is reduced only to showing how classes of things can be related
to one another epistemologically, because the question of the ontological relations of classes is foreclosed by assuming the metaphysical propriety of
distinguishing substances and their qualities.

Edwards refuses to endorse this most ahistorical approach to the question of
certainty, noting that before the question of certainty in knowledge can even be
raised, there has to be a vocabulary of determinate things that can be known.
That vocabulary is established in a divine discourse, whose propositions determine the identity of subjects and predicates in specifically historical terms:

> There must be a certainty in things themselves, before they are certainly known,
> or (which is the same thing) known to be certain. For certainty of knowledge is
> nothing else but knowing or discerning the certainty there is in the things them-

---

16. Edwards, *Freedom of the Will*, 151–52. Cf. David Jacobson, "Jonathan Edwards and the
'American Difference': Pragmatic Reflections on the 'Sense of the Heart'," *Journal of American
Studies* 21 (1987), 377.

selves which are known. Therefore there must be a certainty in things to be a ground of the certainty of knowledge, and to render things capable of being known to be certain. And this is nothing but the necessity of the truth known, or its being impossible but that it should be true; or, in other words, the firm and infallible connection between the subject and predicate of the proposition that contains that truth. All certainty of knowledge consists in the view of the firmness of that connection. So God's certain foreknowledge of the future existence of any event, is his view of the firm and indissoluble connection of the subject and predicate of the proposition that affirms its future existence. The subject is that possible event; the predicate is its future existing; but if future existence be firmly and indissolubly connected with that event, then the future existence of that event is necessary.[17]

The firm and infallible connection between the subject and predicate of a proposition constitutes the truth or philosophical necessity that governs all existence. The divine foreknowledge of a thing is always in terms of that thing's existence as a subject or predicate of a proposition that describes, or rather inscribes, an event. God does not know things apart from knowing them in events; or, to put this more in terms of the logic of supposition, a thing is intelligible in terms of what it supposes as that which provides the rationale for the necessity of its existence.

Such a connection may be a priori, as in the necessity of the existence of being in general: as we have seen before, it is contradictory to suppose absolute nothing. The connection may likewise refer to something that has already occurred (as in the truth of a proposition regarding past events). Or, if it refers to some future event, the necessity of the connection depends on the supposition of one of these other two.[18] In all three forms of philosophical necessity, the same logic of supposition regulates the way in which any thing is considered to be determinate, intelligible, or to have a rationale.

When he applies this way of thinking to the question of the will, Edwards has to struggle to avoid the limitations imposed by the substantialist vocabulary inherent in the distinction of the faculties of the soul. The understanding, he cautions, includes "the whole faculty of perception or apprehension, and not merely what is called reason or judgment."[19] This expansion is necessary to demonstrate how the intellect cannot be understood apart from its ideas. Insofar as the mind exists as the continuity of consciousness communicated by God, the intellect is united to its objects by means of its intentionality. An intellectual judgment of the goodness of a thing is therefore never indifferent, for such a judgment places the self into a relation with the thing. That placement expresses in propositional form the philosophical necessity that mutually identifies the mind and its object.

17. Edwards, *Freedom of the Will*, 264–65. Cf. Miscellany #1039 [1745]. For a comparable treatment of the distinction between certainty and truth by Edwards' contemporary Giambattista Vico, see Stephen H. Daniel, *Myth and Modern Philosophy*, 130–57; and Stephen H. Daniel, "Vico's Historicism and the Ontology of Arguments," *Journal of the History of Philosophy*, forthcoming.
18. See Edwards, *Freedom of the Will*, 152–54.
19. Ibid., 148. Cf. Jenson, *America's Theologian*, 65.

In saying, then, that the will always *is* the greatest apparent good (as opposed to saying is *determined by* the greatest apparent good), Edwards
indicates how the intentionality of intellectual activity links the understanding
intimately to the operation of the will. It does so by identifying the good with
"that which agrees with the inclination and disposition of the mind."[20] To the
extent that "the will always follows the last dictate of the understanding," the
will is the intentionality of the acts that situate a person noetically in existence.[21]
More importantly, as the intentionality of the mind, the will identifies the moral
relation of the self to its objects in virtue of how those intentional objects are
apprehended.

The determination of the will is thus a function of the degree to which the
mind apprehends its objects as good. Those objects are themselves made determinate by means of the mind's apprehension of them as objects to which it
is propositionally related. Their goodness cannot be defined apart from the
mind's apprehension of them as determinate beings. They must be "found out,"
clearly and sensibly, as objects with which the mind is or is not in harmony
before any judgment can be made about them:

> It is not that which appears the greatest good, or the greatest apparent good,
> that determines the will. It is not the greatest good apprehended, or that which
> is apprehended to be the greatest good, but the greatest apprehension of
> good. . . . The having a clear and sensible idea of any good is one way of
> good's appearing, as well as judging that there is good. . . . The degree
> of apprehension of good, which I suppose to determine the will, is composed
> of the degree of good apprehended, and the degree of apprehension. The
> degree of apprehension, again, is composed of the strength of the conception,
> and the judgment.[22]

In accord with Ramist doctrine, a thing must be discovered or "invented" in an
argument before a judgment can be made. In terms of Stoic-Roman law, there
must first be a finding, a "hearing" concerning the thing to be adjudicated. In
apprehending something as good, the mind determines both the thing and
itself as in harmony with one another. That apprehension is not a judgment of
the goodness of the thing; it is merely a determination of the degree to which
a judgment is warranted. The judgment of the goodness of a thing requires
that the thing (now made determinate through the mind's apprehension of it)
be related to the totality of other things. Because the mind by its very nature
is dispositional, inclinational, or intentional, the judgment of a thing in terms
of the totality of being is likewise the mind's self-judgment, an act of conscience. As will be shown below, the acknowledgment or consent implicit in
such a judgment is what Edwards calls *virtue*.

20. Edwards, *Freedom of the Will*, 144. Cf. Edwards, "The Mind," #60 [1728], in *Scientific and Philosophical Writings*, ed. Wallace E. Anderson, 376; and Anderson, ibid., 130.
21. Edwards, *Freedom of the Will*, 148. Cf. Roland A. Delattre, *Beauty and Sensibility in the Thought of Jonathan Edwards: An Essay in Aesthetics and Theological Ethics*, 208.
22. Edwards, "The Mind" #21 (b) [1725], 348. Cf. Ramsey, ed., *Freedom of the Will*, 57.

Divine Decrees and Foreknowledge

No knowledge of any determinate thing in the world is possible apart from the mind's affective engagement with that thing. Whatever comes into our view, even minimally, becomes an object of intentionality or will in virtue of its identification as an object to which we choose to attend. The affects of the mind are discernible by the objects of those affections, just as the objects of such affects are discernible in virtue of the inclinational or volitional activity of the mind or soul:

> In some sense, the affection of the soul differs nothing at all from the will and inclination, and the will never is in any exercise any further than it is affected; it is not moved out of a state of perfect indifference, any otherwise than as it is affected one way or the other, and acts nothing any further. But yet there are many actings of the will and inclination, that are not so commonly called affections: in everything we do, wherein we act voluntarily, there is an exercise of the will and inclination, 'tis our inclination that governs us in our actions: but all the actings of the inclination and will, in our common actions of life, are not ordinarily called affections. Yet, what are commonly called affections are not essentially different from them, but only in the degree and manner of exercise. In every act of the will whatsoever, the soul either likes or dislikes, is either inclined or disinclined to what is in view.[23]

Voluntary actions are by their very nature dis-positional; they posit an object or end over against which they are defined in harmony or disharmony. This act of positing itself is not done "freely," for that would imply an inclination for the will to have an inclination. The will is itself the inclination or disposition of the self's engagement in historical activity. Its affections define it and its relations to all other beings.

The free will issue turns on this question of why the self comes to have just these affections and no others. It cannot be the case that this affective activity is a process of self-constitution, for that would mean that the self is its own cause or rationale. Besides, as with all other things, the self and anything that can be predicated of the self must first be understood as an intelligible event. That is, it must have a cause or rationale for its existence just as it is. The cause of an event provides the rationale for the event. It identifies the event as intelligible specifically in virtue of its position or being posited in a proposition that affirms the event as a cause or reason. As Edwards is careful to note:

> I sometimes use the word 'cause,' in this inquiry, to signify any antecedent, either natural or moral, positive or negative, on which an event, either a thing, or the manner and circumstance of a thing, so depends, that it is the ground and

23. Jonathan Edwards, *Religious Affections,* ed. John E. Smith, 97. See also Edwards, "Concerning God's Moral Government, A Future State, and the Immortality of the Soul," in *Works,* ed. Edward Hickman, 2:511. Cf. Michael J. Colacurcio, "The Example of Edwards: Idealist Imagination and the Metaphysics of Sovereignty," in *Puritan Influences in American Literature,* ed. Emory Elliott, 68.

reason, either in whole, or in part, why it is, rather than not; or why it is as it is, rather than otherwise; or, in other words, any antecedent with which a consequent event is so connected, that it truly belongs to the reason why the proposition which affirms that event, is true.[24]

In affirming an event, a proposition situates that event relative to another event, and in doing so, identifies its rationale. No event exists apart from such an identification, for no event is intelligible apart from its place in a discourse. But even if the affirmation of the event identifies the event as significant or meaningful, there is still the question of what provides the rationale for the affirmation itself. That is why Edwards has to insist that all discourse ultimately be understood as a divine communication (at least from a regenerate perspective); otherwise, there would be no way to equate the meaning of a proposition with its truth.

In rejecting the substantialist assumption that things are intelligible in themselves prior to their appearance in propositional settings, Edwards is forced to search for the a priori conditions or rationale for the intelligibility of propositions. That rationale cannot be based on the inherent intelligibility of things, for to invoke such an inherence is to admit that one cannot provide an explanation for why historical events occur as they do. By showing how events are intelligible only in terms of the propositional expressions of providential history, Edwards reveals how the key for discerning the rationale for expression itself is the acknowledgment of such expressions as functions of divine communication.

The divinity of such a communication consists in its aboriginal, non-referential character; it refers to nothing other than itself for its own legitimacy and intelligibility. The facticity of expression in propositional form identifies with certainty the nature of reality as intelligible; and its truth rests on its own self-validation. In this sense, recognizing the truth of history depends on seeing how the meaning or significance of history consists not in its representation of something other than itself, but rather in its integral participation in the process of displacement and supposition enacted in God's decrees.

Even propositions about future events are intelligible first and foremost in virtue of their truth conditions, which means that even the futurity of events is part of their propositional determination. This is a requirement of the logic of supposition, insofar as the meaning of an event supposes its propositional form as its rationale. Moreover, Edwards observes, the proposition supposes God's decree as that which makes intelligible the possibility that the proposition be true:

It is as perfectly unreasonable to suppose, that this proposition should be true, viz. such a thing will be, or is to be, without a reason why it is true; as it is that this proposition should be true, such a thing actually is, or has been, without some reason why it is true, or why that thing exists. . . . And therefore I draw this consequence, that if there must be some reason of the futurition of the thing,

24. Edwards, *Freedom of the Will*, 180–81.

or why the thing is future; this can be no other than God's decree, or the truth of the proposition, that such a thing will be, has been determined by God. For the truth of the proposition is determined by the supposition.[25]

No event occurs without a cause, for the cause of an event is supposed in the event as its ground or reason. The connection between cause and effect is a necessary relation, because all relations contribute either positively or negatively to the determination or specification of the identity and existence of a thing. A completely contingent being would be a being for whom there is no rationale for being; that is, such a being would not be.

This way of reasoning does not simply assume the causal maxim (every event has a cause) or the principle of sufficient reason (for everything that exists, there is a sufficient reason for its existence). As I have suggested in describing the logic of supposition, Edwards is here appealing to a logic that explains how the causal maxim and the principle of sufficient reason function even in attempts to raise doubts about their legitimacy. For even to posit the possibility of contingent existence is already to define a thing relative to some other thing in terms of which its existence is to be considered.

Attempts (by Hume, for example) to restrict the causal maxim or the principle of sufficient reason to epistemological, as opposed to metaphysical, claims miss the point of the logic of supposition in two ways. First, the very distinction between the epistemological and the metaphysical presumes the logic of substantialist predication that the logic of propositions rejects. Second, the identification of determinate existences and determinate objects of knowledge itself assumes the propriety of some sense of identity which is left unexplicated in a metaphysics of subjectivity. Edwards' reliance on the causal maxim and the principle of sufficient reason reveals how both epistemology and metaphysics employ beliefs for which there ought to be evidence in order to make them intelligible.

Such evidence, of course, is crucial for our being able to know a thing. Even more importantly, the evidence of a thing is what makes it evidently that thing. Thus, for Edwards, evidence is not limited to a question of what we know, but includes what constitutes the truth of the thing. More properly stated, since every thing is defined in terms of a proposition whose truth expresses a divine decree of determinacy, no thing—not even a future thing—can be specifically that thing apart from its necessary connection to its causes or evidence. Not even God would be able to know an absolutely contingent being, for such a being would lack any specific characteristics by which it could be identified:

> For a thing to be certainly known to any understanding, is for it to be *evident* to that understanding: and for a thing to be evident to any understanding, is the same thing, as for that understanding to *see evidence* of it: but no understanding, created or increased, can see evidence where there is none: for that is the same

---

25. Edwards, "Miscellaneous Observations concerning the Divine Decrees in General, and Election in Particular," in *The Works of President Edwards,* ed. Samuel Austin, 5:367–68. Cf. Edwards, *Freedom of the Will,* 213–14.

thing, as to see that to be, which is not. And therefore, if there be any truth which is absolutely without evidence, that truth is absolutely unknowable, insomuch that it implies a contradiction to suppose that it is known. . . . Thus 'tis demonstrated, that there is in the nature of things absolutely no evidence at all of the future existence of that event, which is contingent, without all necessity (if any such event there be); neither self-evidence nor proof. And therefore the thing in reality is not evident; and so can't be seen to be evident, or, which is the same thing, can't be known.[26]

The absolutely unknowable cannot be supposed without contradiction, for the act of supposition is itself the ground for knowledge in virtue of providing evidence or sufficient reason for a thing. To think of "signs or evidences" as accidentally or contingently related to the existence of a thing is to ignore the way that evidence is the basis for not only certain knowledge, but also ontological determination.[27]

In this way the signs or evidences of a thing reveal the thing as the very revelation in terms of which the signification or communication occurs. When a thing is understood in terms of its inherent significance, it is recognized as being necessarily what it is in virtue of the immediacy of the propositional relation in which it is expressed. This occurs the moment a thing is recognized as self-evident, that moment of saintly or prophetic inspiration when "all the Deity appears in the thing, and in everything pertaining to it."

> The prophet has so divine a sense, such a divine disposition, such a divine pleasure, and sees so divine an excellency and so divine a power in what is revealed, that he sees as immediately that God is there as we perceive one another's presence when we are talking together face to face.[28]

A divine disposition is the disposition to see a thing as self-evident; or rather, it is sense of how a thing's evidence consists in the thing's otherness, its disposition. Here the communication does not point beyond its own expressivity for its significance, for its significance is immediately present as the very constitution of its meaning.

This sense of signs or evidences replaces the unregenerate (classical-modern, Aristotelian-Lockean) notion that signs cannot be trusted to identify things, because they are only accidentally related to the things they signify. A divine sense of signs is an affection of the mind whereby the inherent spirituality or intentionality of a thing is recognized.[29] Because the mind is itself the disposition to identify a thing in terms of its evidence or reason, the affections of the mind are nothing more than the specification or determination of intelligible

26. Edwards, *Freedom of the Will*, 258–59; also 155. Cf. Miscellany #1154, in *The Philosophy of Jonathan Edwards,* ed. Harvey G. Townsend, 181–82.

27. Edwards, *Freedom of the Will*, 260. See Miscellany #782 [1738–39], in *Philosophy of Edwards,* 115. Cf. Miklós Vetö, *La Pensée de Jonathan Edwards,* 228.

28. See Edwards, "The Mind" #20 [1725], 346.

29. See Jonathan Edwards, *Images or Shadows of Divine Things,* ed. Perry Miller, 70; and Mason I. Lowance, *The Language of Canaan: Metaphor and Symbol in New England from the Puritans to the Transcendentalists,* 268–70.

objects to which the self is propositionally related.

That process of historical enactment by which the mind or self becomes determinately related to its objects is, as Edwards admits, an activity of God, specifically the Holy Spirit. God acts *on* the self through patterns of regularity and order in nature.[30] Since the self is constituted in virtue of such patterns, the affections that define the self relative to its objects likewise must be functions of divine determination:

> The soul of man undoubtedly, in every instance, does voluntarily determine with respect to his own consequent actions. But this determination of the will of man, or voluntary determination of the soul of man, is the effect determined. This determining act of the soul is not denied, but supposed, as it is the effect we are speaking of, that·the influence of God's Spirit determines.[31]

The determination of the will is precisely what allows human beings to act voluntarily, for without such determination there would be no specification as to the identity of the agent or the aim of the act. Agent and act are defined simultaneously insofar as the intentionality of the event linking them becomes determinate. Without the supposition of God as the ultimate sufficient reason for why such determinations occur, Edwards claims, we would be unable to account for the existence of any particular self. So in addition to being the object to which God's communications are directed, the self must also be understood as the spirituality or intentionality of that communication.

Evidence is thus what gives the self significance. Insofar as the self is by its very nature dispositional, then its self-evidence must consist in its supposition of a rationale for its determinate individuation. But if the self or subject were to be considered as an autonomous individual—that is, as intelligible apart from the rationale it supposes or the evidence it requires—it would lose all meaning. As indicated in the previous chapter, this fall from significance itself could have no cause or rationale, because sin is precisely that for which one can give no rationale. It is the evidence of such an immanent rationale that signals the presence of God *in* the self as a proof of the communicative nature of existence and as an invitation to establish or confirm a moral community.[32]

Proponents of free will note, though, that this suppositional account of the self forces Edwards to explain specific human affections or dispositions ultimately in terms of patterns of regularity and order established by God. They point out that, if that order requires the total depravity and corruption of human nature, then God inconsistently requires human beings to act in ways that they could not have chosen to do otherwise.

Edwards' response to this objection hinges on his insistence that, were it not for the supposition of a universal determining providence necessitating events

---

30. Cf. Smith, ed., *Religious Affections*, 23–24; and James Hoopes, *Consciousness in New England: From Puritanism and Ideas to Psychoanalysis and Semiotic*, 89–90.

31. Edwards, "Miscellaneous Observations concerning Efficacious Grace," in *Works*, ed. Samuel Austin, 5:480–81. See also Edwards, *Religious Affections*, 423.

32. Cf. Jenson, *America's Theologian*, 191–93.

in the world, the notion of freedom itself would be unintelligible. In order to act, one assumes the possibility of there being connections between our choices to act and the acts themselves. Without the divine decrees that establish and maintain those connections, there would be no reason to believe that our actions are linked to our endeavors to act. Besides, if such decrees were not necessary and universal, there would be no reason to pray for the strength of will to do what we know is morally right.[33]

> Means are foregoing things, and effects are following things: and if there were no connection between foregoing things, and following ones, there could be no connection between means and end; and so all means would be wholly vain and fruitless. . . . And if there were no such thing as an established connection, there could be no choice, as to means; one thing would have no more tendency to an effect, than another; there would be no such thing as tendency in the case. . . . I say, no such necessary connection of a series of antecedents and consequents can in the least tend to hinder, but that the means we use may belong to the series; and so may be some of those antecedents which are connected with the consequents we aim at, in the established course of things. Endeavors which we use, are things that exist; and therefore they belong to the general chain of events; all the parts of which chain are supposed to be connected: and so endeavors are supposed to be connected with some effects, or some consequent things, or other.[34]

As in the case of the propositional connection between subject and predicate in philosophical necessity, the connection between antecedent and consequent relies on the supposition of one by the other. Our choices or endeavors are linked to our actions necessarily by means of a divinely established chain of events. That chain is governed by the logic of supposition, in which cause and effect are determined not by temporal priority but by the harmony of divine decrees:

> God decrees all things harmoniously and in excellent order; one decree harmonizes with another, and there is such a relation between all the decrees as makes the most excellent order. Thus God decrees rain in drought because he decrees the earnest prayers of his people; or thus, he decrees the prayers of his people because he decrees rain. I acknowledge, to say God decrees a thing 'because,' is an improper way of speaking; but not more improper than all our other ways of speaking about God. God decrees the latter event because of the former, no more than he decrees the former because of the latter. But this is what we would: when God decrees to give the blessing of rain, he decrees the prayers of his people; and when he decrees the prayers of his people, he very commonly decrees rain; and thereby there is an harmony between these two decrees, of rain and the prayers of God's people.[35]

This doctrine of divine decrees is not simply Edwards' acknowledgment of the fact that God exists outside of time and therefore conceives of two temporally

---

33. See Edwards to Erskine, 3 August 1757, in *Freedom of the Will,* 470.
34. Edwards, *Freedom of the Will,* 366–67; cf. 431–32.
35. Miscellany #29 [1723] in *Philosophy of Edwards,* 154. Cf. Edwards, "Concerning Divine Decrees," in *Works,* ed. Samuel Austin, 5:401–402; and Vetö, *La Pensée,* 80.

and ontologically distinct events simultaneously. Their simultaneity consists in their ontologically mutual self-definitions. Their individual significance or meaning relies on the fact that in the relation each component exists *for the other*. That one event is posited by its displacement by the other constitutes the meaning of the event in terms of its intentionality or dis-position. God's timelessness allows for the simultaneous comparison of prior and subsequent events; but it does not provide the means to explain how those events come to be independently intelligible in the first place.

Edwards recognizes that the problem stems from the assumption that events could somehow be intelligible apart from the matrix of determination established by God's absolute decrees. Even God's foreknowledge of events supposes the certainty created by the event's specification in those decrees.[36] The fact that God knows with absolute certainty every event that occurs in history means little more than that God is the truth presupposed by the determination of every thing that exists. Indeed, because nothing is intelligible apart from its existence in the divinely decreed order of things, nothing can be known as true apart from the supposition that such propositional knowledge is meaningful from the start. The regularity and order of things expressed in the divine decrees provide the a priori conditions for the possibility of historical (i.e., propositional) determinacy.

In saying that "God is truth itself," then, Edwards is hardly invoking one of the standard Neoplatonic transcendentals; rather, he appeals yet again to a logic in which truth "is a consistent supposition of relations between what is the object of the mind." That consistency of supposition is grounded in "that train and series of ideas, that are raised in our minds according to God's stated order and law."[37] For God, all things are self-evident, because all things are defined in terms of the pattern of evidential justification that constitutes intelligibility. God does not really know the truth as much as he makes truth possible by being the space of discourse in which things are made determinate or certain in propositional relations.

Individual human minds exhibit traits of both the orderly constitution of reality by God and the fragmentation of that order in fallen cognition. In terms of the first trait, our knowledge is intuitive, occurring immediately and without reflection; it is determined by fixed positions, propensities, and habits of mind instilled by God, and our ideas exhibit a "mutual attraction," suggesting natural relations to one another unspoiled by subjective experience.[38] The second trait grounds knowledge in artificial truths by definition and inductive generalizations; the mind is the isolated cogito; a tabula rasa lacking any inherent union with the world; and the connections of our ideas of experience are contingent.

36. See Edwards, *Freedom of the Will*, 261.

37. Edwards, "The Mind" #6 [1723], #10 [1724], #15 [1725], and #40 [1725], 340, 341-42, 344-45, 359.

38. Edwards, "Subjects To Be Handled in the Treatise on the Mind," in *Scientific and Philosophic Writings*, 391–92; and Anderson, ibid., 122, 126–27.

By appealing to features of these two traits, Edwards links the discussion of will immediately to the question of truth. If a proposition regarding someone's future act is intelligible, it is either true or false: The person either will or will not do the act. To say that the act is still undecided is to admit that the act is indeterminate, which is to say that it is no specific act at all. Since all acts are causally related according to the determinate order of divine decrees, any proposition that expresses the truth about a future determinate act identifies that act as necessarily following from antecedent causes.

Insofar as volitions are made determinate by the acts that they inform, and insofar as those acts are determined as moments in the order of events that exhibit God's providential involvement in the world, even volitions can be said to be determined:

> Nothing in the state or acts of the will of man is contingent . . . God does decisively, in his providence, order all the volitions of moral agents, either by positive influence or permission . . . if we put these things together, it will follow, that God's assistance or influence, must be determining and decisive, or must be attended with a moral necessity of the event; and so, that God gives virtue, holiness and conversion to sinners, by an influence which determines the effect, in such a manner, that the effect will infallibly follow by a moral necessity; which is what Calvinists mean by efficacious and irresistible grace.[39]

Edwards warns that the expression "irresistible grace" can be misleading if it is understood to imply that the sinner *wants* to resist this grace, but is overwhelmed by God's action. After all, the will of any individual is determined by God, so it makes no sense to speak about willing to resist that by which one wills. For this very reason, Edwards avoids talk of God's determination of volitions as if they were actions. Instead, he argues that volitions unite a person to his or her act by means of specifying the act as a defining feature of the agent.

To the extent that actions draw attention to their dependence on divine decrees, they reveal how the volitions that inform them suppose an order in which the isolation of subjectivity is rejected. This acknowledgment of evidence for a rationale of the self opens up the possibility for discerning a place for the self in providential history. The active affirmation of that possibility is what Edwards identifies as virtue.

Virtue as Consent

From the standpoint of modernist subjectivity, Edwards' doctrine of the will precludes any intelligible theory of moral virtue. If all human actions and volitions are ultimately determined by God through his divine decrees, then there seems to be no point in talking about choosing between actions as morally

---

39. Edwards, *Freedom of the Will*, 433–34. Cf. William J. Wainwright, "Jonathan Edwards and the Language of God," *Journal of the American Academy of Religion* 48 (1980), 38; and Jenson, *America's Theologian*, 168.

good or evil. As I have indicated, though, Edwards rejects the model of moral agency presumed in that account, because it treats volitions and actions as if they were ontologically independent of one another, containing the grounds or rationale for their own self-validation. He substitutes an ontology that explains how individual things are intelligible not in terms of their individuality, but rather in terms of their supposition of that which is other than themselves.

This ontology becomes for Edwards the basis of his theory of virtue, wherein virtue does not refer to characteristics of individuals, but to the displacement of individuality by a conversion of a person to self-effacing humility. Virtue is not something for which any individual is responsible or for which any person can take credit; assigning credit to the individual would only legitimate the principle of insular individuality that disrupts the divine endeavor to reintegrate being. To insist on autonomy as a prerequisite for moral obligation fails to recognize how the fragmentation of meaning or significance cannot be rectified by appealing to the very condition that is thematized in the idea of the Fall.

For Edwards, virtue consists in the supposition of the self by that which gives it meaning or significance. Insofar as an individual's choices are thought to provide the rationale for his or her actions, those choices have meaning only for the individual. But a system of meaning that is limited to a private language-user is no system at all, for the individual cannot guarantee the stability of relations required for intelligibility without appealing to a criterion other than the expressions and actions chosen by the individual. This is why Edwards has to provide a criterion (viz., the habitual performance of good acts) as a means for determining those who are truly virtuous, the recipients of grace.[40] Without such a criterion, he would be open to charges that virtuous choices could be evaluated apart from virtuous acts, and that individuals might be virtuous apart from their communal engagements in terms of which human life is significant.

A virtuous choice, as such, cannot be attributed to the individual, then, because such a choice supposes the displacement of the individual. Virtue is possible only when the individual's choice is not considered the rationale for action. In that event God (as the other to insular subjectivity) is understood as the cause of the choice:

> The nature of virtue being a positive thing, can proceed from nothing but God's immediate influence, and must take its rise from creation or infusion by God. For it must be either from that, or from our own choice and production, either at once or gradually, by diligent culture. But it cannot begin or take its rise from the latter, viz. our choice or voluntary diligence. For if there exist nothing at all of the nature of virtue before, it cannot come from cultivation; for by the supposition there is nothing of the nature of virtue to cultivate, it cannot be by

---

40. See Edwards, *Religious Affections*, 408–56. Cf. John E. Smith, *Jonathan Edwards: Puritan, Preacher, Philosopher*, 49–55; Michael L. Raposa, "Jonathan Edwards' Twelfth Sign," *International Philosophical Quarterly* 33 (1993), 156–59; and Harold P. Simonson, *Jonathan Edwards: Theologian of the Heart*, 59–61.

repeated and multiplied acts of virtuous choice, till it becomes a habit. For there can be no virtuous choice unless God immediately gives it. The first virtuous choice, or a disposition to it, must be immediately given, or it must proceed from a preceding choice.[41]

The habits that come to be identified as comprising the character of a person are themselves the result of choices whose ultimate cause must be God insofar as those choices are positive. To the extent that a choice is that which informs a determinate action as its intentionality, it posits the action as intelligible, as having a cause. But that ultimate cause is not a self-caused cause, for the self is precisely what is not posited in the supposition of a rationale for a thing.

So in saying that God is the cause of a virtuous choice, Edwards does not imply that God is the self responsible for the choice; for the fall into selfhood would mean the annulment of intelligibility. There is no self for God to cause in causing himself, for the individuality of the self marks the termination of significance. The notion of a self-caused cause would be the semiotic equivalent of a cosmic black hole, from which no light of signification or intelligibility ever escapes.

God's choices or decrees are therefore not the acts of a self, but the repudiation of subjectivity. They undercut the possibility of a Spinozan apotheosis of substance by defining the cause of a thing in terms of its communicative significance. Furthermore, the cause of any self's virtuous choices cannot be another self, for virtuous choice entails the supplanting of the mentality of selfhood with a new mentality in which entity or being is intelligible as a function of supposition.

Just as the determination or invention of the self in virtue of choices is a function of the communal and communicative significance of the acts they inform, so is the judgment of those choices as virtuous. Prior to the identification of a thing within an expression or decree, nothing can be said of the thing because no thing has been made a determinate object of communicative significance. Once it is determinately identified in the divinely constituted order of things, its certainty or necessity is guaranteed by its harmony with other things to which it is propositionally associated in providential history.

This association can be understood either as the pattern of relations among already existing things or as the process by which things originally come into being. To emphasize this distinction, Edwards identifies two notions of virtue. Natural virtue is the acknowledgment that the rationale for individual beings lies not in their individuality, but in their position in a causal network of the necessary relations of things. This acknowledgment or consent to the systematic harmony and integrity of beings is what Edwards calls natural conscience.[42] For the person of conscience, the agreement of natural things with one another exhibits such obvious order and intelligibility that there is "no sense of mind

41. Edwards, "Concerning Efficacious Grace," 5:453.
42. Edwards, "The Mind" #39 [1724] and #45 [1726], 356, 365; and Jonathan Edwards, *The Nature of True Virtue*, in *Ethical Writings*, ed. Paul Ramsey, 589–97.

that can be supposed of a contrary nature and tendency."[43] As a result of "common grace," the naturally virtuous individual is able to apprehend and appreciate beings not for how they relate to himself or herself, but for how they invite the individual to transcend the self.[44]

The very nature of mind as tendential and suppositional requires that the dictates of conscience be grounded in an order of things other than themselves. Because conscience does not provide the rationale to legitimate that order, conscientious judgments distinguish virtue from vice, but are unable to provide any self-authorizing justification for doing so.

By contrast, true virtue consists in the acknowledgment of or consent to the intentionality of being itself. Whereas conscience presumes for its judgments of approbation the divine institution of uniform and natural agreements among beings, true virtue is that propensity or consent of the mind to Being as such. As Edwards puts it, "True virtue essentially consists in benevolence to Being in general. Or perhaps to speak more accurately, it is that consent, propensity and union of heart to Being in general, that is immediately exercised in a general good will."[45] Insofar as true virtue is the consent to the character of propensity itself, it is not consent to any being in particular, nor is it consent to the uniform totality of beings.

Without the justification provided by true virtue, dictates of conscience that identify moral propriety are often understood merely as the artificial dictates of God, intended to aid in our survival. Of course, that is no small benefit to beings who, after all, have a sincere interest in their own temporal welfare. But without a basis for evaluating the propriety of conscientious judgments, we cannot know whether specific judgments of virtue and vice have any legitimacy (apart from pragmatic concerns) or how conscientious guidance can have moral authority:

> Approbation of conscience is the more readily mistaken for a truly virtuous approbation, because by the wise constitution of the great Governor of the world (as was observed) when conscience is well informed, and thoroughly awakened, it agrees with the latter fully and exactly, as to the object approved, though not as to the ground and reason of approving. . . . And indeed natural conscience is implanted in all mankind, there to be as it were in God's stead, and to be an internal judge or rule to all, whereby to distinguish right and wrong. . . . But no wonder that by a long continued worldly and sensual life men more and more lose all sense of the Deity, who is a spiritual and invisible Being. The mind being long involved in, and engrossed by sensitive objects, becomes sensual in all its operations, and excludes all views and impressions of spiritual objects, and is unfit for their contemplation. Thus the conscience and general benevolence are

43. Edwards, *True Virtue*, 623.

44. See "A Divine and Supernatural Light" [1734], in *Jonathan Edwards: Representative Selections*, ed. Clarence H. Faust and Thomas H. Johnson, 102–103; and Edwards, *True Virtue*, 616. Cf. Jenson, *America's Theologian*, 174–75.

45. Edwards, *True Virtue*, 540, 559. Cf. Stephen R. Yarbrough and John C. Adams, *Delightful Conviction: Jonathan Edwards and the Rhetoric of Conversion*, 6–10, 87–88.

entirely different principles, and sense of conscience differs from the holy complacence of a benevolent and truly virtuous heart. . . . The present state of the world is so ordered and constituted by the wisdom and goodness of its supreme Ruler, that these natural principles for the most part tend to the good of the world of mankind. . . . But this is no proof that these natural principles have the nature of true virtue. For self-love is a principle that is exceeding useful and necessary in the world of mankind. So are the natural appetites of hunger and thirst, etc. But yet nobody will assert that these have the nature of true virtue.[46]

A truly virtuous heart does not act based on conscience, for conscience does not contain its own legitimation, its own guarantee of moral propriety. By accepting "complacently" the distinction of the self from others—even in a world that exhibits a moral order—the reliance on conscience ignores the question of how that moral order itself is established. The principles of natural reasoning simply begin with the fact that determinate things occupy places in nature relative to one another (com-placements). As to why they occupy those places, natural reason has no clue.

The aboriginal or divine placement of things in "holy complacence" designates their intentionality, their will-to-the-good, their harmony. Recognition of this *benevolence* is not a characteristic that a being has, but is rather what a being is, insofar as it exists at all. To recognize the harmony of beings is thus to be in harmony with them. Such a state is the acknowledgment of the Being of any and all entity, and therefore must be a general benevolence.

The next chapter addresses the topic of benevolence more in the context of Edwards' doctrine of beauty. My reason for delaying that discussion is to show how Edwards permits the Stoic tension between the moral and ontological senses of *virtus* to reverberate with one another. For if we consider virtue solely in terms of human actions, we miss the opportunity to think of it in terms of power (i.e., as a function of being in general). Such an oversight would reintroduce the question of how any subject can consent to virtue.

Faced with this prospect, Edwards (as before) transforms the question: instead of asking how consent is an act of a subject, he suggests that we should ask how subjective agency itself is a function of consent. Given the possibility of our being able to consent to Being in general, he warns, we cannot limit the scope of our investigation to the derivative notion of subjectivity. It is therefore his aim to describe the conditions in terms of which agency is empowered in and as being.

As one might suspect, Edwards describes consent in terms of the same dispositional, suppositional, intentional, or volitional patterns as found in Being itself, for those patterns define the beauty of Being and the harmony of beings. Indeed, it is only in terms of beauty—what I have referred to as discursive significance, intelligibility, or meaning—that the specification or determination of harmony, consent, agency, or being can be expressed at all.

The possibility of moral agency is thus always already implicit in the intentionality of being as the volitional characterization of the consent to or

---

46. Edwards, *True Virtue*, 612–16.

fulfillment of Being in general. Since Being in general is not the totality of beings (but rather the act of Being of those beings), the benevolence that comprises the consent to Being in general ("general or absolute benevolence") must be the intentionality of Being itself. The volitional character of that intentionality is made evident by Edwards' references to the vocabulary of will in speaking about the union of heart to Being in general, the supreme love of God.[47] But because God is himself not a being, but rather the Being of all beings, the love of God cannot be something to which *one* consents.

The change of heart that Edwards requires for true virtue entails a shift from a love of other beings to a sense of love itself. For morally conscientious individuals, such a shift would not necessarily entail any noticeable change in how they (as opposed to persons of natural virtue) live. It is their motivation for action that would change. Instead of consenting to the existence of beings necessarily related to one another through divine decrees, the elect (with apparent ease) would habitually and consistently do good acts, because every thing toward which their actions would be directed would necessarily be related to something other than itself.

That immanent transcendence is the presence of God in and as Being in general. But Being cannot ultimately be anything other than the intentionality to harmonic fulfillment (i.e., excellence) and the rationale for all intentional acts (including choices). Therefore, consistent with patterns of thought developed in his doctrine of will and rehearsed in his epistemology and aesthetics, Edwards concludes that Being in general must be God.

47. See ibid., 544–45, 550, 594–95; and Ramsey, ibid., 27–31.

VII

THE KNOWLEDGE OF BEAUTY

The centrality of a doctrine of beauty in Edwards' philosophy contrasts markedly with the general subordination of aesthetics in modern philosophy. The previous chapter partially indicated why the concept of beauty or excellence plays such a prominent role in his thought. For Edwards, insofar as anything exists at all, it exists as the disposition to that which transcends it and which, in virtue of that transcendence, gives it significance. The beauty or excellence of a thing consists in its relations to others. Since the very existence of a thing consists in those relations, the ontological and aesthetic dimensions of the thing cannot ultimately be differentiated, without reducing its moral relations to mere accidents.

As Edwards demonstrates in his discussions of virtue, the attempt by theorists like Francis Hutcheson to establish a firmer foundation for judgments of value by appealing to a moral sense provides no ontological justification for such a move.[1] What is needed, he suggests, is a theory that explains how virtue not only is recognized, but also contains the grounds for its own validation.

By insisting on this need to identify virtue in terms of that which provides for its rationale, Edwards appeals to an ontology that does not employ terms like virtue, beauty, or excellence without attempting as well to show the a priori conditions for how such terms can have meaning. As Edwards recognizes, to say that virtue is the consent of being to Being or that excellence is the agreement of one thing with another begs not only the question of what is meant by consent or agreement, but also the question of what strategy of thought could justify such definitions.

Accordingly, his explanation of the meanings of consent and agreement rejects the mentality of substantialist predication in terms of which most of his expositors attempt to describe his thought. Within that mentality virtue and beauty become honorific titles mutually applied to one another (as in "the beauty of virtue"). Furthermore, notions of consent, agreement, fitness, proportion, and harmony, are thrown around with such abandon that one often gets the impression that the meanings of such terms must certainly be self-evident.

---

1. On the historical relations of Edwards' moral theory, the most useful sources are: Paul Ramsey, introduction, notes, and appendix 2 ("Jonathan Edwards on Moral Sense, and the Sentimentalists") in Jonathan Edwards, *Ethical Writings*, ed. Paul Ramsey; and Norman Fiering, *Jonathan Edwards's Moral Thought and Its British Context.*

This of course is not the case with all Edwards scholarship: Paul Ramsey's editorial comments in his edition of Edwards' *Ethical Writings* and Roland Delattre's work on Edwards' aesthetics epitomize a sensitivity for coherently fitting together the various components of Edwards' doctrine on beauty. However, in saying that benevolence is the love of being as excellence, or that complacence is delight in being as existence, even studies such as those become so caught up in the internal relations of Edwards' vocabulary that it is difficult to figure out exactly what it all means.[2] Once initiated into the mind-set, of course, all one needs to do is learn the syntax for juxtaposing terms. As Ramsey and Delattre demónstrate, that is no mean task; because they do such a fine job of it, I see no need to duplicate their efforts.

My interest lies in spelling out the presuppositions one must adopt to become initiated into the Edwardsian project; that is, I am less concerned with determining how Edwards' terms like consent or beauty are related to one another than in revealing the rationale for his doctrines of consent or beauty, as such. As I have suggested before, that rationale is not based on modernist or humanist assumptions that consent is something that a mind does, or that harmony refers to a relation between independently intelligible entities. In overthrowing such assumptions, the rationale implicit in Edwards' thought entails syntactic realignments that come to be identifiable as Edwards' discourse. I am interested in discerning why such realignments should occur at all.

Edwards himself is the first to caution us not to assume that he is engaged in a project in which beauty is described in the standard or typical way as some form of harmony or excellence. For example, he begins his early work, "The Mind," by stating that the notion of excellence, in spite of its central place in our lives (and in his thought), has yet to be explained:

> There has nothing been more without a definition than excellency, although it be what we are more concerned with than anything else whatsoever. Yea, we are concerned with nothing else. But what is this excellency? Wherein is one thing excellent and another evil, one beautiful and another deformed? Some have said that all excellency is harmony, symmetry or proportion; but they have not yet explained it. We would know why proportion is more excellent than disproportion, that is, why proportion is pleasant to the mind and disproportion unpleasant.[3]

All other examinations pivot on the examination of excellence, because without a clear notion of proportion or propriety, all justifications for argument are themselves suspect. The importance that Edwards attaches to excellence stems from his recognition that underlying every attempt to provide a rationale for something is the assumption that one knows what it means to give a rationale. Insofar as excellence is the fitness of an account, it identifies the proportion-

2. See Roland A. Delattre, *Beauty and Sensibility in the Thought of Jonathan Edwards: An Essay in Aesthetics and Theological Ethics*, 109–10.
3. Jonathan Edwards, "The Mind" #1 [1723], *Scientific and Philosophic Writings*, ed. Wallace E. Anderson, 332.

ality of the cause to its effect and provides the reason why the account or proportion pleases the mind. Without an explanation of excellence, we have no
explanation of explanation itself.

Edwards is thus not willing to treat excellence simply as that feature of a
thing that establishes its aesthetic character. To do so would mask the significance of the aesthetic in the process of reasoning, by means of merely
substituting one set of terms for another. As if to emphasize just how such a
substitution compounds this search for clarity, he defines excellence as "the
consent of being to being, or being's consent to entity."[4] The very obscurity of
such a definition signals a challenge to the uncritical acceptance of notions of
consent, being, and entity as foundational terms. Instead of providing a self-
evident or clear and distinct idea from which one can reason, such a definition
draws attention to how the relation of consent to entity still eludes determinate explication.

As suggested in the foregoing chapters, Edwards indicates a way out of this
confusion by showing how the search for self-evident notions upon which to
ground explanations overlooks an alternative form of rationality. In terms of
that alternative—what I have referred to as an ontology of supposition—consent to being is the acknowledgment that being consists in the activity of
substitution or displacement of individuality with some other. Accordingly,
Edwards' rhetorical substitution of terms for one another is not an indication
of a halting search for a better way to say the truth. Rather, the truth conditions
for what he says lie in the substitutions of terms that comprise communication.
If we fail to recognize the propriety of this way of reasoning, we can miss the
significance of Edwards' strategy of answering such questions as, What does it
mean to consent? and How is consent possible? by replacing one set of words
with another.

Insofar as Edwards equates the nature of true virtue with "that which renders any habit, disposition, or exercise of the heart truly beautiful," he links
his theory of moral value to his theory of aesthetic value.[5] Because the concept of consent reveals how both enterprises enact his ontology—as volitions
or dispositions, and as relations of beings to one another—it stands as an indictment against any metaphysics or epistemology that ignores its own implicit
moral or aesthetic character. To the extent that modern metaphysics and epistemology lack this sensibility to value, they do not allow for the development of
the regenerate "sense of the heart" that Edwards' philosophy recommends.

The first section of this chapter is concerned with how Edwards' account of
consent to being functions in his treatments of beauty and excellence. Since consent includes both the conscious acknowledgment of the agreement of beings
and the natural proportionality of inanimate things, this discussion retrieves the
concepts of benevolence and complacence, without restricting them to the consideration of will. The second section recognizes how Edwards' flexible notion

---

4. Ibid., 336.
5. Edwards, *True Virtue*, in *Ethical Writings*, 539.

of consent makes problematic the relation between fallen, speculative knowledge and what he calls sensible knowledge, or the sense of the heart. This latter section shows how grace alone accounts for the conversion to a mentality in which benevolence to Being in general or love of God is possible.

Consent

Edwards acknowledges that the word *consent* normally refers to some act of mind, specifically that of will. But because will is the intentionality or spirituality by which the mind is defined in relation to its objects, the will (or consent to being expressed by and as the will) cannot be different from the act of being itself. To be means to be intentionally related, and the expression "consent to being" emphasizes that fact.

Even though intentionality is more commonly associated with minds or spirits, it must apply to bodies as well, insofar as they can be said to exist. The problem with bodies is that they signify the termination of intelligibility or significance. By contrast, minds explicitly point to their own transcendentality in virtue of the inherent intentionality of their ideas: Every idea is an idea *of* something else. Only when the mind is understood as a thing in itself, differentiated from the objects to which it is intentionally related, does it lack significance. That is, only when the mind is thought of as if it were a body does it lose the characteristic inclination or propensity that Edwards refers to as consent to being.

When applied to bodies, then, consent to being is a derivative concept. This does not mean, though, that natural bodies are excluded entirely from relations of consent, for insofar as bodies direct attention away from their own individuality to what provides the rationale or meaning for their existence, they exhibit an "external excellency." In this way bodies can be said to exist, and thus partake of excellence, insofar as they are in agreement with mind (i.e., insofar as they are intelligible):

> When we spake of excellence in bodies we were obliged to borrow the word 'consent' from spiritual things. But excellence in and among spirits is, in its prime and proper sense, being's consent to being. There is no other proper consent but that of minds, even of their will; which, when it is of minds towards minds, it is love, and when of minds towards other things it is choice. . . . When we spake of external excellency, we said that being's consent to being must needs be agreeable to perceiving being.[6]

The internal excellence of the mind refers to the immanent agreement of mind with its objects, by means of which agreement the mind comes to exist in the first place. No such excellence can be ascribed to individual bodies, because

---

6. Edwards, "The Mind" #45 [1726], 362; see also "The Mind" #1, 337. Cf. Thomas A. Schafer, "The Concept of Being in the Thought of Jonathan Edwards," 346, 354.

the individuality of bodies signals the disruption of the need for a rationale for bodies. Insofar as the very notion of a rationale for the individuation of bodies is contradictory, any excellence that bodies exhibit must be external to their existence; that is, any excellence of bodies must consist in how they occasion in some mind ideas that draw the mind away from the body to that which provides the rationale for the existence of bodies in general.[7] In turn, the mind is drawn to a consideration of its own activity and finally to the activity of consideration itself.

Edwards' characterization of this process as happiness is as perplexing as anything one finds in Hegel. "Happiness," he says, "consists in the perception of these three things: of the consent of being to its own being; of its own consent to being; and of being's consent to being."[8] In other words, in order for something to be happy, it first must exist: this is the identification or consent of being to its own being. But no being can be happy without finding its place in the order of all beings: this is its consent to being relative to the rest of being. Finally, in order to be happy, a being must be able to perceive the rationale for more than its own particular existence relative to other beings: it seeks a rationale for existence itself. The affirmation of such a rationale constitutes being's consent to being.

The consent to being thus encompasses at least three meanings. First, it refers to the affirmation of specific existence. I have referred to this meaning as the determination of a thing in a proposition. This is the moment in a Stoic-Ramist ontology in which a subject is identified or found ("invented") as a *topos* within an argument. Its intelligible existence relies on the communicative exchanges that lay out the vocabulary of the universe.

Second, it refers to the validation or judgments of such topics in the course (and court) of history. The divinely established order of things provides a basis on which the significance and meaning of individual things can be explained in terms of cause and effect, types and antitypes. In this second sense, the consent to being is the acknowledgment that no particular being includes the justification for its own existence.

Third, the consent to being refers to the supposition of a rationale for the first two forms of consent: consent, like existence in general, must have a rationale that consists in nothing other than the intentionality or supposition of consent itself. Consent in this last sense becomes the basis for explaining how individual *topoi* or places in discourse are possible and how there can be a divine order of things. It recognizes the a priori conditions for considering the possibility of existence.

The first sense demonstrates why Edwards' aesthetic ontology requires relations of beauty to be understood as essentially spiritual. It specifies the character of intentionality assumed by the other two forms of consent or

7. See Edwards, "Beauty of the World" [1726] and "The Mind" #1, in *Scientific and Philosophic Writings*, 305, 337–38; and Miscellany #108.
8. Edwards, "The Mind" #1, 338.

agreement. Insofar as it is concerned with the possibility of consent in general, it does not identify the criteria by which relations of beauty in particular are described and perceived.

The second and third forms define the differences between secondary or natural beauty and primary, spiritual, or moral beauty. Natural beauty refers to how things in nature exhibit a fitness, propriety, or "uniformity and mutual correspondence." Moral or spiritual beauty refers to the way things in the world are perceived—not as individual objects ordered wisely by a benevolent creator, but as internally related and mutually defining components of the mind itself:

> That consent, agreement, or union of being to being, which has been spoken of, viz. the union or propensity of *minds* to mental or spiritual existence, may be called the highest, and first, or primary beauty that is found among things that exist: being the proper and peculiar beauty of spiritual and moral beings, which are the highest and first part of the universal system for whose sake all the rest has existence. Yet there is another, inferior, secondary beauty, which is some image of this, and which is not peculiar to spiritual beings, but is found even in inanimate things: which consists in a mutual consent and agreement of different things in form, manner, quantity, and visible end or design; called by the various names of regularity, order, uniformity, symmetry, proportion, harmony, etc.[9]

The harmony revealed in natural beauty is pleasing and inspiring, but it does not engage the heart of the observer, because the heart does not share in the determination of those objects. In contrast, spiritual beauty is the agreement of the mind and the heart, in which the disposition or affections of the mind determine the object of experience as an intentional object for the mind. The mind's apprehension of spiritual beauty, though, is not based on any subjective interest or self-love, for the very notion of subjectivity or of the self as distinct from its objects is undermined by recognizing how mind has (and is) the inherent propensity of an object to be united to or in agreement with another.

Apprehension of the spiritual beauty or excellence of a thing does not, therefore, begin with the assumption of the ontological independence of the thing; it is not a thing first and only afterwards designated as beautiful. Rather, its excellence consists in its not being considered as an "it" at all, but as a plurality:

> One alone, without any reference to any more, cannot be excellent; for in such a case there can be no manner of relation no way, and therefore, no such thing as consent. Indeed, what we call 'one' may be excellent, because of a consent of parts, or some consent of those in that being that are distinguished into a plurality some way or other. But in a being that is absolutely without plurality there cannot be excellency, for there can be no such thing as consent or agreement.[10]

9. Edwards, *True Virtue*, 561–62; also 564–65. Cf. Miscellany #782, in Jonathan Edwards, *The Philosophy of Jonathan Edwards*, ed. Harvey G. Townsend, 122; and Delattre, *Beauty and Sensibility*, 18–21, 109–10, 211–12.
10. Edwards, "The Mind" #1, 337.

Consent or agreement is what allows us to be able to talk intelligibly about a unit. Apart from a context in which a unit is identified relative to other units, it is pointless to imagine how such unity is to be understood. This restriction on intelligibility is not simply a function of our limited human intellects, but is a requirement of the discursive character of being.

Contrary to Neoplatonic claims, then, the One cannot serve as the ultimate principle for intelligibility or being, for its very designation as a unit demands its placement in a discursive or semiotic matrix. Thus, Edwards remarks that the intelligibility and excellence of God himself depends on the plurality of the Trinity, for significance requires the possibility of signification, which in turn requires the differentiation between signifier and signified. "Therefore if God is excellent," he concludes, "there must be a plurality in God; otherwise, there can be no consent in him." [11] If God is a simple unit, he is simply unintelligible and thus cannot be excellent.

As with every other intelligible thing, God's consent is not something that he does as much as it is something that he is. A signifier does not choose its signified; rather, "it" exists as a function of the discursive exchanges in terms of which it is intelligible and identifiable. Insofar as signifier and signified are thought of as independent units, they are unintelligible and unimaginable, just as the persons of the Trinity cannot be conceived apart from their relations to one another. Accordingly, only a mistaken or fallen notion of person or self would describe the spiritual agreement of persons as a consent those persons choose to have.

In terms of the fallen discourse of subjectivity, it makes sense to speak about loving oneself—as though one could choose not to love oneself. But in Edwards' view, it makes no sense even to imagine not loving oneself, for that would imply that the self is distinct from the affections in terms of which the self is defined. Self-love cannot therefore be an affection of the self, for the love of the self is the intentionality of being, whereby the self simply is. Mere self-love must arise "simply and necessarily from the nature of a perceiving, willing being." [12] Insofar as any being perceives or wills, it consents to or loves itself as the product of those intentional acts. Its consent to or love of itself is the product of those intentional acts, for the intentionality of those acts is not something the self has as much as it is what the self is.

Simple self-love is an instance of consent to being in the first sense. Edwards contrasts it with what he calls compounded self-love, that is, the consent to or love of the regularity or order of things to which the self belongs and in virtue of which the self experiences delight or pleasure. As with simple self-love, compounded self-love exhibits the intentionality of perception and will; but in compounded self-love, the self is understood as linked

---

11. Miscellany #182 [1725]. Cf. Robert W. Jenson, *America's Theologian: A Recommendation of Jonathan Edwards*, 91.

12. Miscellany #530 [1731–32], in *Philosophy of Edwards*, 203. Cf. "The Mind" #1, 337; and Miklós Vetö, *La Pensée de Jonathan Edwards*, 96–97.

to other beings. This link accounts for feelings of sympathy, pity, and general affection for others:

> There is . . . a compounded self-love, which is exercised in the delight that a man has in the good of another: it is the value that he sets upon that delight. This I call compounded self-love, because it arises from a compounded principle. It arises from the necessary nature of perceiving and willing being, whereby he takes his own pleasure or delight; but not from this alone, but it supposes also another principle, that determines the exercise of this principle, and makes that to become its object which otherwise cannot: a certain principle uniting this person with another, that causes the good of another to be its good. The first arises simply from his own being, whereby that which agrees immediately and directly with his own being, is his good; the second arises also from a principle uniting him to another being, whereby the good of that other being does in a sort become his own. This second sort of self-love is not entirely distinct from love to God, but enters into its nature.[13]

The consent to the being of oneself in the well-being of another depends on the second sense of consent described above. It still assumes the propriety of individuation, but it recognizes that the intelligibility of individual existence consists in being related to others in virtue of a divinely established harmony. This second sort of self-love enters into the love of God, because it draws the mind to the recognition that the rationale for one's own existence and well-being involves others.

By acknowledging a dependence on others, the individual consents to a relation that justifies or explains the individual in terms other than itself. The individual's situation relative to others is what makes the individual intelligible. Inasmuch as the individual is intelligible as an individual, it must be related to other individuals. God's establishment of order or agreement among individuals aids fallen human intellection in its attempt to overcome the individuality that stands in the way of the appreciation of spiritual beauty. But it does not cure the mind of its weakness and passivity or its reliance on its perception of things as individuals.

However, the perception of natural beauty does draw the mind's attention to the experience of its own pleasure. That experience of the mind's being pleased with its ideas is what constitutes will or choice.[14] To the extent that the mind is intentionally related to its objects—that is, to the extent that it is informed by will—the mind identifies those objects as its own. This awareness of its own active engagement with its objects is the consent to being that Edwards refers to as love.

The mind's apprehension of objects as things distinct from itself, but with which it is in harmony, is the experience of natural beauty; and the affection of mind that characterizes this experience is the love of complacence.[15] This

---

13. Miscellany #530, in *Philosophy of Edwards*, 203. Cf. Ramsey, ed., *Ethical Writings*, 14–18; Fiering, *Edwards's Moral Thought*, 157–60; and Vetö, *La Pensée*, 186–87.

14. See Edwards, "The Mind" #67 [mid-1740s], 384.

15. See Edwards, *True Virtue*, 542–44; and Miscellany #530, in *Philosophy of Edwards*, 204.

form of love is delight in a person or being in virtue of its beauty as an individual in harmony with other things; it is the affection of mind associated with the second sense of consent.

The apprehension of the union or identity of mind with its objects is the experience of spiritual beauty. The affection characterizing this experience is the love of benevolence. "Love of *benevolence*," writes Edwards, "is that affection or propensity of the heart to any being, which causes it to incline to its well being, or disposes it to desire and take pleasure in its happiness."[16] Such love can hardly be said to be an affection of the mind, for the mind cannot be conceived apart from its objects. So Edwards identifies the love of benevolence as the sense of the heart, a felt union of perceiver and perceived.

This form of love is the third sense of consent, in which consent is an acknowledgment that the intelligibility of the totality of existents is grounded in the apprehension of Being in general. Particular beings can exist intelligibly only in virtue of their integration into the divine order of things; and the divine order of things is intelligible only in the displacement or supposition of individuality. Without some means to relate the analogies in nature that Edwards' typology thematizes, though, those analogies are significant only in themselves and signify nothing beyond themselves.

For this reason Edwards concludes that the experience of primary or spiritual beauty provides the a priori conditions for the experience of the harmony or consent that defines natural beauty. As he says in *Religious Affections*, "Moral excellency is the excellency of natural excellencies."[17] The a priori conditions for the experience of spiritual beauty are, in turn, merely the reflections of the conditions for the apprehension of or consent to being. Since being itself is intelligible or excellent only in relation to such apprehension or consent, all being is in one sense or another beautiful:

> Existence or entity is that into which all excellency is to be resolved. Being or existence is what is necessarily agreeable to being; and when being perceives it, it will be agreeable perception; and any contradiction to being or existence is what being, when it perceives, abhors.[18]

The contradiction to being that being abhors is the contradiction implicit in the assumption that perception might not entail an agreement, that is, that it might not be united to or identified with something other than itself. Without such agreement or excellence "all the world is empty, no better than nothing, yea worse than nothing."[19] Indeed, because a thing exists only in virtue of its harmonious relations to an other, apart from such relations it is like a term removed from all propositional settings. It is literally less than nothing, for even nothing would have some meaning relative to something.

16. Edwards, *True Virtue*, 542. Cf. Sang Hyun Lee, *The Philosophical Theology of Jonathan Edwards*, 154.

17. Jonathan Edwards, *Religious Affections*, ed. John E. Smith, 257.

18. Edwards, "The Mind" #62, 381. Cf. Delattre, *Beauty and Sensibility*, 59, 65.

19. *Religious Affections*, 274. Cf. Vetö, *La Pensée*, 306.

This rather involved way of describing things as related to one another in essentially aesthetic terms indicates just how strange Edwards' account is when compared with humanist attempts to speak of consent. For Edwards, consent is not only part of the epistemology of beauty; it also inscribes the parameters for delineating the mind and its objects. No implicit idealism underlies the contrasts between benevolence and complacence, primary and secondary beauty, or the love of excellence and the delight in existence, because it is precisely in these terms that notions of mind or idea are formulated. Since no such idealism can be imported justifiably into his account, Edwards' vocabulary of beauty remains suspiciously foreign to the modernist reader.

In Edwards' aesthetics, cordial consents, benevolence, and love no longer describe subjective states; nor is a subjective sensitivity to natural beauty necessarily linked to the appreciation of spiritual or moral beauty.[20] Consent, benevolence, and love actually undercut the premise upon which subjectivity is based. Likewise, the recognition of God's arbitrary association of natural and spiritual beauty undermines any notion that either is intelligible in itself.

By means of this approach, Edwards emphasizes how that which is appropriate or proper for being, or what "agrees" with being, is the propriety of being itself. To say that being is proper means that it is itself; but to say that it is itself is already to imply that its intelligibility consists in its displacement or supposition of (and thus relation to) an other, even if the proposition in terms of which it is related is one of identity or equality.

Thus the relation of identity (e.g., A is A)—a relation often dismissed in substantialist metaphysics as trivially true—is crucial for Edwards, for it provides the foundation for the intelligibility or beauty of what a thing properly is, namely, a term whose meaning (even as an individual) is a function of the proposition of which it is a part:

> This simple equality, without proportion, is the lowest kind of regularity, and may be called simple beauty; all other beauties and excellencies may be resolved into it. . . . All beauty consists in similarness, or identity of relation. In identity of relation consists all likeness, and all identity between two consists in identity of relation. . . . And so in every case, what is called correspondency, symmetry, regularity and the like, may be resolved into equalities; though the equalities in a beauty in any degree complicated are so numerous that it would be a most tedious work to enumerate them. There are millions of these equalities. . . . Therefore the lowest and most simple kind of beauty is equality or likeness, because by equality or likeness one part consents with but one part. But by proportion one part may sweetly consent to ten thousand different parts, all the parts may consent with all the rest, and not only so, but the parts taken singly may consent with the whole taken together.[21]

Self-identity is always the identity of a self for an other, the identification of a self relative to an other. It is the supposition of an other to which it can be re-

---

20. See Edwards, *True Virtue*, 544–48. Cf. Delattre, *Beauty and Sensibility*, 196–99, 206.
21. Edwards, "The Mind" #1 and #62, 333–35, 380.

lated at least in terms of identity. In other words, identity is intelligible only in terms of the discursive matrix that displaces the self. Apart from its own self-identity, no being is intelligible as a being except as being what it is. Without the assurance of that determination (whereby a being is identical to itself), no being can be even minimally beautiful.

The more ways that a being can be identified in terms of its equalities or proportions, the more extensive is its beauty. To the extent that a being cannot be identified with the totality of things (i.e., the system of the universe), it exhibits a particular or false beauty. But to the extent that a thing is viewed "with regard to all its tendencies, and its connections with everything it stands related to," it has "a generally extended excellence and a true beauty."[22] The tendencies or dispositions of a thing define it as a being and constitute the conditions for its beauty. The extent or degree to which the thing is defined in terms of everything else in the universe comprises its greatness or grandeur.[23]

Consent to the totality of beings makes a being great. True virtue, however, is not the consent or benevolence to the totality of beings. Rather, it is the union of the heart to Being in general; it is the identity or agreement of a being with the inherently suppositional or dispositional character not only of its being, but also of all beings. Since this agreement is an agreement of identity, it is not an act of an individual mind, but is rather the self-appreciation of the Being of beings.

Insofar as the Being of beings is God, this conclusion might seem to imply that true virtue is God's self-love or appreciation. But the very notion of a self is precisely what Edwards' relational definition of being precludes. Therefore, Edwards has to find a way to describe the identity between an individual being and the being by which it and all else has being, without at the same time implying that this relation legitimates individuality.

The solution to this problem lies in Edwards' concept of the sense of the heart. Such a sense is not knowledge that any individual has as an individual. Instead it is the knowledge of the identity of a thing with itself without the presupposition that the thing is distinguishable from that knowledge or that that knowledge is distinguishable from the thing. This rejection of the distinction between mind and its objects by means of recognizing each in terms of one another signals just how radical a challenge Edwards' sense of the heart is to the classical-modern theory of knowledge.

Knowledge and Grace

As with other aspects of his philosophy, Edwards' epistemology includes accounts of knowledge from the perspective of fallen, sinful humanity, as well

---

22. Edwards, *True Virtue*, 540; "The Mind" #14 [1725], 344. Cf. Stephen R. Yarbrough, "Jonathan Edwards on Rhetorical Authority," *Journal of the History of Ideas* 47 (1986), 400; and Anderson, ed., *Scientific and Philosophic Writings*, 81–82.

23. See Edwards, "The Mind" #64 [mid-1740s], 382. Cf. Vetö, *La Pensée*, 287.

as from the perspective of the regenerate. The former perspective is epitomized in the thought of Locke and is the focus of Edwards' comments about signs, especially in his *Religious Affections*, Miscellany #777, and what Miklòs Vetö refers to as the "great" Miscellany #782. The latter perspective transforms the former notion of signification by emphasizing how the inherent intentionality or spirituality of being provides the basis for a new sense of knowing, a sense of the heart. Together the two perspectives constitute Edwards' theory of knowledge; and together their different presentations of the functions of signs make up the epistemological character of Edwards' semiotics.

With the exception of Christ, who knows beings immediately as signs of God (i.e., as suppositions of Being itself), all beings rely on signs for what they know. Such signs, Edwards observes, include the ways in which things are images of or resemble one another; words or motions that communicate another person's "voluntary significations"; causes and effects; and the a priori connections among antecedents and consequents in arguments.[24] These signs comprise the sensible vocabulary for thinking and, as such, represent things both as external to our thoughts and as substitutions for ideas themselves:

> Those signs that we are wont to make use of in our thoughts for representatives of things, and to substitute in the room of the actual ideas themselves, are either the ideas of the names by which we are wont to call them or the ideas of some external sensible thing that some way belongs to the thing—some sensible image or resemblance, or some sensible part, or some sensible effect, or sensible concomitant, or a few sensible circumstances. We have the ideas of some of these excited, which we substitute in the room of those things that are most essential, and use 'em as signs as we do words, and have respect to 'em no further in our discourse.[25]

To the extent that signs are considered as representations of things instead of as parts of the things themselves, they function either as names arbitrarily associated with those things or as indications of the externality of the objects of thought. When we think using signs rather than the actual ideas of things themselves, we think in terms of representation. Relations of representation are based on connections such as resemblance, cause and effect, and concomitant or circumstantial association. Representation requires us to assume a real distinction between a thing and the sign that represents it. Insofar as a sign is understood as a substitute for the actual idea of a thing, the presence of the sign stands as a marker for the thing's externality to thought. To say that a sign represents a thing already designates the thing as external and as not being essentially united to the activity of its apprehension.

Edwards' evaluation of the place of the sign hinges on the extent to which relations of signification necessarily entail a representational epistemology. Certainly, the arbitrary assignment of a name to a thing signals the externality of

24. See Miscellany #777 [1738–39]. Cf. Perry Miller, ed., *Images or Shadows of Divine Things*, by Jonathan Edwards, 32.
25. Miscellany #782, in *Philosophy of Edwards*, 116.

the relation between the two; but this is less an indictment of the possibility of essential relations between words and things than it is a caution against thinking that the assignment of such relations overcomes the gap between idea and thing, assumed in a representational notion of signification.

The problem with using signs as we do words is that we assume that discourse involves simply substituting one thing for another—as if the things themselves were not already defined precisely in virtue of just such substitutions. "Our" discourse assumes the externality of things without recognizing how that very assumption of subjectivity forestalls all subsequent attempts to retrieve a union with objects of knowledge.

The obvious artifice of simply linking signs to one another, "wherein we don't directly view the things themselves by the actual presence of their ideas or . . . sensation of their resemblances," is what Edwards calls *mere cogitation or notional knowledge.* Mere cogitation is possible only to the extent that the terms or signs used in discourse comprise a form of "mental reading wherein we don't look on the things themselves but only on those signs of them that are before our eyes."[26] This kind of knowledge is simply a familiarity with how concepts or ideas are typically related as signs to one another in discourse. Since those signs are associated to the things to which they refer only accidentally, they provide no grounds for any true knowledge. However, the sensible immediacy of the manipulation of signs in mere cogitation hints at what would constitute an ideal form of understanding, namely, one wherein the mind has a direct apprehension of its object.

A more perspicuous distinction can be formulated, therefore, between knowledge associated with the understanding and the immediacy of experience that Edwards calls the sense of the heart. In understanding, the proper activity of signs is to represent objects external to themselves. Knowledge of the first kind includes mere cogitation or speculation, as well as any other apprehension in which things are identified in terms of something apart from that with which the mind is actually engaged. Knowledge of the second kind treats a thing as that which is apprehended immediately and understood as an object of intentionality or will, and in which the significance of the thing consists precisely in that apprehension. The immediacy of the thing as an intentional object of will or inclination distinguishes the way it is known from speculative knowledge, in that it is felt or sensed rather than simply understood. Just as understanding what pain is differs from feeling pain, so understanding the meaning of a thing in terms of something other than the experience of understanding it differs from appreciating its significance firsthand:

> Hence arises another great distinction . . . 1. that understanding which consists in mere SPECULATION or the understanding of the head; or 2. that which consists in the SENSE OF THE HEART. The former includes all that understanding that is without any proper ideal apprehension or view or all understanding of mental things of either faculty that is only by signs. And also all ideal views of

26. Ibid., 118.

things that are merely intellectual or appertain only to the faculty of understanding, i.e. all that understanding of things that don't consist in or imply some
motion of the will or, in other words (to speak figuratively) some feeling of the
heart, is mere speculative knowledge, whether it be an ideal apprehension of
them or no. But all that understanding of things that does consist in or involve
such a sense or feeling is not merely speculative but sensible knowledge. . . . This
distribution of the human knowledge into SPECULATIVE and SENSIBLE, though
it seems to pertain [to] only one particular kind of the objects of our knowledge—
viz. those things that appertain or relate to the will and affections—yet indeed
may be extended to all the knowledge we have of all objects whatsoever. For
there is no kind of thing that we know but what may be considered as in some
respect or other concerning the wills or hearts of spiritual beings.[27]

Insofar as the classical-modern mentality raises the prospect of a gap between
the mind and its objects (especially if those objects are considered external to
the mind), the significance of things known in terms of such a mentality (i.e.,
notions) remains purely speculative. Indeed, as notions, the objects of our
knowledge are never more than the meanings of the things we know, since
they do not provide a guarantee for their own truth.

Even God's revelations, in the words of the Bible and in the signs of nature,
indicate only the topics with which an ideal and sensible knowledge is concerned.[28] They do not prove their truth because they do not necessarily change
the conditions by which something is understood as a thing. Only when there
is a change in the way that something is seen as a sign—that is, only when
the classical-modern separation of word, idea, and thing is replaced by a sense
of excellence in which things are related formally—is the possibility of truth
regained:

The word of God is only made use of to convey to the mind the subject matter
of this saving instruction: and this indeed it doth convey to us by natural force
or influence. It conveys to our minds these and those doctrines; it is the cause
of the notions of them in our heads, but not of the sense of the divine excellency of them in our hearts. Indeed a person cannot have spiritual light without
the word. But that does not argue, that the word properly causes that light. The
mind cannot see the excellency of any doctrine, unless that doctrine be first in
the mind; but the seeing of the excellency of the doctrine may be immediately
from the Spirit of God; though the conveying of the doctrine or proposition itself
may be by the word. So that the notions that are the subject matter of this light,
are conveyed to the mind by the word of God; but that due sense of the heart,
wherein this light formally consists, is immediately by the Spirit of God.[29]

27. Ibid., 119–20. Cf. Edwards, *Religious Affections*, 96, 272; Smith, ibid., 32; and Vetö, *La Pensée*,
228–41.

28. See Miscellany #782, in *Philosophy of Edwards*, 124; and *True Virtue*, 571–72. Cf. Yarbrough,
"Rhetorical Authority," 401–403.

29. Jonathan Edwards, "A Divine and Supernatural Light," in *Jonathan Edwards: Representative
Selections*, ed. Clarence H. Faust and Thomas H. Johnson, 110–11. Cf. Jenson, *America's Theologian*,
66–70; and Perry Miller, "Jonathan Edwards on the Sense of the Heart," *Harvard Theological Review*
41 (1948), 127.

This sense of the heart undercuts the prospect of skepticism by challenging the modernist presumption that knowledge is the agreement of our ideas either with external referents (to which they correspond) or with one another (with which they are coherent). To assume that ideas themselves are ontologically independent of either their referents or one another opens a breach between content and conviction that no divine revelation can overcome.

What makes conviction possible is therefore nothing less than the possibility of a change of heart, a change in the assumptions about the relation between the mind and its objects. Such a change involves the recognition that notional knowledge does not supply the grounds for its own conviction and therefore cannot provide the ideal and sensible apprehension of spiritual excellence. As disconnected contents of consciousness, notions embody the disruption of knowledge.

In contrast to the basic elements of consciousness identified in the propositional logic of supposition, notions are not inherently united to or defined by their relations to other ideas. Even when notions are associated contingently with other ideas through relations of agreement or disagreement, they do not provide grounds for knowledge, since they still signal the presumption of their ontological independence. "Knowledge," Edwards insists, "is not the perception of the agreement or disagreement of ideas, but rather the perception of the union or disunion of ideas."[30] Apart from such unions, ideas are mere notions unable to guide thought in any way that would provide certainty. Knowledge does not begin with the assumption that ideas are intelligible prior to their union. If they were meaningful apart from their union, then the perception of such a union would be arbitrary or, at least, contingent. That, in turn, would undermine any possibility for the mind's being able to distinguish truth from falsity other than in terms of convention.

With this strategy, Edwards grounds truth in reality instead of in the apprehension of relations of ideas. The intentionality of existence marks all reality as inherently ideational or spiritual. That union of ideas with reality which typically identifies claims of truth is thus made possible by a redefinition of idea and reality in essentially suppositional terms. In those terms knowledge is the perception of ideas as suppositionally united to their objects as the forms of ideas linked to their contents.

In supposing that there are things outside our ideas, we cannot suppose that they are outside all ideation, because supposition is itself the ideational character of being. The truth about supposed external things consists in the agreement of our ideas with the determinate pattern by which they are revealed to us by God. Thus, truth is the perception of the agreement of our ideas with the sequence of ideas God communicates to us. But since that communication constitutes not only the order of the objects we perceive, but also the character of the mind itself, the truth of what we know and the nature and existence of mind are ultimately identified as the agreement or union of the

30. Edwards, "The Mind" #71 [after 1748], 385. Cf. Schafer, "Concept of Being," 208.

mind with its objects. Those objects, in turn, exist as intelligible insofar as they enact the suppositional displacements typical of divine communication:

> After all that has been said and done, the only adequate definition of truth is the agreement of our ideas with existence. To explain what this existence is, is another thing. In abstract ideas, it is nothing but the ideas themselves; so their truth is their consistency with themselves. In things that are supposed to be without us, 'tis the determination, and fixed mode, of God's exciting ideas in us. So that truth in these things is an agreement of our ideas with that series in God. 'Tis existence, and that is all that we can say.[31]

To say that something exists *means* that that thing is united through its intentionality to other things whose determination is fixed through God's exciting ideas in us. But since "we" are functions within that semiotic matrix, our understanding of things in terms of their intentionality is simply an affirmation of how their existence and intelligibility depend on their "consistency" with one another.

God does not, therefore, excite individual ideas in individual minds. Rather, God is the lure beyond individuality, the immanent excitement of ideation. The agreement of our ideas with existence is the consistency of those ideas with what makes them intelligible, that is, their deference to an other. Because such deference expresses itself in and as the communication of the other, it is the inherent power or Stoic fire of the intentionality of being. In describing truth as the consistency of ideas with themselves or with the pattern of God's communication, Edwards is not implying that there is an intelligible distinction between the two. The whole point of his redefinition of existence as immanent intentionality is to undercut talk of what is internal and external.

Admittedly, for those who continue to labor under the fallen condition thematized by original sin, there is no immediately obvious connection between our ideas and the order of the world; hence, error and skepticism. In terms of the "spiritual" mentality of the elect, however, things are understood not as mere objects before the mind, but as instances of the mind's own inclinations toward integration with its objects. The sensible knowledge of the heart identifies things (and, reflexively, the mind itself) in terms of their inherent harmonies and connections. In such a view, to say of things that they are real is to understand them in terms of relations that are unintelligible apart from their engagements with one another and with the mind:

> There is such a thing as an appearing real, that is, a conviction of the reality of a thing, that is incommunicable, that cannot be drawn into formal arguments or be expressed in words, which is yet the strongest and most certain conviction. We know how things appear that are real, with what an air; we know how those things appear which we behold with waking eyes. They appear real, because we have a clear idea of them in all their various mutual relations, concurring

---

31. Edwards, "The Mind" #15 [1725], 344–45.

circumstances, order, and dispositions—the consent of the simple ideas among themselves, and with the compages of beings, and the whole train of ideas in our minds, and with the nature and constitution of our minds themselves: which consent and harmony consists in ten thousand little relations and mutual agreements that are ineffable.[32]

The apprehension of the myriad agreements that constitute reality forms the basis for the mind's ability to distinguish truth and falsehood. That ability cannot be a function of speculative knowledge, because speculative knowledge does not provide a means for determining whether the objects with which it deals are real. Insofar as the objects of speculative knowledge are not affective apprehensions—that is, insofar as they are not apprehended with conviction—they do not serve as the bases for action.

According to Edwards, this pragmatic commitment to action and the firmness of resolve implicit in sensible knowledge can characterize views of both natural individuals and the regenerate.[33] The sensation of sounds in harmony or the pleasure of reflecting on one's own happiness allows natural individuals to experience directly their relation to the order of the world. This appreciation differs substantially from the speculative consideration by natural individuals of their place in the world, because through sensible knowledge individuals come to know in virtue of their associations with other things, not in virtue of their private mastery of subjective ideas.

Sensible knowledge thus identifies the associations upon which the love of complacence is based. In virtue of sensible knowledge, natural individuals are motivated to act conscientiously. Moreover, in times of spiritual inspiration or illumination, when God imparts speculative knowledge to the soul, those individuals experience affectively and with conviction the religious significance of the common operation of the Spirit of God.

The saints likewise experience the heartfelt sense or apprehension of the unity and excellence of things. Additionally, they enjoy the ability or grace to transcend the inclination to interpret things in terms of themselves. This "evangelical humiliation" of the self cannot be justified by appealing to any natural affections, for all natural relations assume the propriety of individuation.[34] Such an effacement of the self subverts the natural sense of propriety by undermining the intelligibility of distinctions between things. Because the grace that effects this displacement of the self cannot be the result of anything for which the self is responsible, it marks the displacement of the self by the activity or presence of God.

---

32. Miscellany #201 [1726], in *Philosophy of Edwards*, 246–47. See also Miscellanies #397 [1729] and #408 [1729–30], ibid., 249.

33. See Miscellany #782, in *Philosophy of Edwards*, 120–25; and Edwards, *Religious Affections*, 270–71, 296. Cf. James Hoopes, *Consciousness in New England: From Puritanism and Ideas to Psychoanalysis and Semiotic*, 82.

34. See Edwards, *Religious Affections*, 311–12. Cf. Vetö, *La Pensée*, 251–59; and Wayne Proudfoot, "From Theology to a Science of Religions: Jonathan Edwards and William James on Religious Affections," *Harvard Theological Review* 82 (1989), 156–57.

In explaining how sanctifying or efficacious grace requires an ontological revision of how we speak of the saints, Edwards no longer feels restricted by natural assumptions about moral agency. For example, he does not have to assume that agents exist prior to their actions. In the case of the elect, the discourse of individuality (in terms of which self-interested agency is intelligible) is displaced by the space or matrix of divine discourse. Such displacement radically changes what discourse or communication means. For as repudiations of subjectivity, the saints exemplify how communication can be redefined as the semiotic context for intelligibility instead of being merely the means by which individuals overcome their cognitive and practical isolation from one another.

Not surprisingly, then, Edwards' doctrine of efficacious grace circumvents the need to suppose that God is another subject, by portraying God not as a moral agent, but rather as the rationale for the possibility of there being determinate moral agents in the first place.

> In efficacious grace we are not merely passive, nor does God do some, and we do the rest. But God does all, and we do all. God produces all, and we act all. For that is what he produces, viz., our own acts. God is the only proper author and fountain; we only are the actors. We are, in different respects, wholly passive and wholly active.[35]

Efficacious grace replaces the mentality of natural determination with an ontology in which the elect no longer think of themselves as subjects linked by predication to discrete objects of intellectual apprehension. By efficacious grace the elect are no longer properly considered as subjects at all, so their union with God does not entail their being absorbed into another subject (God). For the regenerate, existence is no longer conceivable as something that might or might not have been predicated of discrete subjects, since anything that is truly intelligible has to be comprehended in terms of its adumbration of Providence. Their transformation through grace retrieves for the elect the possibility of the prelapsarian unity of all things with God, by recalling the prospect of an ontology of supposition.

In that ontology the existence of a thing is defined by its union with (or love of) that which displaces its insular subjectivity. Grace allows the saint to think of things in terms of the dispositions or intentionality of their actions, rather than in terms of a complacence resigned to accept things as discriminate identities. This benevolence or love of a thing for the sake of its own being differs from the love of complacence, because benevolence does not assume that intelligible existence (or excellence) is first and foremost a solitary unity.

As I have suggested before, this point alone should be enough to demonstrate the distinctly non-Neoplatonic character of Edwards' philosophy, in that

---

35. "Miscellaneous Observations concerning Efficacious Grace," in *The Works of President Edwards*, ed. Samuel Austin, 5:473. See also Jonathan Edwards, *Freedom of the Will*, ed. Paul Ramsey, 435. Cf. Michael J. Colacurcio, "The Example of Edwards: Idealist Imagination and the Metaphysics of Sovereignty," in *Puritan Influences in American Literature*, ed. Emory Elliott, 61.

it rejects the assumption that God or the One is intelligible apart from the acts or dispositions by which God is in virtue of being excellent. To imagine something beyond that which makes God intelligible—for example, to imagine God as sublime—is already to appeal to the very conditions of intelligibility or rationality identified with the excellence of God. This excellence consists in his unity with or consent to being in general. Insofar as being in general is nothing other than God himself, even the intra-trinitarian differentiation of being as the object of divine intentionality can serve no other purpose than to indicate the aboriginal character of this logic in Edwards' understanding of being.[36]

Though benevolence in God is the consent to being in general, it is not the consent to particular beings (which is God's complacence). In creating, God identifies a being first as the displacement of himself and second as the displacement of other beings.[37] Each being is originally excellent, insofar as it is a consent to its own displacement or humiliation. The Fall is the substitution of this sense of displacement with a notion of existence that ignores the process of how something determinate comes into being precisely as a displacement or supposition.

Retrieving the prelapsarian "enlargedness of soul" in terms of which the elect *comprehend* all other creatures, grace discloses how beings come into existence always already pointing to their own transcendentality.[38] The saint never experiences a mere natural object without at the same time experiencing the relations of intentionality in terms of which the object is intelligible. For the saint, consent to being is only indirectly a love of particular beings, because the relationship of the saint with those beings is not concerned with those beings in their particularity, but with what makes them intelligible as existents. The saint experiences things not as complacently ordered in the world, but as united benevolently and aesthetically through the intentionality of their being.

Edwards' doctrines of the excellence of God and the moral beauty of the saint are therefore united in virtue of their mutual insistence that benevolence is less the act of an intelligible subject than the supposition of what designates intelligibility itself. If existence is intelligible, significant, or rational, it must be characterized in the same suppositional or transcendental terms that characterize the identification of excellence or beauty. In such a characterization every existent has being in virtue of its harmonious placement in the discursive exchange of which it is a part.

The discourse of subjective and autonomous actions, by contrast, draws on a different tradition, one in which the aesthetic character of existence is erased

36. See Edwards, "The Mind" #45, 364; and *True Virtue*, 542–44, 621. Cf. Delattre, *Beauty and Sensibility*, 147.
37. See Edwards, *Dissertation concerning the End for which God Created the World*, in *Ethical Writings*, 438–39.
38. See Edwards, *Charity and Its Fruits*, in *Ethical Writings*, 253. Cf. John E. Smith, *Jonathan Edwards: Puritan, Preacher, Philosopher*, 102.

by means of dismissing as unintelligible questions of the emergence of intelligibility. This discourse refuses to consider how substances come to be considered as intelligibly differentiated. Consequently, it provides no means for explaining why some individuals and not others would be chosen by God as recipients of saving grace.

Of course, doubts about God's dispensation of efficacious grace or about God's election of the saints strike Edwards simply as instances of how an entrenched metaphysics of subjectivity misses the point of what is required for a comprehensive understanding of intelligibility. Experience is not possible unless there is something that makes it intelligible. Even to question whether experience is ultimately intelligible or whether existence is ultimately absurd is to imagine the absence of precisely what is necessary to identify such an inquiry as intelligible. In Edwards' account, the recognition of that absence would itself justify the inquiry by fulfilling the expectation of a termination of thought in an other.

Thus the very nature of thought, like the nature of existence, disrupts the modernist impulse to dissociate being and value, immanence and transcendence. For Edwards, knowledge and existence are thoroughly aesthetic, because all beings are significant in virtue of their immanent transcendentality. Just as no theory of beauty can ignore the metaphysical or epistemological implications of aesthetic judgments, so no legitimate ontology can be developed without recognizing how the concern for significance or meaning guides it. That concern appears in Edwards' recurring references to communicative, discursive, or semiotic themes, and it drives Edwards to place his theory of excellence at the heart of his philosophy.

CONCLUDING REMARKS

THE PROPRIETY OF CHRIST

The mere prospect of Christ, the God-man, is an embarrassment to the substantialist metaphysics that Edwards' philosophy throws into doubt. For if God and human beings are substances, and substances cannot be predicated of one another, then something cannot be two substances at the same time. It comes as no surprise, then, that from the standpoint of the classical-modern mentality, the incarnation is a mystery. By not disrupting that mystery, Edwards acknowledges the fact that, for a fallen, unregenerate mind, the Christ event is unintelligible. However, Edwards' use of the ontology of supposition indicates how, for the elect, the incarnation presents no more of a theoretical difficulty than the appreciation of the significance of anything else in the world.

The key to this insight lies in revising the sense in which existence is properly understood. Once Edwards examines the presuppositions for intelligibility or significance in which the inquiry about existence is couched, he discovers that the same requirements for the intelligibility of the inquiry hold for the significance of existence. This recognition opens up the issue of propriety itself; and it is there that Edwards' doctrine of Christ reveals the patterns of thought that inform the regenerate mind.

In spite of the modernist inclination to identify him as such, the Christ that Edwards describes is not properly an individual—at least not in the way that modernity defines an individual as the subject of predication. In Edwards' thought, Christ is a challenge to the notion of an individual proper; or rather, Christ is a challenge to the propriety of individuality. Both divine and human, Christ subverts ontologies (including emanationist theories) in which substantialistic individuality becomes the mark of existential legitimacy. Christ's existence emphasizes his deference to others, instead of his own individuality. That act of self-displacement is at the heart of the ontology of supposition that permeates all of Edwards' philosophy.

By concluding this book with a note on Edwards' doctrine of Christ, I do not intend simply to acknowledge at the last minute the overwhelmingly religious character or theological cast of Edwards' thought. Edwards' Christianity is so central to his thinking that to ignore the figure of Christ, in order to avoid mixing his theology with his philosophy, is to accept the very bifurcation of mentalities that his work attempts to overcome. Instead, my retrieval

of Edwards' concept of Christ indicates how Christ embodies an ontology of
aboriginal signification that is lost by insisting on the distinction of theology
and philosophy in the first place.

Accordingly, these final remarks on Edwards' position identify neither a philosophy nor a theology of Christ, for they do not assume the propriety of such
a disciplinary distinction without at the same time questioning the nature of
the object of such studies. To assume first that Christ is some determinate thing
or person who can be studied in different ways is already to fall into the substantialist mentality that Edwards' project discounts. Nor can we begin with the
assumption that theology studies one kind of object and philosophy another,
in hopes of explaining why their portraits of Christ differ; that would not explain what legitimates their original differences in strategy. Only by allowing
for the possibility that topics of study themselves undermine the disciplinary
strategies in terms of which they are first identified can we understand the
complete revision in mentality or change of heart that characterizes the saint's
fixation on Christ.

For Edwards, to see all things in Christ is to understand things as Christ is
understood, namely, as an image—the image of God. But no image is intelligible apart from that of which it is the image. If it were intelligible apart from
that of which it is the image, it would be a distinct substance, but not a
"proper" image. A proper image is not distinct from that of which it is the
image, because its being consists in its pointing beyond itself as signifier to
that significance or meaning that transcends it and yet is of its essence.

This transcendentality of every thing in terms of which it is significant constitutes its spirituality. Insofar as a thing is the image of that which identifies it
as something significant, it is identified as something proper. Its propriety consists in its spirituality or transcendence of its materiality (i.e., of that which
would make the image conceivable apart from that of which it is the image).
Since everything is conceivable only in terms of—that is, as the supposition
of—another, sheer materiality cannot be conceived at all.

Only spiritual things are therefore intelligible. To say that something is
spiritual and thus intelligible in virtue of its being an image, however, does not
guarantee the propriety of its being an image. Insofar as it is conceived as a
distinct spiritual thing, its very distinction contradicts the spirituality in virtue
of which it is properly an image and capable of being intelligible:

> There is no other properly spiritual image but idea, altho there may be another
> spiritual thing that is exactly like [it]. Yet one thing's being exactly like another
> don't make it the proper image of that thing. If there be one distinct spiritual
> substance exactly like another, yet [it] is not the proper image of the other; this
> one made after the other, yet it is not any more an image of the first, than the
> first is of the last.[1]

---

1. Miscellany #260.

What makes a spiritual being *like* another (as opposed to being an image of it) is the fact that that being is not understood as immanently united to or defined by its other. The sheer possibility of being exactly like another spiritual thing reveals the way that the thing itself has the possibility of being a proper image.

To say that a thing is a proper image, though, is not to say that it is a perfect image. Though a proper image or signifier is inherently linked to what it signifies as a requirement for its intelligibility, it can always be misconceived as a notion lacking any significance. That possibility is the legacy of original sin. Even the saint's recognition of the significance of natural things as images, types, or shadows of their spiritual fulfillment does not eliminate the saint's cognizance of the differentiation of those things. As such, not even the saint achieves a perfect idea of the spiritual significance of a being, for a perfect idea of the spirituality of a thing is exactly the same thing as a perfect idea of existence itself. And that would amount to nothing less than having a perfect idea of God.

Christ, on the other hand, as the exemplar for signification itself, is a perfect image, God's perfect idea of himself. As the *Logos* or Word of divine communicability, Christ is the image or idea of the intentionality of existence.[2] The Word is the complex of the discursive practices in terms of which the existence of the world is intelligible, meaningful, or significant. The prospect that the world can have a rationale validated as divine truth or as God's perfect understanding of himself is the "Amen" that Edwards notes is another name for the Son of God.[3]

The sanctification of humanity and the world in general thus culminates for Edwards in the realization of the integrity of existence. That integrity is possible because existence itself is a system of signification. As part of that system of divine discourse, the human soul is beautiful or beatified insofar as it becomes a proper image of the excellence of Christ.[4] That transformation of mind in the elect reinstates the sense of the inherently communicative character of existence.

By appealing to the Stoic-Ramist ontology or semiotics on which such a move is based, Edwards reaffirms the importance of Christ for philosophic discourse. More importantly, he describes an alternative to classical-modern philosophies. That alternative undermines the personalist assumptions of modernity and resists the inclination to limit rhetorical, moral, or aesthetic features of existence to expressions of subjectivity.

That this way of thinking is unfamiliar to modernist readers of philosophy accounts, no doubt, for why Edwards continues to be considered both

2. See Miscellany #94, in *The Philosophy of Jonathan Edwards,* ed. Harvey G. Townsend, 255; Miscellanies #260, #766, #777, and #1358 [after 1755]; and Jonathan Edwards, *An Unpublished Essay of Edwards on the Trinity,* ed. George P. Fisher, 91–92.
3. See Miscellany #260; and *Essay on the Trinity,* 91. Cf. Jonathan Edwards, *Freedom of the Will,* ed. Paul Ramsey, 287, 289.
4. See Miscellany #108. Cf. Paul Ramsey, ed., *Ethical Writings,* by Jonathan Edwards, 529n.

geographically and thematically peripheral to the study of most modern philosophy. Indeed, since presuppositions about the nature of philosophy and its historiography are today couched primarily in the very terms that Edwards undermines, it seems unlikely that he will soon be accorded the attention given his modernist contemporaries.

Still, the development of poststructuralist strategies allows us to identify those historiographic presuppositions as products of the hegemony of classical modernity, putting us in a much stronger position to appreciate how he highlights the strictures of modernity. Through such poststructuralist analyses of his philosophy, we are alerted to his cautions about how desire and power function in classical-modern liberalism, especially in the attempt to impose the humanistic enshrinement of subjectivity onto divine discourse. It has been my aim to indicate how contemporary work in poststructuralist and semiotic thought contribute to that reexamination of the limits of modernity by pointing to the alternative mentality on which Edwards draws.

BIBLIOGRAPHY

Published Materials

Aarsleff, Hans. *From Locke to Saussure: Essays on the Study of Language and Intellectual History*. Minneapolis: University of Minnesota Press, 1982.

Adams, John C. "Alexander Richardson's Philosophy of Art and the Sources of the Puritan Social Ethic." *Journal of the History of Ideas* 50 (1989): 227–47.

_____. "Alexander Richardson's Puritan Theory of Discourse." *Rhetorica* 4 (1986): 255–74.

_____. "Ramist Concepts of Testimony, Judicial Analogies, and the Puritan Conversion Narrative." *Rhetorica* 9 (1991): 251–68.

Addis, Laird. *Natural Signs: A Theory of Intentionality*. Philadelphia: Temple University Press, 1989.

Adriaens, Mark. "Ideology and Literary Production: Kristeva's Poetics." In *Semiotics and Dialectics: Ideology and Text*, edited by Peter V. Zima. Amsterdam: John Benjamins, 1981.

Ames, William. *Technometry*. Translation and commentary by Lee W. Gibbs. Philadelphia: University of Pennsylvania Press, 1979.

Anderson, Paul R., and Fisch, Max H. *Philosophy in America: From the Puritans to James*. New York: Octagon Books, 1969.

Anderson, Wallace E. "Immaterialism in Jonathan Edwards' Early Philosophical Notes." *Journal of the History of Ideas* 25 (1964): 181–200.

_____. Introduction to "Images of Divine Things" and "Types" Notebook, in *Typological Writings*, by Jonathan Edwards. Edited by Wallace E. Anderson and Mason I. Lowance, Jr., with David Watters. New Haven: Yale University Press, 1993.

_____. Introduction to *Scientific and Philosophical Writings*, by Jonathan Edwards. Edited by Wallace E. Anderson. New Haven: Yale University Press, 1980.

Bannet, Eve Tavor. *Structuralism and the Logic of Dissent: Barthes, Derrida, Foucault, Lacan*. Urbana and Chicago: University of Illinois Press, 1989.

Bercovitch, Sacvan. *The American Jeremiad*. Madison: University of Wisconsin Press, 1978.

Boehner, Philotheus. *Medieval Logic*. Chicago: University of Chicago Press, 1952.

Brown, David. *Continental Philosophy and Modern Theology*. New York: Basil Blackwell, 1987.

Brumm, Ursula. "Jonathan Edwards and Typology." In *Early American Literature*, edited by Michael T. Gilmore. Englewood Cliffs, N.J.: Prentice-Hall, 1980.

Bryant, Louise May, and Patterson, Mary. "The List of Books Sent by Jeremiah Dummer . . ." In *Papers in Honor of Andrew Keogh, Librarian of Yale University*, edited by the Yale University Library Staff. New Haven: Yale University Press, 1938.

Burgersdijck, Franco. *Institutionum logicorum libri duo*. Cantabrigiae: Roger Daniel, 1645.

_____. *Monitic Logica*. London: R. Cumberland, 1697.

Cherry, Conrad. *Nature and Religious Imagination: From Edwards to Bushnell*. Philadelphia: Fortress Press, 1980.

_____. *The Theology of Jonathan Edwards: A Reappraisal*. Garden City, N.Y.: Anchor Books, 1966.

Colacurcio, Michael J. "The Example of Edwards: Idealist Imagination and the Meta-physics of Sovereignty." In *Puritan Influences in American Literature*, edited by Emory Elliott. Urbana: University of Illinois Press, 1979.

Colapietro, Vincent M. *Peirce's Approach to the Self: A Semiotic Perspective on Human Subjectivity*. Albany: State University of New York Press, 1989.

Cooey, Paula M. *Jonathan Edwards on Nature and Destiny: A Systematic Analysis*. Lewiston, N.Y.: Edwin Mellon Press, 1985.

Corcoran, John. "Remarks on Stoic Deduction." In *Ancient Logic and Its Modern Interpretations*, edited by John Corcoran. Boston: D. Reidel, 1974.

Croll, Oswald. *Signatures of Internal Things*, bound with Croll's *Basilica Chymica*. Translated by John Hartman. London: John Stukey and Thomas Passenger, 1669–70.

Culler, Jonathan. *The Pursuit of Signs: Semiotics, Literature, Deconstruction*. Ithaca, N.Y.: Cornell University Press, 1981.

Daniel, Stephen H. *Myth and Modern Philosophy*. Philadelphia: Temple University Press, 1990.

———. "Vico's Historicism and the Ontology of Arguments," *Journal of the History of Philosophy*, forthcoming.

Davidson, Edward H. "From Locke to Edwards." *Journal of the History of Ideas* 24 (1963): 355–72.

———. *Jonathan Edwards: The Narrative of a Puritan Mind*. Cambridge: Harvard University Press, 1968.

Davis, Thomas M. "The Traditions of Puritan Typology." In *Typology and Early American Literature*, edited by Sacvan Bercovitch. Amherst: University of Massachusetts Press, 1972.

Debus, Allen G. *The Chemical Philosophy: Paracelsian Science and Medicine in the Sixteenth and Seventeenth Centuries*. 2 vols. New York: Science History Publications, 1977.

Deely, John. "John Locke's Place in the History of Semiotic Inquiry." In *Semiotics 1986*, edited by John Deely and Jonathan Evans. Lanham, Md.: University Press of America, 1987.

Delattre, Roland A. *Beauty and Sensibility in the Thought of Jonathan Edwards: An Essay in Aesthetics and Theological Ethics*. New Haven: Yale University Press, 1968.

De Prospo, Richard C. *Theism in the Discourse of Jonathan Edwards*. Newark: University of Delaware Press, 1985.

Derrida, Jacques. *Positions*. Translated by Alan Bass. Chicago: University of Chicago Press, 1981.

Eco, Umberto. "Looking for a Logic of Culture." In *The Tell-Tale Sign: A Survey of Semiotics*, edited by Thomas Sebeok. Lisse, Netherlands: De Ridder, 1975.

———. *The Role of the Reader*. Bloomington: Indiana University Press, 1979.

Edwards, Jonathan. *Ethical Writings*. Edited by Paul Ramsey. New Haven: Yale University Press, 1989.

———. *Freedom of the Will*. Edited by Paul Ramsey. New Haven: Yale University Press, 1957.

———. *Images or Shadows of Divine Things*. Edited by Perry Miller. New Haven: Yale University Press, 1948.

———. *Jonathan Edwards: Representative Selections*. Edited by Clarence H. Faust and Thomas H. Johnson. New York: Hill and Wang, 1962.

———. *Original Sin*. Edited by Clyde A. Holbrook. New Haven: Yale University Press, 1970.

———. *The Philosophy of Jonathan Edwards*. Edited by Harvey G. Townsend. Eugene: University of Oregon Press, 1955.

———. *Religious Affections*. Edited by John E. Smith. New Haven: Yale University Press, 1959.

_____. *Scientific and Philosophical Writings.* Edited by Wallace E. Anderson. New Haven: Yale University Press, 1980.

_____. *Sermons and Discourses, 1720–1723.* Edited by Wilson H. Kimnach. New Haven: Yale University Press, 1992.

_____. *Typological Writings.* Edited by Wallace E. Anderson and Mason I. Lowance, Jr., with David Watters. New Haven: Yale University Press, 1993.

_____. *An Unpublished Essay of Edwards on the Trinity.* Edited by George P. Fisher. New York: Charles Scribner's Sons, 1903.

_____. *The Works of Jonathan Edwards.* 2 vols. Edited by Edward Hickman. 1834. Reprint, Edinburgh and Carlisle, Pa.: Banner of Truth Trust, 1974.

_____. *The Works of Jonathan Edwards.* Edited by Perry Miller, John E. Smith, et al. New Haven: Yale University Press, 1957–.

_____. *The Works of President Edwards.* 8 vols. Edited by Samuel Austin. Worchester, Mass.: Isaiah Thomas, 1808–09.

_____. *The Works of President Edwards.* 10 vols. Edited by Sereno E. Dwight. New York: Carvill, 1829–30.

Edwards, Rem B. *A Return to Moral and Religious Philosophy in Early America.* Washington, D.C.: University Press of America, 1982.

Ellis, Joseph J. *The New England Mind in Transition: Samuel Johnson of Connecticut, 1696–1722.* New Haven: Yale University Press, 1973.

Erdt, Terence. *Jonathan Edwards: Art and the Sense of the Heart.* Amherst: University of Massachusetts Press, 1980.

Fiering, Norman. *Jonathan Edwards's Moral Thought and Its British Context.* Chapel Hill: University of North Carolina Press, 1982.

_____. "The Rationalist Foundations of Jonathan Edwards's Metaphysics." In *Jonathan Edwards and the American Experience*, edited by Nathan O. Hatch and Harry S. Stout. New York: Oxford University Press, 1988.

Flower, Elizabeth, and Murphey, Murray G. *A History of Philosophy in America.* 2 vols. New York: Capricorn Books, 1977.

Foucault, Michel. *The Archaeology of Knowledge.* Translated by A. M. Sheridan Smith. New York: Harper and Row, 1972.

_____. "Nietzsche, Freud, Marx." In *Transforming the Hermeneutic Context: From Nietzsche to Nancy*, edited by Gayle L. Ormiston and Alan D. Schrift. Albany: State University of New York Press, 1990.

_____. *The Order of Things.* New York: Random House, 1970.

Frede, Michael. *Essays in Ancient Philosophy.* Minneapolis: University of Minnesota Press, 1987.

_____. "The Original Notion of Cause." In *Doubt and Dogmatism: Studies in Hellenistic Epistemology*, edited by Malcolm Schofield, Myles Burnyeat, and Jonathan Barnes. New York: Oxford University Press, 1980.

Galdon, Joseph A. *Typology and Seventeenth-Century Literature.* The Hague: Mouton, 1975.

Gale, Theophilus. *The Court of the Gentiles.* 2d ed. Oxford: Thomas Gilbert, 1672.

Gibbs, Lee W. Introduction to *Technometry*, by William Ames, translated by Lee W. Gibbs. Philadelphia: University of Pennsylvania Press, 1979.

Gracia, Jorge J. E. *Philosophy and Its History: Issues in Philosophical Historiography.* Albany: State University of New York Press, 1992.

Graeser, Andreas. "The Stoic Theory of Meaning." In *The Stoics*, edited by John M. Rist. Berkeley: University of California Press, 1978.

Guelzo, Allen C. *Edwards on the Will: A Century of American Theological Debate.* Middletown, Conn.: Wesleyan University Press, 1989.

Hatch, Nathan O., and Stout, Harry S., eds. *Jonathan Edwards and the American Experience.* New York: Oxford University Press, 1988.

Helm, Paul. "John Locke and Jonathan Edwards: A Reconsideration." *Journal of the History of Philosophy* 7 (1969): 51–61.

Holbrook, Clyde A. Introduction to *Original Sin*, by Jonathan Edwards. Edited by Clyde A. Holbrook. New Haven: Yale University Press, 1970.

———. "Jonathan Edwards on Self-Identity and Original Sin." *The Eighteenth Century: Theory and Interpretation* 25 (1984): 45–63.

Hoopes, James. "Calvinism and Consciousness from Edwards to Beecher." In *Jonathan Edwards and the American Experience*, edited by Nathan O. Hatch and Harry S. Stout. New York: Oxford University Press, 1988.

———. *Consciousness in New England: From Puritanism and Ideas to Psychoanalysis and Semiotic.* Baltimore: Johns Hopkins University Press, 1989.

Howell, Wilbur Samuel. *Logic and Rhetoric in England, 1500–1700.* Princeton: Princeton University Press, 1956.

Jackson, B. Darrell. "The Theory of Signs in St. Augustine's *De Doctrina Christiana*." In *Augustine: A Collection of Critical Essays*, edited by R. A. Markus. Garden City, N.Y.: Anchor Books, 1972.

Jacobson, David. "Jonathan Edwards and the 'American Difference': Pragmatic Reflections on the 'Sense of the Heart'." *Journal of American Studies* 21 (1987): 377–85.

Jenson, Robert W. *America's Theologian: A Recommendation of Jonathan Edwards.* New York: Oxford University Press, 1988.

Johnson, Samuel. *Samuel Johnson, President of King's College: His Career and Writings.* 4 vols. Edited by Herbert Schneider and Carol Schneider. New York: Columbia University Press, 1929.

Johnson, Thomas H. "Jonathan Edwards's Background of Reading." *Colonial Society of Massachusetts: Transactions* 28 (1930–31): 193–222.

Kennedy, Rick. "The Alliance between Puritanism and Cartesian Logic at Harvard, 1687–1735." *Journal of the History of Ideas* 51 (1990): 549–72.

Kimnach, Wilson H. Introduction to *Sermons and Discourses, 1720–1723*, by Jonathan Edwards. Edited by Wilson H. Kimnach. New Haven: Yale University Press, 1992.

———. "Jonathan Edwards's Pursuit of Reality." In *Jonathan Edwards and the American Experience*, edited by Nathan O. Hatch and Harry S. Stout. New York: Oxford University Press, 1988.

Knight, Janice. "Learning the Language of God: Jonathan Edwards and the Typology of Nature." *William and Mary Quarterly*, 3d ser. 48 (1991): 531–51.

Kretzmann, Norman. "The Main Thesis of Locke's Semantic Theory." In *Locke on Human Understanding: Selected Essays*, edited by I. C. Tipton. Oxford: Oxford University Press, 1977.

Kristeva, Julia. *Desire in Language.* Edited by Leon S. Roudiez. Translated by Thomas Gora, Alice Jardine, and Leon S. Roudiez. New York: Columbia University Press, 1980.

———. *The Kristeva Reader.* Edited by Toril Moi. New York: Columbia University Press, 1986.

———. *Revolution in Poetic Language.* Translated by Margaret Waller. New York: Columbia University Press, 1984.

Kuklick, Bruce. *Churchmen and Philosophers: From Jonathan Edwards to John Dewey.* New York: Yale University Press, 1985.

Lee, Sang Hyun. *The Philosophical Theology of Jonathan Edwards.* Princeton: Princeton University Press, 1988.

Liszka, James Jakob. *The Semiotic of Myth: A Critical Study of the Symbol.* Bloomington: Indiana University Press, 1989.

Locke, John. *An Essay concerning Human Understanding.* Edited by Peter H. Nidditch. Oxford: Clarendon Press, 1975.

Long, A. A. *Hellenistic Philosophy: Stoics, Epicureans, Sceptics.* 2d ed. Berkeley: University of California Press, 1986.

———. "Language and Thought in Stoicism." In *Problems in Stoicism*, edited by A. A. Long. London: Athlone Press, 1971.

Losonsky, Michael. "Leibniz's Adamic Language of Thought." *Journal of the History of Philosophy* 30 (1992): 523–43.

Lowance, Mason I. "'Images or Shadows of Divine Things' in the Thought of Jonathan Edwards." In *Typology and Early American Literature*, edited by Sacvan Bercovitch. Amherst: University of Massachusetts Press, 1972.

_____. Introduction to "The Types of the Messiah," in *Typological Writings*, by Jonathan Edwards. Edited by Wallace E. Anderson and Mason I. Lowance, Jr., with David Watters. New Haven: Yale University Press, 1993.

_____. *The Language of Canaan: Metaphor and Symbol in New England from the Puritans to the Transcendentalists.* Cambridge: Harvard University Press, 1980.

Lyttle, David. "Jonathan Edwards on Personal Identity." *Early American Literature* 7 (1972–73): 163–71.

Major-Poetzl, Pamela. *Michel Foucault's Archaeology of Western Culture.* Chapel Hill: University of North Carolina Press, 1983.

Markus, R. A. "St. Augustine on Signs." In *Augustine: A Collection of Critical Essays*, edited by R. A. Markus. Garden City, N.Y.: Anchor Books, 1972.

Mates, Benson. *Stoic Logic.* Berkeley: University of California Press, 1961.

McDermott, Gerald R. *One Holy and Happy Society: The Public Theology of Jonathan Edwards.* University Park: Pennsylvania State University Press, 1992.

Miller, Perry. Introduction to *Images or Shadows of Divine Things*, by Jonathan Edwards. Edited by Perry Miller. New Haven: Yale University Press, 1948.

_____. *Jonathan Edwards.* New York: William Sloane Assoc., 1949.

_____. "Jonathan Edwards on the Sense of the Heart." *Harvard Theological Review* 41 (1948): 123–45.

_____. *The New England Mind: The Seventeenth Century.* Cambridge: Harvard University Press, 1939.

Moody, Ernest A. *Studies in Medieval Philosophy, Science and Logic.* Berkeley: University of California Press, 1975.

Morgan, Michael L. "Authorship and the History of Philosophy." *Review of Metaphysics* 42 (1988): 327–55.

Morris, William S. "The Genius of Jonathan Edwards." In *Reinterpretation in American Church History*, edited by Jerald C. Brauer. Chicago: University of Chicago Press, 1968.

_____. *The Young Jonathan Edwards: A Reconstruction.* New York: Carlson Publishing Co., 1991.

Murphy, Arthur E. "Jonathan Edwards on Free Will and Moral Agency." *Philosophical Review* 68 (1959): 181–202.

Nagy, Paul J. "Jonathan Edwards and the Metaphysics of Consent." *The Personalist* 51 (1970): 434–46.

Norton, Arthur O. "Harvard Text-Books and Reference Books of the Seventeenth Century." *Colonial Society of Massachusetts: Transactions* 28 (1930–31): 361–438.

Ong, Walter J. *Ramus: Method, and the Decay of Dialogue.* Cambridge: Harvard University Press, 1958.

Opie, John, ed. *Jonathan Edwards and the Enlightenment.* Lexington, Mass.: Heath, 1969.

Ormsby-Lennon, Hugh. "Rosicrucian Linguistics: Twilight of a Renaissance Tradition." In *Hermeticism and the Renaissance: Intellectual History and the Occult in Early Modern Europe*, edited by Ingrid Merkel and Allen G. Debus. Washington, D.C.: Folger Shakespeare Library, 1988.

Pachter, Henry M. *Paracelsus: Magic into Science.* New York: Henry Schuman, 1951.

Pagel, Walter. *Paracelsus: An Introduction to Philosophical Medicine in the Era of the Renaissance.* 2d ed. New York: Karger, 1982.

Peirce, Charles S. *Collected Papers.* 8 vols. Edited by C. Hartshorne, P. Weiss, and A. Burks. Cambridge: Harvard University Press, 1931–58.

_____. *New Elements of Mathematics.* 4 vols. Edited by C. Eisele. The Hague: Mouton, 1976.

_____. *Peirce on Signs.* Edited by James Hoopes. Chapel Hill: University of North Carolina Press, 1991.

Pippin, Robert B. *Modernism as a Philosophical Problem.* Cambridge: Mass.: Basil Blackwell, 1991.

Proudfoot, Wayne. "From Theology to a Science of Religions: Jonathan Edwards and William James on Religious Affections." *Harvard Theological Review* 82 (1989): 149–68.

Ramsey, Paul. Introduction to *Ethical Writings,* by Jonathan Edwards. Edited by Paul Ramsey. New Haven: Yale University Press, 1989.

_____. Introduction to *Freedom of the Will,* by Jonathan Edwards. Edited by Paul Ramsey. New Haven: Yale University Press, 1957.

Raposa, Michael L. "Jonathan Edwards' Twelfth Sign." *International Philosophical Quarterly* 33 (1993): 153–62.

Robinson, Charles F., and Robinson, Robin. "Three Early Massachusetts Libraries." *Colonial Society of Massachusetts: Transactions* 28 (1930–31): 107–75.

Rorty, Richard. *Contingency, Irony, and Solidarity.* Cambridge: Cambridge University Press, 1989.

Ross, Stephen David. *Metaphysical Aporia and Philosophical Heresy.* Albany: State University of New York Press, 1989.

Rupp, George. "The 'Idealism' of Jonathan Edwards." *Harvard Theological Review* 62 (1969): 209–26.

Saunders, Jason L. *Justus Lipsius: The Philosophy of Renaissance Stoicism.* New York: Liberal Arts Press, 1955.

Sebeok, Thomas A. "'Semiotics' and Its Congeners." In *Frontiers in Semiotics,* edited by John Deely, Brooke Williams, and Felicia E. Kruse. Bloomington: Indiana University Press, 1986.

Shea, Daniel B. "Deconstruction Comes to Early 'America': The Case of Edwards." *Early American Literature* 21 (1986–87): 268–74.

Silverman, Kaja. *The Subject of Semiotics.* New York: Oxford University Press, 1983.

Simonson, Harold P. *Jonathan Edwards: Theologian of the Heart.* Grand Rapids, Mich.: William B. Eerdmans, 1974.

Smith, Claude A. "Jonathan Edwards and 'The Way of Ideas'." *Harvard Theological Review* 59 (1966): 153–73.

Smith, John E. Introduction to *Religious Affections,* by Jonathan Edwards. Edited by John E. Smith. New Haven: Yale University Press, 1959.

_____. "Jonathan Edwards as Philosophical Theologian." *Review of Metaphysics* 30 (1976): 306–24.

_____. *Jonathan Edwards: Puritan, Preacher, Philosopher.* Notre Dame: University of Notre Dame Press, 1992.

Smith, Philip A. "Bishop Hall, 'Our English Seneca'." *PMLA* 63 (1948): 1191–1204.

Stein, Stephen J. "The Spirit and the Word: Jonathan Edwards and Scriptural Exegesis." In *Jonathan Edwards and the American Experience,* edited by Nathan O. Hatch and Harry S. Stout. New York: Oxford University Press, 1988.

Stempel, Daniel. "Blake, Foucault, and the Classical Episteme," *PMLA* 96 (1981): 388–407.

Storms, C. Samuel. *Tragedy in Eden: Original Sin in the Theology of Jonathan Edwards.* Lanham, Md.: University Press of America, 1985.

Todorov, Tzvetan. *Theories of the Symbol.* Translated by Catherine Porter. Ithaca, N.Y.: Cornell University Press, 1982.

Vetö, Miklós. *La Pensée de Jonathan Edwards.* Latour-Maubourg: Cerf, 1987.

Vickers, Brian. "Analogy Versus Identity: The Rejection of Occult Symbolism, 1580–1680." In *Occult and Scientific Mentalities in the Renaissance,* edited by

Brian Vickers. New York: Cambridge University Press, 1984.

Vico, Giambattista. *On the Most Ancient Wisdom of the Italians.* Translated by Lucia M. Palmer. Ithaca: Cornell University Press, 1988.

Wainwright, William J. "Jonathan Edwards and the Language of God." *Journal of the American Academy of Religion* 48 (1980): 519–30.

Weddle, David. "Jonathan Edwards on Men and Trees, and the Problem of Solidarity." *Harvard Theological Review* 67 (1974): 155–75.

Yarbrough, Stephen R. "The Beginning of Time: Jonathan Edwards' *Original Sin.*" In *Early American Literature and Culture: Essays Honoring Harrison Meserole,* edited by Kathryn Zabelle Derounian. Newark: University of Delaware Press, 1992.

———. "Jonathan Edwards on Rhetorical Authority." *Journal of the History of Ideas* 47 (1986): 395–408.

Yarbrough, Stephen R., and Adams, John C. *Delightful Conviction: Jonathan Edwards and the Rhetoric of Conversion.* Westport, Conn.: Greenwood, Press, 1993.

Zeman, J. Jay. "Peirce's Theory of Signs." In *A Perfusion of Signs,* edited by Thomas A. Sebeok. Bloomington: Indiana University Press, 1977.

Unpublished Materials

Ames, William. "Theses Physiologiae." William Partridge's handwritten copy. Beinecke Library, Yale University.

Anderson, Wallace E. MS correspondence and materials regarding the Yale edition of Edwards' typological writings. Office of *The Works of Jonathan Edwards,* Yale Divinity School, New Haven.

Edwards, Jonathan. "Miscellanies." Eight volumes of transcriptions prepared by Thomas A. Schafer based on Edwards' manuscripts. Beinecke Library, Yale University.

Schafer, Thomas A. "The Concept of Being in the Thought of Jonathan Edwards." Ph.D. diss., Duke University, 1951.

INDEX

Abraham, 40
Act, 102, 136–37, 168; divine, 108, 116–19, 130; free, 152–61, 171–76
Adam, 130, 135–41, 151; and posterity, 130–35, 141–50
Aesthetics. *See* Beauty
Affections: mental, 164, 167–68, 182–85, 189–90, 193; natural, 72–77
Agency, 110, 136, 152, 168; moral, 153, 155–56, 159, 171–72, 194
Agreement, 177, 191; natural, 71, 173–74, 179; of self to objects, 100, 153, 180–83
Agricola, Rudolph, 68, 75, 77–79, 81
Alchemy, 74–77
Allegory, 49–50, 61–62
Ames, William, 73–74, 77, 82
Analogy, 32–33, 37–38, 71–74, 185
Anderson, Wallace, 7, 11–18, 40, 69
Arguments, Ramist, 70, 73–74, 79–83, 88, 91, 160
Aristotelianism, 24, 79, 147, 158; predicate logic, 85; on signs, 25–26, 45, 167
Arminianism, 153, 155
Arnauld, Antoine, 70
Astrology, 67–68, 71, 74–77
Atomism, 69–70, 80–81, 94, 98–99
Augustine, St., 26, 77n, 81, 132
Author, 3, 9, 18, 25, 67n
Autonomy, 150, 153, 155–58, 172

Barrow, Isaac, 81
Beauty, 36, 153, 175, 177–79, 196; natural vs. spiritual, 182–87
Being, 73, 175–77, 188; as consent, 174–76, 179–80, 185–86; intentionality of, 91, 103, 107, 117–20, 127; and nothing, 84; as space, 87–88
Benevolence, 174–77, 179–80, 185–87, 194; divine, 195
Bercovitch, Sacvan, 7
Berkeley, George, 65, 84
Body, 28, 67, 70, 73, 91–93, 129, 140–43; excellence of, 180–81; and mind, 100–101
Book of nature, 5, 19, 22, 32, 34; and medicine, 76, 82; and typology, 41–42, 57–60
Boyle, Robert, 69
Brumm, Ursula, 7
Burgersdijck, Franco, 68, 72, 73, 79

Calvinism, 17, 77n, 132, 153, 171
Cambridge Platonists, 68
Cartesianism, 3, 68; reasoning, 70, 77–78; on self, 26, 69, 105, 136, 148
Causality, 6, 72, 83–86, 97–98, 115, 125, 136, 164–66, 181; and choices, 152, 155, 167–70; divine, 89–93, 172–73
Certainty, 160–62, 165, 167, 170
Chauncy, Charles, 75
Cherry, Conrad, 62
Choice, 106, 133, 136–38, 143, 151–60. *See also* Will
Christ, 10, 40, 51, 188; and metaphysics, 197–99; Son of God, 96, 128–29, 198–99; new Adam, 134–35, 141, 146, 150–51
Chrysippus, 78
Church, 128–29, 141
Cicero, Marcus Tullius, 79, 81
Classical episteme: Edwards' use of, 40, 78; Foucault on, 19–20, 24–25, 30–31, 38–39, 66
Classical modernity, vii–viii, 2–4, 101, 118, 155; on Christ, 197; as fallen mentality, 21–22, 46, 91, 131; logic of, 77, 85, 108; on self, 30, 102–106, 140, 143; on signs, 70; on typology, 43, 64–65
Clement of Alexandria, 105
Commonplace, 67, 79–84, 107–108, 181; mind or person as, 98, 134, 150–51; rhetorical heritage of, 67, 88–91, 161; as supposition, 92–94, 100
Communication. *See* Discourse
Community, 42–43, 149–50, 156, 168
Complacence, 175, 178–79, 184–85, 194; divine, 195
Concept, 25–30, 44–45
Condillac, Étienne Bonnot de, 16
Conscience, 163, 173–76, 193
Consciousness, 88; continuity of, 148–49, 162; fallen, 143
Consent, 175–77; kinds of, 181–85; to Being, 53, 72–73, 101, 104, 126, 179–81, 186–87, 195
Contingency, 69, 157, 166; of actions, 156, 159, 161
Convenience of things, 33, 37, 72–73
Cooey, Paula, 45, 62–63, 104
Creativity, 30; divine, 53, 104, 108, 120

STEPHEN H. DANIEL, Professor of Philosophy and Humanities at Texas A&M University, is author of *Myth and Modern Philosophy* and *John Toland: His Methods, Manners, and Mind.*